Trafficking of Human Beings from a Human Rights Perspective

International Studies in Human Rights

Volume 89

The titles in this series are listed at the end of this volume.

Trafficking of Human Beings from a Human Rights Perspective: Towards a Holistic Approach

Tom Obokata

MARTINUS NIJHOFF PUBLISHERS
LEIDEN • BOSTON

A C.I.P. Catalogue record for this book is available from the Library of Congress.

Printed on acid-free paper.

ISBN 90 04 15405 1

Koninklijke Brill NV incorporates the imprints Brill Academic Publishers, Martinus Nijhoff Publishers and VSP.

http://www.brill.nl

Printed and bound in The Netherlands.

Table of Contents

Acknowledgements

The completion of this research monograph would not have been possible without the assistance of a number of individuals and organisations. It is based on my doctorate thesis completed at the University of Nottingham, where I was supervised by Patrick Twomey. He spent long hours reading and commenting on my many drafts. I would also like to express my gratitude to my examiners, Professors Robert McCorquodale and Ryszard Piotrowicz, who gave me helpful suggestions with regard to the final version of this monograph. In addition, I would like to thank the scholars, representatives of governments, non-governmental organisations and inter-governmental organisations around the world, all of whom are too many to list. They have provided me with valuable information and continuing support.

My study at the University of Nottingham was partially funded by the School of Law and International Office. The School of Law also provided me with financial assistance to attend conferences and conduct research trips to Bangkok (Thailand), Brussels (Belgium), Geneva (Switzerland) and London. I would also like to express my gratitude to the Carnegie Trust for the Universities of Scotland, which funded my follow-up visit to Thailand in the summer of 2005.

Finally, I would like to thank my family and friends. The completion of my education and this research monograph would not have been possible without the continuing support and encouragement of my parents. My friends and colleagues at the Universities of Nottingham and Dundee have also been a source of invaluable help. Special thanks to Ed Goodwin, Julie Self, Pamela Ferguson, Fiona Raitt, and Elizabeth Kirk for proof-reading and giving me guidance on completing this monograph. All errors and omissions remain mine alone.

Tom Obokata

Acknowledgements

Table of Cases

I. International Cases

European Court of Justice

Inter-American Court of Human Rights

II. National Cases

United Kingdom

United States of America

Table of Treaties and other International Instruments

Introduction

Background

Trafficking of human beings is a widespread practice in the modern world. It has been estimated that between 600,000 and 800,000 people, the majority of whom are women and children, are trafficked worldwide each year.[1] Virtually all States are affected by trafficking,[2] and traffickers are believed to make approximately $ 9.5 billion annually from trafficking business.[3] The origins of trafficking can be traced back to the ancient practices of slavery and the slave trade.[4] However, trafficking of human beings has acquired a different meaning since the beginning of the Twentieth Century. While slavery and the slave trade were commonly associated with transporting African slaves to Europe and North America, trafficking was initially understood to take place for prostitution and sexual exploitation of white women and girls within Europe.

The growth of trafficking business in modern times has been fuelled by a wide variety of factors. The end of the Cold War and the fall of the iron curtain saw the surge of trafficking business from Eastern Europe. As newly independent States struggled to establish their own structure for governance, and due to a lack of effective law enforcement and border control, Eastern European States

1 U.S. Department of State, *Trafficking in Persons Report 2005*, p. 6 (hereinafter Trafficking Report 2005).

2 Ryf, K.C, 'The First Modern Anti-Slavery Law: The Trafficking Victim Protection Act 2000,' 34 *Case Western Reserve Journal of International Law* 45 (2002), p. 47; and Shannon, S, 'Prostitution and the Mafia: The Involvement of Organized Crime in the Global Sex Trade,' in Williams (ed.), *Illegal Migration and Commercial Sex: The New Slave Trade* (New York: Frank Cass)(1999), p. 122.

3 Trafficking Report 2005, *supra*, p. 13. See also UNICEF UK, *End Child Exploitation: Stop Traffic!* (London: UNICEF UK)(2003), p. 11.

4 Iselin, B, *Trafficking in Human Beings: New Patterns for an Old Phenomenon* (Paper Presented to "Trafficking in Persons: Theory and Practice in Regional and International Cooperation"), Bogota, Colombia (November 2003), pp. 2 and 3.

became vulnerable to criminal activities, including trafficking of human beings.[5] The process of globalisation, particularly advancement in communication and transportation, has also made it easier for traffickers to traffic people.[6] These developments have coincided with the adoption of restrictive immigration laws and policies by developed States, all of which are popular destinations for trafficked people. This, however, has proven to be counterproductive, as a lack of means for legal migration has compelled people to use the services provided by traffickers.[7]

People are trafficked by land, sea and air generally from poor States into developed ones, and certain trafficking routes have been identified. From Russia, for instance, people are trafficked through the Balkan region, Poland and the Czech Republic into Western Europe.[8] Italy and Greece have been identified as common destinations for people from the Middle East.[9] In addition, people from Africa are trafficked not only into Western Europe, [10] but also into the United States and Canada.[11] In a similar vein, traffickers traffic people from China and South East Asian States into North America through the Atlantic Trafficking Route.[12]

A wide variety of individuals and groups is known to take part in trafficking. An important aspect of modern day trafficking is the involvement of organised criminal groups. Groups such as the *Snakeheads* (China), *Yakuza* (Japan), and *Russian Mafia* are known to actively engage in trafficking. Family members, friends and prominent figures in local communities also lure potential victims into the process.[13] Moreover, there is evidence to suggest that members of peace-

5 Rijken, C, *Trafficking in Persons, Prosecution from a European Perspective* (The Hague: T.M.C. Asser Press)(2003), p. 3.

6 *Ibid.*, p. 6. Other major causes of trafficking will be explored in Chapter 2 on national case studies of Thailand, Poland and the United Kingdom.

7 Schloenhardt, A, 'Organised Crime and the Business of Migrant Trafficking: An Economic Analysis,' 32 *Crime, Law and Social Change* 203 (1999), p. 212.

8 National Criminal Intelligence Service (NCIS), *UK Threat Assessment of Serious and Organised Crime 2003*, p. 38.

9 *Ibid.*

10 *Ibid.*

11 Lederer, L. J, *Trafficking Route from Africa* (Baltimore: Protection Project)(2000).

12 Lederer, L.J, *Atlanta Trafficking Routes* (Baltimore: Protection Project)(2000). Further information is available at http://www.protectionproject.org.

13 U.S. Department of State, *Trafficking in Persons Report 2003*, p. 7 (hereinafter Trafficking Report 2003).

keeping missions and other inter-governmental organisations (IGOs) also take part in trafficking business.[14]

The rapid growth in trafficking of human beings and its transnational nature have prompted the international community to take urgent action, and a major step was taken when the United Nations adopted the *Protocol to Prevent, Suppress and Punish Trafficking in Persons, Especially Women and Children* (Trafficking Protocol), attached to the *United Nations Convention against Transnational Organised Crime* (Organised Crime Convention)[15] in December 2000. One key aspect of the Trafficking Protocol is that it adopted a definition of trafficking for the first time under international law. Article 3 (a) provides:

> "Trafficking in persons" shall mean the recruitment, transportation, transfer, harbouring, or receipt of persons, by means of threat or use of force or other forms of coercion, of abduction, of fraud, of deception, of the abuse of power or of a position of vulnerability or of the giving or receiving of payments or benefits to achieve the consent of a person having control over another person, for the purpose of exploitation. Exploitation shall include, at the minimum, the exploitation of the prostitution of others or other forms of sexual exploitation, forced labour or services, slavery or practices similar to slavery, servitude or removal of organs.[16]

The adoption of this definition is an important development because it provides a general guidance to different actors, such as scholars, governments, non-governmental organisations (NGOs), and IGOs to examine and respond to trafficking.

This definition reflects different views held recently by these actors at the national, regional and international levels. Some actors, particularly States, maintain a strong link between trafficking and illegal migration, while others, such as women's groups, focus their attention on prostitution as a form of subsequent exploitation inherent in the practice. Despite these differences in views, they hold one thing in common. They generally agree that the trafficking of human beings is a human rights issue.[17] Many of those trafficked are coerced or

---

14 *Written Statement of Human Rights Advocates International*, E/CN.4/2004/NGO/95; Human Rights Watch, *Hopes Betrayed: Trafficking of Women and Girls to the Post-Conflict Bosnia and Herzegovina for Forced Prostitution*(2002); and UN Interregional Crime and Justice Research Institute (UNICRI), *Trafficking, Slavery and Peacekeeping: The Need for a Comprehensive Training Program (Conference Report)*(May 2002).

15 A/RES/55/25 (2001), Annexes I and II. See Annex 1.

16 *Ibid.*

17 Trafficking Report 2005, *supra*, p. 13; *Reports of the Secretary General on Trafficking in Women and Girls*, E/CN.4/2002/80 and E/CN.4/2003/74; *Informal Note by*

deceived into the process and experience acts amounting to slavery and forced labour once they reach their destination, as the definition above clearly suggests. Therefore, it is easy to regard trafficking as a serious violation of human rights.

However, addressing the human rights aspects of the phenomenon has proven to be difficult in practice. At the national level, a criminal justice response characterised by crime and immigration control dominates, and promotion of a human rights approach remains a secondary concern. At the regional and international levels, although the importance of addressing the human rights aspects of trafficking is widely recognised, IGOs have not been able to do so effectively. The activities of key IGOs, such as the United Nations, focus predominantly on the supply side of trafficking in States of origin, and do not adequately deal with the demand for trafficked people and other pertinent issues in States of destination. In other words, they have so far failed to take a holistic approach which addresses wider issues surrounding the phenomenon.

One reason why it is difficult to promote a human rights approach is that a comprehensive analysis of trafficking and related issues in light of human rights norms and principles established under international human rights law has not been fully developed. The Office of the United Nations High Commissioner for Human Rights has adopted the *Recommended Principles and Guidelines on Human Rights and Human Trafficking*.[18] However, these Principles and Guidelines are not legally binding and do not fully articulate applicable human rights norms and principles to the practice. As a result, the nature and the extent of

---

the United Nations High Commissioner for Human Rights, A/AC.254/16; *Note by the Office of the United Nations High Commissioner for Human Rights, the United Nations Children's Fund and the International Organisation for Migration on the Draft Protocols Concerning Migrant Smuggling and Trafficking in Persons*, A/AC.254/27; Becki, Y, 'Trafficking of Humans Across the United States Borders: How United States Laws Can Be Used to Punish Traffickers and Protect Victims,' 13 *Georgetown Immigration Law Journal* 73 (1998); Global Alliance Against Trafficking in Women (GAATW), *Human Rights and Trafficking in Persons: A Handbook* (Bangkok: GAATW)(2001); Inglis, S.C, 'Expanding International and National Protections against Trafficking for Forced Labour Using a Human Rights Framework,' 7 *Buffalo Human Rights Law Review* 55 (2001); Corrigan, K, 'Putting Brakes on the Global Trafficking of Women for the Sex Trade: An Analysis of the Existing Regulatory Schemes to Stop the Flow of Traffic,' 25 *Fordham International Law Journal* 151 (2001); Hartsough, T, 'Asylum for Trafficked Women: Escape Strategies Beyond the T Visa,' 13 *Hastings Women's Law Journal* 77 (2002); Obokata, T, 'Human Trafficking, Human Rights, and the Nationality, Immigration and Asylum Act 2002,' 4 *European Human Rights Law Review* 410 (2003); and Murray, J, 'Who Will Police the Peace-Builders? The Failure to Establish Accountability for the Participation of the United Nations Civilian Police in Trafficking of Women in Post-Conflict Bosnia and Herzegovina,' 34 *Columbia Human Rights Law Review* 475 (2003).

18 E/2002/68/Add.1. See Annex 3.

obligations imposed upon States and non-State actors are not entirely clear, and a human rights discourse in relation to trafficking remains without much substance.

The purpose of this book, then, is to go further than simply recognising that trafficking is a human rights issue. It attempts to establish a human rights framework to analyse and address the act by identifying applicable human rights norms and principles from the beginning to the end of the trafficking process, such as the rights to life, work, health, as well as freedom from torture and slavery. It then articulates key obligations under international human rights law, including the obligations to prohibit trafficking, punish traffickers, protect victims, and to address the causes and the consequences of the practice.

Research Design

A wide variety of sources have been consulted in the research behind this book with the use of different research methods. Chapter 1, which examines the evolution of trafficking, is based on an examination of material sources of the law, which include treaties and *travaux préparatoires,* as well as non-binding instruments at the regional and international levels; official papers and reports produced by States and IGOs; and literature of scholars and NGOs.

In relation to Chapters 2 (National Case Studies of Thailand, Poland, and the United Kingdom) and 3 (The Role of IGOs), relevant legislation, policies, official documents and reports of States, IGOs and NGOs were relied upon in the first instance. The statistical data on the number of people trafficked and law enforcement practices primarily come from these actors, although investigative reports produced by local media were also used. In addition, field trips were conducted in Bangkok (Thailand), London (United Kingdom), Brussels (Belgium), and Geneva (Switzerland) between 2001 and 2005, and several interviews were held with the representatives of the governments, NGOs, the European Union, the United Nations and other IGOs. Finally, electronic and written correspondence from different actors has also been relied upon.

Chapters 4 and 5 were largely based upon an examination of human rights norms and principles developed and elaborated by the UN Charter mechanisms including Special Rapporteurs on Violence against Women and on Sales of Children, and the Working Group on Contemporary Forms of Slavery as well as Treaty Monitoring mechanisms such as the Human Rights Committee, Committee on Economic, Social and Cultural Rights and the Committee on the Elimination of Discrimination Against Women. The jurisprudence established by these mechanisms as well as others such as the European Court of Human Rights, the Inter-American Court of Human Rights, the International Criminal Tribunals for the Former Yugoslavia and for Rwanda, and the International Court of Justice have also been analysed not only to articulate human rights obligations imposed upon States, but also to address those of non-State actors such as organised criminal groups. The growing body of literature by human rights scholars has also provided insights into the development of international human rights law relevant to trafficking of human beings.

Structure

Chapter 1 illustrates how the understanding of trafficking has evolved over time. It begins with an overview of the ancient practices of slavery and the slave trade, followed by an analysis of early instruments on trafficking of human beings adopted in the first part of the Twentieth Century. It will be shown that these instruments are mainly concerned with trafficking for prostitution or sexual exploitation of women and children. The Chapter continues with contemporary views on trafficking of human beings. A detailed analysis of the definition of trafficking under the Trafficking Protocol is provided in the following contexts: migration, gender, organised crime and human rights. The distinction between trafficking and smuggling of human beings and its policy implications are also illustrated. An examination reveals that trafficking is increasingly viewed from a human rights perspective. It is also argued that a human rights framework is beneficial because it not only allows different actors to pay close attention to the plight of victims, but also promotes a holistic approach to trafficking in which due consideration is given to wider issues such as the causes and consequences of the practice.

Chapter 2 introduces national case studies of Thailand, Poland, and the United Kingdom. These States are chosen as they can be designated as typical States of origin, transit and destination. The main observation made is that although Thailand, Poland and the United Kingdom recognise the need to address the human rights aspects of trafficking, they primarily focus on a criminal justice response to trafficking with much emphasis on punishment of traffickers and those trafficked by way of crime and immigration control. While NGOs pay more attention to the plight of victims of trafficking, their performance is affected by a number of obstacles such as a lack of funding and of co-operation from different sectors, and duplication of work.

Chapter 3 continues with an analysis of the role played by IGOs. It begins with an examination of the European Union (EU). It was selected as an example of a regional organisation because the policies and programmes adopted in relation to the phenomenon have been more extensive than others. The Chapter then illustrates an initiative known as the United Nations Inter-Agency Project on Trafficking in Mekong Sub-region (UNIAP). An analysis of the UNIAP is useful as it provides insights into the reality of co-ordination and co-operation among different agencies working in the field. The Chapter continues with an examination of two more pertinent organisations: the International Organisation for Migration (IOM) and the International Labour Organisation (ILO). The main conclusion reached is that IGOs have failed to take a holistic approach to trafficking and therefore that a human rights framework is not being promoted effectively.

The main purpose of Chapters 4 is to identify applicable human rights norms and principles from the beginning to the end of the trafficking process, such as the rights to life, work, health, as well as freedom from inhuman or degrading acts and slavery. It then attempts to articulate human rights obligations imposed upon non-State actors by analysing the current development of international human rights law. Two main observations are made. First, although non-State actors do not have legal obligations and therefore cannot be held directly accountable under international human rights law, a horizontal application of human rights norms and principles can be sought at the national level through criminal and civil proceedings. Second, at the international level, it is submitted that trafficking can be regarded as a crime against humanity, and therefore the principle of individual criminal responsibility can be applied. In short, indirect enforcement of human rights norms and principles is at least a possibility.

Chapter 5 in turn explores certain human rights obligations which can be imposed upon States. While a wide variety of obligations exist, this book focuses on the following four key obligations imposed upon all States regardless of their status as States of origin, transit or destination: obligations to prohibit trafficking, punish traffickers, protect victims and address the causes and consequences of the phenomenon. It will be shown that these are firmly established under international human rights law. Further, the potential of the Trafficking Protocol to promote a human rights framework, as well as implications of the interaction between different branches of international law, such as international human rights law, international criminal law and transnational criminal law, will be examined. The general conclusion reached is that a human rights framework can make a valuable contribution to the global action against trafficking.

Chapter 1

Understanding Trafficking

1.1 Introduction

This Chapter analyses how our understanding of trafficking has evolved over time. A starting point is an examination of slavery and the slave trade in ancient times[1] as the origin of trafficking can be traced back to those practices. The key elements of slavery and the slave trade were the ownership of human beings for subsequent exploitation with the use of violence and threat, and deprivation of their liberties and freedoms.[2] The Chapter continues with an illustration of early views on trafficking of human beings. This is done through an examination of five key international treaties on the phenomenon which were adopted in the first part of the Twentieth Century.

The second part of this Chapter presents our contemporary understanding of trafficking. The most important development in modern times is the adoption of the Trafficking Protocol. This Chapter identifies core elements in the definition of trafficking under the Trafficking Protocol by comparing it with that of smuggling of human beings adopted by the *Protocol Against the Smuggling of Migrants by Land, Sea and Air* (Smuggling Protocol).[3] The Chapter then

1 For studies of slavery and the slave trade in general, see Patterson, O, *Slavery and Social Death: A Comparative Study* (Cambridge: Harvard University Press)(1982); Solow, B.L (ed.), *Slavery and the Rise of the Atlantic System* (Cambridge: Cambridge University Press)(1991); Bradley, K, *Slavery and Society at Rome* (Cambridge: Cambridge University Press)(1994); Bush, M. L, *Serfdom and Slavery: Studies in Legal Bondage* (London: Longman)(1996); Drescher, S, and S. L. Engerman (eds.), *A Historical Guide to World Slavery* (Oxford: Oxford University Press)(1998); Lovejoy, P. E, *Transformation in Slavery: A History of Slavery in Africa* (2nd ed.)(Cambridge: Cambridge University Press)(2000); and McKeown, N, *The Invention of Ancient Slavery* (London: Duckworth)(2002).

2 *Updated Review of the Implementation of and Follow-up to the Conventions on Slavery: Working paper by Mr. David Weissbrodt and Anti-Slavery International*, E/CN.4/Sub.2/2000/3, paras. 17-20 (hereinafter Updated Review).

3 A/RES/55/25 (2001), Annex III. See Annex 2.

provides a detailed analysis of the core elements of trafficking in the contexts of migration, gender, organised crime and human rights through a review of literature. Wherever these contemporary views come from, it is concluded that the scope of the definition under the Trafficking Protocol is wide enough to accommodate most of these different perspectives. It is further noted that different actors are in agreement that trafficking is fundamentally a matter of human rights.

1.2 Historical Background

Slavery and the slave trade can be seen as the origins of modern day trafficking. Although the practices were common in the ancient civilisations of the Middle East and Mediterranean, they became more prominent during the period of the Roman Empire, and the legacy left by that Empire was said to have influenced subsequent practices in Europe and North America.[4] Under the Roman law, slaves were treated as private property or chattels of owners or masters[5] and were commonly used as maids, guards, cooks, partners in sex or prostitutes, and manufacturers of pottery, glassware, jewels, etc.[6] They were usually placed under harsh conditions and did not enjoy legal personality.[7] Towards the end of the Roman Empire (Fifth and Sixth Centuries A.D.), the practices of slavery and the slave trade declined as masters/owners started emancipating their slaves. Some freed slaves for moral reasons influenced by Christianity.[8] Others let them go as the cost of holding them was high.[9] Some slaves were also able to buy freedom from their masters by accumulating some wealth.[10]

The legacy of Roman slavery and the slave trade, however, was inherited by the successive Byzantine Empire (eastern portion of the Roman Empire). The clear evidence of this is the Roman Law codified by the Emperor Justinian. The Code consisted of a mixture of senatorial legislation, imperial decrees and opinions of jurists, and existed until the Byzantine Empire ceased to exist.[11] A section of the Code stated that "slaves are in the power of their masters; for we find that among all nations slave owners have the power of life and death over

4 Phillips, W. D, *Slavery From Roman Times to the Early Transatlantic Trade* (Manchester: Manchester University Press)(1985), pp. 3 and 16.

5 Blackburn, R, *The Making of New World Slavery: From the Baroqu to the Modern 1492-1800* (London and New York: Verso)(1997), p. 35.

6 Phillips, *supra*, pp. 24 and 25.

7 *Ibid.*, p. 27.

8 *Ibid.*, p. 35.

9 Meltzer, M, *Slavery: A World History, Volume I* (New York: Da Capo Press)(1993), p. 183.

10 Phillips, *supra*, p. 35.

11 *Ibid.*, p. 38.

their slaves, and whatever a slave earns belongs to his master."[12] This passage was used to justify the use of slaves. The Code was retained throughout the Middle Ages, and served as a basis for legal codes of many European kingdoms.

The practices of slavery and the slave trade were common not only in Europe, but also in the Islamic world (i.e. Middle East and North Africa). Slavery was an established institution under the *Koran*, and the Islamic States were among the first to acquire slaves from Africa.[13] The use of African slaves was common during the reign of the Ottoman Empire, and they were regarded as desirable among the Islamic and Arab States.[14] Those African slaves were mainly used as gold and copper miners, sugar plantation workers, or domestic servants, similar to the case of the Roman slaves.[15]

Although slavery and the slave trade existed during the early part of the Middle Ages in Europe, the most significant expansion occurred in the Fifteenth Century, when the Portuguese made an advance into Africa with the initial aim of gaining access to gold. When they reached West Africa for the first time, they acquired a dozen Africans to be presented before Prince Henry as gifts.[16] The Portuguese then started establishing themselves in the trade of both gold and slaves from Africa.[17] From this point on, slavery and the slave trade of Africans spread to many parts of Europe, such as Russia, the Caucasus, the Balkans, and Norman England.[18]

The general attitude of slave traders and owners towards the slaves was not positive. The slaves were portrayed as ugly beings, infidels, or beasts[19] and those characterisations served as a justification for the use of violence and other cruel means to maintain control over them. [20] When slavery and the slave trade of Africans became prominent, a racial element was added to people's perception on slavery, in that their race and skin colour were commonly identified and associated with the status of slavery.[21] This perception of slaves was prevalent not only in Europe and the Islamic World,[22] but also in the United States.[23] Slav-

12 Blackburn, *supra*, p. 35.

13 *Ibid.*, p. 79.

14 *Ibid.*

15 *Ibid.*, p. 80.

16 Meltzer, *supra*, *Volume II*, p. 1.

17 Blackburn, *supra*, p. 102.

18 *Ibid.*, p. 81.

19 *Ibid.*, p. 105.

20 Bales, K, *New Slavery: A Reference Handbook* (Santa Barbara: ABC-CLIO Inc.)(2000), p. 10.

21 Blackburn, *supra*, pp. 14 and 15.

22 Phillips, *supra*, p. 72.

23 Bales, *supra*, p. 10.

ery and the slave trade of black people later came to be known as the old or the traditional form of slavery.[24]

The prohibition of slavery in the United States is worth noting in this regard. The Thirteenth Amendment to the Constitution of the United States, adopted in December 1865, abolished slavery.[25] In interpreting the Thirteenth Amendment in *Civil Rights Cases*, the United States Supreme Court made a distinction between Roman slavery and American slavery, and stated that while the former was about enslaving whites, the latter related only to black Africans.[26] This illustrates that race was perceived as a defining element of slavery in the United States.[27]

It is useful at this point to analyse definitions of slavery and the slave trade under international law in order to identify core elements. The key international instrument on slavery is the *Slavery Convention* 1926.[28] Article 1(1) defines slavery as "the status or condition of a person over whom any or all of the power attaching to the right of ownership are exercised."[29] Article 1(2) then describes the slave trade as:

> all acts involved in the capture, acquisition or disposal of a person with intent to reduce him to slavery; all acts involved in the acquisition of a slave with a view to selling or exchanging him; all acts of disposal by sale or exchange of a slave acquired with a view to being sold or exchanged, and, in general, every act of trade or transport in slaves.[30]

---

24 Rassam, A. Y, 'Contemporary Forms of Slavery and the Evolution of the Prohibition of Slavery and the Slave Trade Under Customary International Law,' 39 *Virginia Journal of International Law* 303 (1999), p. 319; and Demleitner, N, 'Forced Prostitution: Naming an International Offense,' 18 *Fordham International Law Journal* 163 (1994), p. 192.

25 USCA CONST. amend. XIII, § 1. It reads "Section 1. Neither slavery nor involuntary servitude, except as a punishment for crime whereof the party shall have been duly convicted, shall exist within the United States, or any place subject to their jurisdiction."

26 Quoted in Holland, K. M, ' Equality and the Constitution: A Study in the Transformation of a Concept,' in Goldwin and Kaufman (eds.) *Slavery and Its Consequences: The Constitution, Equality and Race* (Washington D.C.: American Enterprise Institute for Public Policy Research)(1988), p. 95.

27 See further Finkelman, P, 'The Constitution and the Intention of the Framers: The Limits of Historical Analysis,' 50 *University of Pittsburgh Law Review* 349 (1989).

28 60 LNTS 253.

29 *Ibid.*

30 *Ibid.*

In analysing these definitions under the Slavery Convention, in conjunction with a brief history of slavery and the slave trade illustrated above, several common characteristics can be identified. First, slavery entailed ownership/control over another human being. Slaves were treated as commodities of the owners or slave masters and lacked legal personality. Second, the ownership of slaves was life-long or permanent in character. Third, deprivation of personal rights and freedoms, such as the freedom of movement, and rights to liberty and property, was also an important feature of slavery. It will be shown below that trafficking in modern times shares some of these characteristics.

1.3 Early Views on Trafficking

Trafficking of human beings in the first part of the Twentieth Century was understood to take place for the purpose of prostitution and/or sexual exploitation. This becomes clear in analysing five international instruments adopted during this period. The first international legal instrument directly related to the subject matter was the *International Agreement for the Suppression of the White Slave Traffic* 1904 (1904 Agreement).[31] This Agreement was adopted mainly due to the stagnant economic conditions in Europe which led to the sale of women into prostitution,[32] and thirteen European States saw the necessity to suppress such a practice.[33]

The term "white slave traffic" merits further explanation. The term was used to describe trafficking in the first instance, as the process itself resembled that of the traditional form of slavery and the slave trade.[34] However, this term has a different meaning. The traditional form of slavery and the slave trade entailed the transport of black people from the continent of Africa to Europe and the United States for a variety of purposes as shown above. The term "white slave," however, has its origin in describing female factory workers in England, and was later used to describe slavery of white women in Europe for the purpose of prostitution.[35] Therefore, the 1904 Agreement was inapplicable firstly to men and boys, and secondly to women and girls of races other than whites.

Despite differences between the traditional form of slavery and white slave traffic, an examination of the provisions of the 1904 Agreement reveals that

31 24 UKTS 1.

32 Demleitner, *supra*, p. 167.

33 Those States were Belgium, Denmark, France, Germany, Italy, The Netherlands, Norway, Portugal, Russia, Spain, Sweden, Switzerland, and the United Kingdom. Beckman, M. D, 'The White Slave Traffic Act: The Historical Impact of a Criminal Law Policy on Women,' 72 *Georgetown Law Journal* 1111(1984), p. 1113.

34 Demleitner, *supra*, p. 165.

35 *Ibid.*, pp. 165 and 166. See also, Nadelmann, E. A, 'Global Prohibition Regimes: The Evolution of Norms in International Society,' 44 *International Organisation* 479 (1990).

slavery, the slave trade, and trafficking share many characteristics. Under Article 1 of the Agreement, the act of trafficking was described as the "procuring of women or girls for immoral purposes abroad."[36] The term "procure" in an ordinary sense means "obtaining" or "acquiring" and is therefore in conformity with the definition of the slave trade described above. The element of subsequent exploitation is also evident, as women and girls were to be trafficked for immoral purposes. In addition, the term "abroad" suggests international movement of women and girls. Other treaties related to trafficking also include these elements.

The 1904 Agreement, however, did not contribute much to the suppression of white slave traffic, as provisions on law enforcement were non-existent. While the Agreement obliged States to adopt measures in the areas of information exchange,[37] identification of victims,[38] and supervision of employment agencies,[39] no provision touched upon enhancement of law enforcement. Consequently, trafficking continued to flourish.[40]

This prompted the adoption of another treaty, the *International Convention for the Suppression of the White Slave Traffic* 1910 (1910 Convention).[41] The scope of application was the same as the 1904 Agreement, as the link between trafficking and prostitution and/or sexual exploitation of white women was maintained. A major difference was that the 1910 Convention urged States to suppress the act and punish those responsible in stronger terms. Article 1 of the Convention provided:

> Whoever, in order to gratify the passions of another person, has procured, enticed, or led away, even with her consent, a woman or girl under age, for immoral purposes, shall be punished, notwithstanding that the various acts constituting the offence may have been committed in different countries. [42]

The punishment of offenders was to be facilitated by amendment of national legislation to punish offenders and extradition.[43]

---

36 1904 Agreement, *supra*.

37 Articles 1 and 2, *ibid.*

38 Articles 3 and 4, *ibid.*

39 Article 5, *ibid.*

40 Demleitner, *supra*, p. 168 (quoting Harris, H. W, *Human Merchandise: A study of the International Traffic in Women* (1928), p. 38). See also, *Report of the Special Rapporteur on Violence against Women, Its Causes and Consequences on Trafficking in Women, Women's Migration and Violence against Women.* E/CN.4/2000/68, para. 18 (hereinafter Special Rapporteur on Women (2000)).

41 20 UKTS 269.

42 *Ibid.*

43 Articles 3 and 5, *ibid.*

The description of trafficking, however, was more extensive under the 1910 Convention. While the 1904 Agreement focused on the procurement of women and girls, the 1910 Convention went further to use such terms as "enticing." The term "enticing" suggests, among other things, the use of deception.[44] The element of coercion was also included under the 1910 Convention. Article 2 spoke of trafficking with the use of violence, threats, and abuse of authority.[45] It is important to stress here that the use of coercion was one of the characteristics of slavery and the slave trade as described earlier. Moreover, the 1910 Convention added a phrase "even with her consent," meaning that trafficking could either be voluntary or involuntary.

The 1910 Convention was designed to address the process of the procurement and transportation of women and girls, and it did not specifically deal with the end purpose of prostitution. The retention of women and girls in brothels was excluded from application of the 1910 Convention because it was considered to be a matter of domestic jurisdiction.[46] Although States were required to criminalise trafficking, they were under no obligation to do the same with prostitution. Therefore, the 1910 Convention was criticised for its limited scope.[47]

After World War I, the League of Nations regarded the problem of trafficking as serious and decided to include a provision on trafficking in the text of the Covenant of the League of Nations.[48] Under the auspices of the League of Nations, two more international agreements on trafficking were adopted. The first was the *International Convention for the Suppression of the Traffic in Women and Children* 1921 (1921 Convention).[49] This Convention endorsed the description of trafficking under the 1910 Convention.[50] Therefore, prostitution and sexual exploitation were treated as an important part of trafficking. How-

44 It is worth noting that under the *Polish Penal Code*, the term "enticing" is interpreted to include this element. Centre for Reproductive Law and Policy, *Women of the World: Laws and Policies Affecting Their Reproductive Lives (East Central Europe)* (New York: Centre for Reproductive Law and Policy)(2000), p. 117. See Chapter 2 for the case study of Poland.

45 1910 Convention, *supra*.

46 United Nations Department of Economic and Social Affairs, *Study on Traffic in Persons and Prostitution*, ST/SOA/SD/8, p. 1(hereinafter 1959 Study). See also, Demleitner, *supra*, p. 169.

47 Chuang, J, 'Redirecting the Debate over Trafficking in Women: Definitions, Paradigms and Contexts,' 11 *Harvard Human Rights Journal* 65 (1998), pp. 74 and 75.

48 Article 23.1(c) of the Covenant of League of Nation, quoted in Farrior, S, 'The International Law on Trafficking in Women and Children for Prostitution: Making it Live Up to its Potential,' 10 *Harvard Human Rights Journal* 213 (1997), pp. 216 and 217.

49 9 LNTS 15.

50 Article 1, *ibid*.

ever, there are some differences in comparison with previous instruments. For instance, the term "white slave" was omitted from the title of the Convention. This is important as it shows the recognition by the international community that women and children of any race could be subjected to trafficking. Further, 1921 Convention applies to children of both sexes, unlike previous instruments which only applied to girls.

The second instrument was the *International Convention for the Suppression of the Traffic in Women of Full Age* 1933 (1933 Convention).[51] Trafficking was described in a similar language as the 1910 and 1921 Conventions, with the main focus once again placed upon prostitution and sexual exploitation.[52] In addition, the 1933 Convention retained the international character of trafficking, as it covered acts carried out in another State.[53] These two treaties adopted by the League of Nations were also ineffective, mainly because they continued to treat prostitution as a matter of domestic concern, and therefore did not oblige States to abolish the practice.[54]

The League of Nations recognised the fact that one of the contributing factors to the expansion of trafficking was the existence of brothels.[55] There was also a growing awareness that prostitution should not merely be a matter of domestic jurisdiction. As a result, in order to promote international action for abolition of brothels, and the prosecution and punishment of people managing them, the League of Nations prepared a draft convention in 1937, which was to be concluded in 1940. The convention was never adopted, due to the outbreak of World War II.

After World War II, the Economic and Social Council of the United Nations, in resolution 43 (IV)(1947), requested the Secretary-General to restart the study of the League of Nation's draft convention of 1937, make any amendments, and introduce necessary improvements.[56] This eventually led to the adoption of the *Convention for the Suppression of the Traffic in Persons and the Exploitation of the Prostitution of Others* 1949 (1949 Convention).[57] This instrument was a consolidated version of all of the treaties mentioned earlier. Nevertheless, the 1949 Convention was different from earlier treaties in some respects. For instance, it made an explicit connection between trafficking and exploitation of prostitu-

51 150 LNTS 431.

52 Article 1, *ibid.*

53 *Ibid.*

54 1959 Study, *supra*, pp. 1and 2; Demleitner, *supra*, p. 170; and Chuang, *supra*, p. 75. See also, Lassen, N, 'Slavery and Slavery-like Practices: United Nations Standards and Implementation,' 57 *Nordic Journal of International Law* 197 (1988).

55 1959 Study, *ibid.*, p. 2.

56 *Ibid.*

57 96 UNTS 271.

tion, as can be seen from the title of the Convention. This also is an instrument which is neutral in gender, and therefore recognises that men and boys can be trafficked for prostitution. In addition, the 1949 Convention covers trafficking that takes place both within and across national frontiers.

The 1949 Convention has been criticised on several grounds. It urged States Parties to suppress trafficking and to punish those who owned brothels.[58] Nevertheless, it did not specifically require States to prohibit prostitution itself. Article 6 provided that:

> Each Party to the present Convention agrees to take all the necessary measures to repeal or abolish any existing law, regulation or administrative provision by virtue of which persons who engage in or are suspected of engaging in prostitution are subject either to special registration or to the possession of a special document or to any exceptional requirements for supervision or notification.[59]

One reason for inclusion of this provision was that the drafters of the 1949 Convention feared "that prohibition would drive prostitution underground, and that laws designed to punish both the clients and the prostitutes, in practice, would be selectively enforced only against prostitutes."[60] In addition, the Convention was criticised on the ground that it did not take into account "modern forms of prostitution" such as sex tourism[61] and other forms of sexual exploitation which include, but are not limited to, forced labour and marriage.[62]

To summarise, the gender perspective with particular reference to prostitution dominated early views on trafficking. Although it has its roots in slavery and the slave trade, trafficking requires a distinct approach as it involves practices distinct from slavery and the slave trade. Therefore, it has also been dealt with separately from these practices under international law. Five instruments on trafficking were adopted from the beginning of the Twentieth Century, compared to two on slavery and slave trade.[63] Arguably, the international community

---

58 Articles 1 and 2, 1949 Convention, *supra*.

59 *Ibid.*

60 Demleitner, *supra*, p. 177. See also, *Report of the Working Group on Contemporary Forms of Slavery*, E/CN.4/Sub.2/1991/41.

61 Reanda, L, 'Prostitution as a Human Rights Question: Problems and Prospects of United Nations Action,' 13 *Human Rights Quarterly* 202 (1991), p. 210.

62 Special Rapporteur on Women (2000), *supra*, paras. 22 and 23. Although the Special Rapporteur gave this criticism in analysing 1949 Convention, it also applies to other earlier treaties, as they focused on prostitution and/or sexual exploitation.

63 In addition to the Slavery Convention, *Supplementary Convention on the Abolition of Slavery, the Slave Trade, and Institutions and Practices Similar to Slavery*, 226 UNTS 3, was adopted in 1956.

has made a moral distinction and regarded trafficking of women for prostitution to be a greater priority than slavery and the slave trade of African people.

1.4 Contemporary Views on Trafficking

1.4.1 Preliminary Consideration

Contemporary views on trafficking of human beings mark a departure from earlier views. As knowledge of the subject matter deepened, a wide variety of views on, and definitions of, trafficking have been advanced by different actors. Trafficking in modern times is commonly regarded as a "contemporary form of slavery."[64] The term denotes that it is different from the old or traditional form of slavery described above. While there is no internationally accepted definition of the "contemporary form of slavery," there is a set of characteristics which separate it from the traditional form of slavery. For instance, legal ownership of people is not a defining attribute under the contemporary form of slavery.[65] Under the traditional form of slavery, the ownership of slaves was legally registered to allow owners to protect their investments. However, it has been maintained that legal ownership has become less important in modern times because slaves can be replaced easily.[66] It is also the case that the contemporary form of slavery is less permanent. In addition, racial bias is not the key justification for enslavement under the contemporary form of slavery. While "ethnic and racial differences were used in the past to explain and excuse slavery," the profit to be made from slavery and the slave trade has become a more important consideration in modern times.[67]

Alongside this notion of trafficking as the contemporary form of slavery, the most important development in relation to trafficking is the adoption of the Trafficking Protocol. The drafting of this Protocol was set in motion when the United Nations General Assembly adopted a resolution establishing an Ad Hoc Committee to develop instruments on organised crime, including trafficking in 1999.[68] Not only States, but also other actors such as NGOs played an important

---

64 See for example, Rassam, *supra*; Section 102(a), *Victims of Trafficking and Violence Protection Act of 2000* (106th Congress of the United States of America), H.R. 3244; and *Reports of the Working Group on Contemporary Forms of Slavery*, E/CN.4/Sub.2/1995/28/Add.1, E/CN.4/Sub2/1999/17, and E/CN.4/Sub.2/2001/30.

65 Bales, *supra*, p. 9.

66 *Ibid*, p. 7.

67 *Ibid.*, pp. 10 and 11. See also, Hartsough, *supra*, p. 83.

68 A/RES/53/111 (Transnational Organised Crime). For the political and legal developments leading to the adoption of the Organised Crime Convention, see Vlassis, D, *The United Nations Convention Against Transnational Organized Crime and its Three Protocol: Development and Outlook*.

part in developing these instruments.[69] After a series of sessions, the Committee finalised the Organised Crime Convention and Trafficking and Smuggling Protocols, which were subsequently adopted in Palermo, Italy in December 2000. Article 3 of the Trafficking Protocol stipulates that:

> (a) "Trafficking in persons" shall mean the recruitment, transportation, transfer, harbouring, or receipt of persons, by means of threat or use of force or other forms of coercion, of abduction, of fraud, of deception, of the abuse of power or of a position of vulnerability or of the giving or receiving of payments or benefits to achieve the consent of a person having control over another person, for the purpose of exploitation. Exploitation shall include, at the minimum, the exploitation of the prostitution of others or other forms of sexual exploitation, forced labour or services, slavery or practices similar to slavery, servitude or removal of organs;
>
> (b) The consent of a victim of trafficking in persons to the intended exploitation set forth in the subparagraph (a) of this article shall be irrelevant where any of the means set forth in the subparagraph (a) have been used;
>
> (c) The recruitment, transportation, transfer, harbouring or receipt of a child for exploitation shall be considered "trafficking in persons" even if this does not involve any of the means set forth in subparagraph (a) of this article;
>
> (d) "Child" shall mean any person under eighteen years of age.[70]

The relationship between trafficking and slavery/enslavement is critical. While it may be easy to treat these two acts synonymously, trafficking and slavery are not necessarily the same. This becomes clear in analysing the meaning of enslavement and slavery. The key element of slavery as stipulated in the Slavery Convention is the right of ownership. In the context of trafficking of human beings, subsequent exploitation can effectively amount to slavery[71] because the right of ownership is fully exercised and retained when people are exploited in the sex and other industries in States of destination.

Such an interpretation is consistent with the opinion of the International Criminal Tribunal for the Former Yugoslavia (ICTY) in the *Kunarac* case,[72] which elaborated on the meaning of slavery and enslavement under interna-

69 Potts, L. G, 'Global Trafficking in Human Beings: Assessing Success of the United Nations Protocol to Prevent Trafficking in Persons,' 35 *George Washington International Law Review* 227 (2003), pp. 238 and 239.

70 Trafficking Protocol, *supra*.

71 Rijken, *supra*, p. 75.

72 *Prosecutor v. Kunarac,* IT-96-23, Trial Judgement, 22 February 2001.

tional law. The Trial Chamber noted that a mere ability, among others, to buy, sell, or trade people, although an important factor to be taken into consideration, is in itself insufficient in determining whether or not the enslavement is committed.[73] This suggests that something more than transporting is necessary. Trafficking, then, may be treated as slavery simultaneously mainly when people are exploited afterwards by traffickers themselves as this ensures the continuous exercise of the right of ownership. In other words, if people are exploited by those other than traffickers when they reach their destination, the continuous exercise of ownership on the part of traffickers is terminated, and therefore trafficking may not be easily regarded as slavery. In this respect, the Trial Chamber held that "the duration of the suspected exercise of powers attaching to the right of ownership is another factor that may be considered when determining whether someone was enslaved." [74]

A question may also be raised whether or not subsequent exploitation of people is a necessary element of trafficking. It has been maintained that for an act to constitute trafficking, the element of subsequent exploitation must be present.[75] This may, however, turn out to be problematic, because not all trafficked people are exploited afterwards, due to an early interception by the law enforcement authorities in States of destination, for example. Under such circumstances, an act may not be regarded as trafficking even when victims experience a wide variety of human rights abuses during the process. An alternative approach is to treat subsequent exploitation a sufficient, but not a necessary, element of trafficking. Such an interpretation of trafficking seems to be in conformity with the definition under the Trafficking Protocol. The phrase "for the purpose of" can be interpreted merely to mean *mens rea* to facilitate exploitation. This makes the offence of trafficking intact even when people are not exploited afterwards, provided that *mens rea* on the part of traffickers is established. A similar view is supported by some commentators.[76]

In addition, the definition of trafficking should not to be confused with "smuggling of human beings." The adoption of the Smuggling Protocol illustrates that these two acts are different. Article 3 of the Smuggling Protocol defines smuggling as:

---

73 *Ibid.*, para. 543.

74 *Ibid.*, para. 542.

75 Piotrowicz, R, 'European Initiatives in the Protection of Victims of Trafficking Who Give Evidence Against Their Traffickers' 14 *International Journal of Refugee Law* 263 (2000), p. 266.

76 Chuang, *supra*, p. 79, quoting the separate definitions of trafficking and subsequent exploitation (forced labour and slavery-like practices) adopted by the Global Alliance Against Trafficking in Women (GAATW), and Rijken, *supra*, pp. 57-61.

> The procurement, in order to obtain, directly or indirectly, a financial or other material benefit, of illegal entry of a person into a State Party of which the person is not a national or permanent resident.[77]

The following key elements of trafficking can be identified in comparing these two definitions. First, unlike trafficking, smuggling does not entail coercion or deception, indicating that smuggling is a voluntary act on the part of those smuggled.[78] Second, the services of smugglers end when those smuggled have reached their destination, while trafficking can result in people being subsequently exploited. Third, smuggling entails international movements, whereas trafficking can take place both within and across national frontiers. Fourth, smuggling entails illegal entry into a given State, and entry can both be legal and illegal in the case of trafficking. Smuggling, therefore, can be summarised as an act of facilitating illegal migration.[79]

The distinction between trafficking and smuggling is more likely to result in separate legislative and law enforcement responses.[80] The use of coercion or deception by traffickers as well as subsequent exploitation have the effect of portraying those trafficked as victims of human rights abuses,[81] and this reinforces a case for their protection even when they enter into a State and/or stay illegally. However, the definition of smuggling means that those smuggled are willing participants in illegal migration[82] and this may provide a justification for States to apply strict enforcement measures such as arrest, detention and deportation against them.[83] As will be shown later, however, smuggling of human beings has

77 Smuggling Protocol, *supra*.

78 Twomey, P, 'Europe's Other Market: Trafficking in People,' 2 *European Journal of Migration and Law* 1 (2000), p. 7.

79 For *Travaux Preparatoires* of the Smuggling Protocol, see A/AC.254/4/Add.1/Rev. 1- 6, and A/55/383/Add.1.

80 Hyland, K. E, 'Protecting Human Victims of Trafficking: An American Framework,' 16 *Berkeley Women's Law Journal* 29 (2001), p. 34.

81 *Smuggling and Trafficking in Persons and the Protection of Their Human Rights: Note by the Secretary-General*, E/CN.4/Sub.2/2001/26, para. 22; Miller, A, and A. N. Stewart, 'Report from the Roundtable on the Meaning of "Trafficking in Persons": A Human Rights Perspective,' 20 *Women's Rights Law Reporter* 11 (1998), p. 17; and Hartsough, *supra*, p. 95.

82 Cooper, B, 'A New Approach to Protection and Law Enforcement under the Victims of Trafficking and Violence Protection Act,' 51 *Emory Law Journal* 1041 (2002), p. 1047; and Piotrowicz, *supra,* p. 266, footnote 10.

83 Gallagher, A, 'Human Rights and the New UN Protocols on Trafficking and Migrant Smuggling: A Preliminary Analysis,' 23 *Human Rights Quarterly* 975 (2001), p. 1000.

human rights dimensions, and therefore the distinction between trafficking and smuggling can undermine the human rights of those smuggled.

These core elements of trafficking may be better understood by analysing them through different aspects of the practice: migration, gender, organised crime and human rights. These aspects are chosen as trafficking in modern times is commonly identified and analysed through these lenses by different actors involved. These aspects, however, should not be treated in isolation, because they overlap with one another. Therefore, a clear line cannot be drawn among them. The key questions which will be examined are whether or not the scope of the definition under the Trafficking Protocol is broad enough to accommodate different views held by actors, and the extent to which its provisions reflect some or all of the diverse and sometimes competing perspectives.

1.4.2 Trafficking and Migration

1.4.2.1 Illegal Migration

A starting point is to analyse the relationship between trafficking and illegal migration. Some actors, particularly States,[84] emphasise this aspect. This inevitably limits the scope of trafficking to international movements. Although illegal migration may be one aspect of trafficking, it is not an accurate illustration of the phenomenon.[85] To begin with, in some cases, traffickers arrange authentic travel documents and visas, and migrants enter into a State legally. Consequently, migration itself is not illegal. A study on trafficking of women from Central and Eastern Europe, conducted by the International Organisation for Migration (IOM) in 1995, illustrated that women often entered legally into Belgium, the Netherlands, and Switzerland as entertainers.[86] In addition, people can be trafficked internally. As will be shown in Chapter 2, transporting of Thai nationals as well as hill tribe people from rural areas to large cities such as Bangkok for prostitution and sexual exploitation is regarded as trafficking by some of those concerned, particularly NGOs.

---

84 See Chapter 2 on case studies of the Thailand, Poland and the United Kingdom. See further Secretariat of the Budapest Group, *The Relationship between Organised Crime and Trafficking in Aliens* (Vienna: International Centre for Immigration Policy and Development(ICMPD))(1999), p. 2.

85 Drew, S, 'Human Trafficking: A Modern Form of Slavery?' 4 *European Human Rights Law Review* 481 (2002), p. 489.

86 IOM, *Trafficking and Prostitution : The Growing Exploitation of Migrant Women from Central and Eastern Europe (Migration Information Programme)* (Budapest: IOM)(1995)(hereinafter IOM (1995)). The evidence of legal entry can also be found in Austria (IOM, *Trafficking of Women into Austria for Sexual Exploitation (Migration Information Programme)* (Vienna: IOM and Austrian Ministry of Women's Affairs)(1996)) and Italy (IOM, *Trafficking of Women into Italy for Sexual Exploitation (Migration Information Programme)*(Geneva: IOM)(1996)).

Many actors recently recognised that confining trafficking to illegal international movement limits the understanding of the phenomenon, and have accordingly adopted wider definitions. For instance, the Council of Europe adopted the following definition, in *Recommendation R (2000)11* on action against trafficking in human beings for the purpose of sexual exploitation:

> the procurement by one or more natural or legal persons and/or the organisation of the exploitation and/or transport or migration – legal or illegal – of persons, even with their consent, for the purpose of their sexual exploitation, *inter alia* by means of coercion, in particular violence or threats, deceit, abuse of authority or of a position of vulnerability. [87]

The view that trafficking involves both legal and illegal migration is also shared by the United States[88] and the IOM.[89]

These views are reflected in the Trafficking Protocol. During the drafting stage of this Protocol, a discussion arose as to whether or not trafficking should be confined to international movement. It is worth noting in this respect that all drafts of the Protocol contained the term "international trafficking."[90] Many delegates felt the necessity for this inclusion in order to make the Protocol compatible with the Organized Crime Convention.[91] Nevertheless, the view was increasingly taken that inclusion of the term "international" limited the scope of the instrument and that it failed to protect all persons who were victims of trafficking.[92] This latter view prevailed.

However, the scope of the definition is constrained by Article 4 of the Trafficking Protocol. It provides that the offence of trafficking must be transnational

---

87 Adopted by the Committee of Ministers on 19 May 2000 at the 710th meeting of Ministers' Deputies.

88 Section 102(b)(5), *Victims of Trafficking and Violence Protection Act of 2000*, *supra*.

89 IOM, *Trafficking in Migrants: IOM Policy and Responses*, MC/EX/INF/58 (10/5/99) (hereinafter IOM Policy on Trafficking). The IOM's working definition of trafficking stipulates that the phenomenon can occur when 1) a migrant is illicitly engaged (recruited, kidnapped, sold, etc) and/or moved either within national or across international borders; and 2) intermediaries (traffickers) during any part of this process obtain economic or other profit by means of deception, coercion and/or other forms of exploitation under conditions that violate the fundamental human rights of migrants. See Chapter 3 for an analysis of activities of the IOM.

90 From first through seventh drafts A/AC.254/Add.3/Rev.1 through 7.

91 A/AC.254/4/Add.3/Rev.5, footnote 18.

92 *Ibid.*

in nature.[93] Under Article 3 of the Organised Crime Convention, trafficking can be regarded as transnational in nature if:

(a) It is committed in more than one State,
(b) It is committed in one State but a substantial part of its preparation, planning, direction, or control takes place in another State;
(c) It is committed in one State but involves an organized criminal group that engages in criminal activities in more than one State; or
(d) It is committed in one State but has substantial effects in another State.[94]

This Article excludes certain forms of trafficking which take place within national borders. For instance, when the preparation and planning are conducted within a State, internal transportation cannot be considered as trafficking under subparagraph (b). Subparagraph (c) also suggests that an act is not within the ambit of the Protocol definition if it is carried out by individual traffickers and/or when activities of the organised criminal groups do not extend beyond national borders. Moreover, internal transportation is likely to be excluded from the scope of the definition under subparagraph (d), if it does not have substantial effects in another State.

An added complication can also be found in smuggling of human beings. As clearly illustrated by the definition above, smuggling is an intermediary function which facilitates illegal crossing of borders.[95] Although smugglers may arrange false passports, driving licences, visas, and other documents in order to assist individuals to migrate, an entry may not be totally illegal at all times. There are cases where smugglers assist individuals in arranging authentic travel and identity documents and visas, and receive a large sum of money in return.[96] As for

93 *supra.*

94 Organized Crime Convention, *ibid.*

95 See further, Pomodoro, L, 'Trafficking and Sexual Exploitation of Women and Children,' in Williams and Vlassis (eds.), *Combating Transnational Crime: Concepts, Activities and Responses* (London: Frank Cass)(2001), p. 238; Jordan, A, 'Trafficking in Human Beings: The Slavery That Surrounds Us,' *Arresting Transnational Organized Crime: An Electronic Journal of U.S. Department of States.* Vol. 6, No.2 (2001), at http://usinfo.state.gov/journals/itgic/0801/ijge/gj05.htm; O'Neill Richard, A, *International Trafficking in Women to the United States: A Contemporary Manifestation of Slavery and Organised Crime* (Washington D.C.: Center for Study of Intelligence(CIA))(2000), p. v; and Emerton, R, *Trafficking of Women into Hong Kong for the Purpose of Prostitution: Preliminary Research Findings* (Occasional Paper No. 3)(Hong Kong: Centre for Comparative and Public Law)(2000), p. 2.

96 The author's experience as a legal clerk at the United Nations High Commissioner for Refugees Regional Office of Japan and the Republic of Korea between February and September 2000.

those smuggled, turning to smugglers, as opposed to regular travel agencies, may be a preferred alternative, as activities of smugglers are clandestine and they can avoid direct contacts with State authorities. This benefits those who would face persecution if they come in contact with their governments, for example.

1.4.2.2 Coercion and Lack of Consent

Another important element of migration is coercion. This element in the definition under the Trafficking Protocol makes it clear that people cannot be trafficked voluntarily, and some commentators also support this view.[97] However, the meaning of coercion can be complex. For instance, the scope of coercion is broad in that it can be physical (visible) or psychological (less visible),[98] and terms such as threat/use of force, violence, and abuse of authority in the definition under the Trafficking Protocol do not necessarily have distinctions. A question has also been raised as to whether or not deception forms part of coercion.[99]

Although the definition of trafficking suggests that coercion or deception are used by traffickers when they are recruiting and transporting people from States of origin to destination, some causal factors behind trafficking should also be interpreted as coercive. In addition to economic hardship in their States of origin, which is one of the major causes of trafficking, many escape from persecution by States, armed conflicts, and terrorism.[100] Although traffickers may not be directly responsible for triggering these causes of trafficking, they do take advantage and profit from them. It has been argued in this regard that the definition of trafficking under the Trafficking Protocol is broad enough to include these causal factors.[101]

---

97 Salt, J, and J. Hogarth, 'Definitions of the Concepts of Trafficking, Smuggling, and Organized Crime,' in Laczko and Thompson (eds.), *Migrant Trafficking and Human Smuggling in Europe: A Review of the evidence with case studies from Hungary, Poland and Ukraine* (Geneva: IOM)(2000), p. 21; and Inglis, *supra*, p. 67.

98 Chiang, L, 'Trafficking in Women,' in Askin and Koening (eds.), *Women and International Human Rights Law Volume I* (New York: Transnational Publishers)(1999), p. 324.

99 *Ibid.*

100 *Refugee Protection and Migration Control: Perspectives from UNHCR and IOM, Global Consultation on International Protection*, E/GC/01/11 (May 2001), para. 29.

101 Malone, L. A, 'Economic Hardship as Coercion under the Protocol on International Trafficking in Persons by Organised Crime Elements,' 25 *Fordham International Law Journal* 54 (2001), pp. 89-91. Chuang also discusses the possibility of treating economic hardship as a form of coercion, *supra*, pp. 93-94. However, Rijken notes that "the use of coercion by the traffickers will be more difficult to prove if economic circumstances can be seen as a form of coercion," *supra*, p. 62.

Moreover, with respect to the distinction between trafficking and smuggling, coercion attached to trafficking risks portraying those smuggled as willing participants. This can be problematic, as many people experience coercion during the process of smuggling. Many of them are placed under harsh conditions and are subjected to torture and other inhuman or degrading treatments during their journey.[102] Further, many people lose their lives during the smuggling process. In 2001, for instance, an overcrowded ship with smuggled migrants on board sank off the coast of Indonesia and 356 people died as a result.[103] Such cases of fatalities have also been reported in Ireland, Libya, Mexico, Niger, the United Kingdom and the United States of America.[104]

Also relevant to the element of coercion is a lack of consent. Subparagraph (b), Article 3 of the Trafficking Protocol stipulates that consent is irrelevant if any of the means to achieve trafficking described in subparagraph (a) are used. This widens the scope of protection of individuals.[105] Not only those who are forcibly trafficked, but also those who give their initial consent but later withdraw it also can be included. Nevertheless, the element of consent also raises conceptual difficulties. For example, it is an element which can make one a victim or a collaborator of trafficking. In many cases, people are coerced and/or deceived into trafficking without any knowledge of subsequent exploitation. Under these circumstances, they can clearly be seen as victims and therefore it becomes easier for different actors to provide protection. Nevertheless, many do have some knowledge of what trafficking involves, and yet agree to be part of it. Ghosh notes that some migrants turn to traffickers deliberately in order to elude immigration laws and regulations and to pursue economic gains.[106] In other cases, people are aware of the subsequent exploitation. Many Eastern European women trafficked to Western Europe, for instance, know that they are being recruited for prostitution.[107] Under these circumstances, those trafficked can be treated as collaborators by States as they willingly participate in the process and even co-operate with traffickers.[108] In sum, the existence of consent can be used to distinguish between those who require protection and those who do not.

102 Tessier, K, 'The New Slave Trade: The International Crisis of Immigrant Smuggling,' 3 *Global Legal Studies Journal* 261 (1995-1996), p. 261.

103 *Report of the Special Rapporteur on Migrants*, E/CN.4/2002/94, para. 32 (hereinafter Special Rapporteur on Migrants 2002).

104 *Written Statement Submitted by Human Rights Advocates International*, E/CN.4/2002/NGO/45, paras. 4-14 (hereinafter Human Rights Advocate (2002)).

105 Chuang, *supra*, p. 89.

106 Ghosh, B, *Huddled Masses and Uncertain Shores: Insights into Irregular Migration* (The Hague: Kluwer Law International)(1998), p. 23.

107 IOM (1995), *supra*.

108 For more discussion on the matter, see Chuang, *supra*.

1.4.3 Trafficking and Gender

It was shown above that early views on trafficking focused mainly upon prostitution and/or sexual exploitation of women and girls. Some organisations and commentators in modern times strongly maintain this link.[109] One modern contributing factor for this is the emergence of stronger advocacy for women's human rights.[110] Since the creation of the United Nations in 1945, protection of women's rights has been high on its agenda. This is evident in the adoption of more than 20 different instruments which include provisions on the status and treatment of women.[111] In the case of trafficking, because women and girls have been the primary victims for prostitution and sexual exploitation, it has been treated as an issue affecting women's human rights,[112] particularly as a form of violence against them.[113]

Such a link does reflect the reality to some extent. Prostitution and sexual exploitation are still common forms of subsequent exploitation. It has been estimated that the annual profit made by trafficking of women for prostitution and sexual exploitation amounts to between $ 7 and 12 billion.[114] Compared to drug or arms trafficking, trafficking in women is said to be relatively low-risk and highly profitable,[115] because the detection capabilities of the law enforcement agencies are not as strong as those adopted to tackle other forms of trafficking, and the penalties are less severe.[116]

Nevertheless, people are also trafficked for purposes other than prostitution and sexual exploitation. It has been reported that about one quarter of

---

109 Hughes, D. M, 'The "Natasha" Trade: The Transnational Shadow Market of Trafficking in Women,' 53 *Journal of International Affairs* 625 (2000), pp. 627 and 628; Demleitner, *supra*; Dolgopol, U, 'Women's Voice, Women's Pain,' 17 *Human Rights Quarterly* 127 (1995); Barry, K, 'Female Sexual Slavery: Understanding the International Dimensions of Women's Oppression,' 3 *Human Rights Quarterly* 44 (1981); and Farrior, *supra*.

110 See below for the linkage between trafficking and human rights in general.

111 Toepfer, S. J, and B. S. Wells, 'The Worldwide Market for Sex: A Review of International and Regional Legal Prohibitions Regarding Trafficking in Women,' 2 *Michigan Journal of Gender & Law* 83 (1994), p. 93.

112 Chiang, *supra*, p. 324.

113 See, for example, *Vienna Declaration and Programme of Action* (A/CONF.157/23)(1993), para. 13; and *Report of the Special Rapporteur on Violence against Women*, E/CN.4/2001/73.

114 Hughes, *supra*, pp. 625 and 628 .

115 *Ibid.*, p. 625.

116 Office of the High Commissioner for Human Rights (OHCHR), 'Trafficking in People: The Human Rights Dimension,' in Williams and Vlassis (eds.), *Combating Transnational Crime*, *supra*, p. 245.

the entire population of those trafficked are exploited sexually.[117] This suggests that the majority are trafficked for other purposes. The need to pay attention to other forms of exploitation is recognised by the UN Special Rapporteurs on Violence against Women and on Sales of Children, Child Prostitution and Child Pornography,[118] NGOs such as the Foundation Against Trafficking in Women, the International Human Rights Law Group, and the Global Alliance Against Trafficking in Women,[119] and the Organisation for Security and Co-operation in Europe (OSCE).[120]

Another problem is that the debates on trafficking from a gender perspective tend to focus more on prostitution rather than on the process of trafficking. Scholars and women's organisations typically fall into two distinct groups in dealing with prostitution. One group condemns both voluntary and involuntary prostitution on the ground that prostitution is never entirely consensual and reduces all women to nothing more than pure sex objects.[121] The other group accepts the right of women to choose prostitution as a career and condemns sex trafficking only when the career choice is non-consensual or when the conditions imposed on a consensual sex worker are inhumane or unanticipated.[122] Whichever view one takes, focusing too much on prostitution and/or sexual exploitation can be to the detriment of a comprehensive analysis of trafficking, particularly because subsequent exploitation is a sufficient, but not necessary, element of the practice as noted earlier.

---

117 Hughes, *supra*, p. 628, quoting an estimate given by the United Nations.

118 Special Rapporteur on Women (2000), *supra*, para. 13; and *Report of the Special Rapporteur on Sales of Children, Child Prostitution and Child Pornography*, E/CN.4/1999/71, paras. 53-86.

119 GAATW, 'Appendix A: Human Rights Standard for the Treatment of Trafficked Persons,' in *Human Rights and Trafficking in Persons: A Handbook, supra.*

120 OSCE. *ODIHR Background Paper 1999/3, Trafficking in Human Beings: Implications for the OSCE* at http://www.osce.org/documents/odihr/1999/09/1503_en.html. This definition is based on the definition used or recommended by the UN Special Rapporteur on Violence Against Women, the Human Rights Caucus, and the President's Inter-Agency Council on Women (United States). It should be noted, however, that after the adoption of the Trafficking Protocol in December 2000, the OSCE adopted the definition given in that Protocol. See Kartusch, A, *Reference Guide Anti-Trafficking Legislative Review with Particular Emphasis on South Eastern Europe* (Warsaw: OSCE/ODIHR) (2001), p. 9.

121 Tiefenbrun, S, 'The Saga of Susannah a U.S. Remedy For Sex Trafficking in Women: The Victims of Trafficking and Violence Protection Act of 2002,' *Utah Law Review* 107 (2002), p. 124

122 *Ibid.* See also, Hague, C. H, 'Prostitution of Women and International Human Rights Law: Transforming Exploitation into Equality,' 8 *New York International Law Review* 23 (1995), pp. 24 and 25

In this respect, the definition in the Trafficking Protocol is neutral in gender. During the drafting stage, a question was raised as to whether or not it should only address women and children. Argentina, one of the proponents of the draft Protocol, expressed a view in support of a focus specifically on women and children, with an explicit link to prostitution and/or sexual exploitation.[123] Nevertheless, at the Second Session of the Ad Hoc Committee, held in March 1999, almost all States expressed the view that the Protocol should address all persons.[124] Consequently, at the Fourth Session of the Ad Hoc Committee, a revised version of the Protocol was submitted, and the language was changed from "women and children" to "all persons, especially women and children."[125]

The need to include all persons regardless of gender is also reflected in the content of subsequent exploitation under the Trafficking Protocol. During the drafting stage, more and more participating States were of the opinion that other forms of exploitation should be included. Australia and Canada, for instance, proposed that the term "forced labour," under the definition contained in the *Forced Labour Convention* 1930, should be added.[126] Belarus was also of the opinion that the removal of organs and organic tissues should also be included as a form of exploitation.[127] This willingness to widen the scope of exploitation was the result of numerous discussions held on the matter by different actors in modern times.

1.4.4 Trafficking and Organised Crime

Another important aspect of trafficking is its linkage with organised crime. Although organised crime has existed for a long time, it was only recently that the need to address it has been expressed at the national, regional and international levels.[128] The growth of organised criminal activities in modern times is a by-product of globalisation. The globalised economy has provided new opportunities not only for business in licit markets, but also criminal and/or underground enterprises in the black or illicit markets.[129] While advancement

123 A/AC.254/4/Add.3/Rev.1.

124 A/AC.254/4/Add.3/Rev.2. International organisations as well as NGOs also shared the same view. Gallagher, *supra*, p. 983.

125 *Ibid.*

126 *Ibid.*

127 A/AC.254/5/Add.19. On this subject, see Morelli, M.N, 'Organ Trafficking: Legislative Proposals to Protect Minors, ' 10 *American University Journal of International Law and Policy* 917 (1995); and Krueger, J, 'Life Coming Bravely of Death: Organ Donation Legislation across European Countries,' 18 *Wisconsin International Law Journal* 321 (2000).

128 Secretariat of the Budapest Group, *supra*, pp. 5-10.

129 Williams, P, and G. Baudin-O'Hayon, 'Global Governance, Transnational Organized Crime and Money Laundering' in Held and McGrew (eds.), *Governing Globali-*

of technology in communication, transportation, financial transaction may be regarded as positive aspects of globalisation, these are simultaneously exploited by organised criminal groups in promoting illegal business.[130]

What is an organised crime? The Organised Crime Convention does not provide a specific definition. Instead, organised crime is understood as "serious crimes" committed by "organised criminal groups." According to Article 2(a) of the Convention,

> "Organised criminal group" shall mean a structured group of three or more persons, existing for a period of time and acting in concert with the aim of committing one or more serious crimes or offences established in accordance with this Convention, in order to obtain, directly or indirectly, a financial or other material benefit.[131]

"A structured group" means "a group that is not randomly formed for the immediate commission of an offence and that does not need to have formally defined roles for its members, continuity of its membership or a developed structure" while "serious crime" is "conduct constituting an offence punishable by a maximum deprivation of liberty of at least four years or a more serious penalty."[132]

The involvement of organised criminal groups in trafficking has become more apparent in modern times. It has been noted that this marks the transition from the traditional form of slavery to modern trafficking of human beings.[133] One of the reasons why organised criminal groups engage in trafficking is the high profit they can make and low risks of carrying it out. The demand for trafficked people exists in the States of destination,[134] and organised criminal groups quickly respond to it by supplying people. For those wishing to travel, they rely on traffickers because of the reduced possibilities for legal migration in States of destination, and they are able to arrange clandestine long- distance travel.[135]

---

zation: *Power, Authority and Global Governance* (Cambridge: Polity Press)(2002), p. 131.

130 *Ibid.*, pp. 131and 132.

131 Organised Crime Convention, *supra*.

132 Articles 2 (b) and (c), *ibid.*

133 Iselin, *supra*, pp. 4 and 6.

134 Secretariat of the Budapest Group, *supra*, p. 16.

135 *Ibid.*, pp. 14 and 15.

Organised criminal groups such as *Triad* (Hong Kong) and *Yakuza* (Japan)[136] are infamous for engaging in trafficking operations.[137] The profits made from trafficking of human beings in turn are used to finance other criminal activities such as extortion, racketeering, money laundering, bribery of public officials, drug use, gambling, loan sharking, and document forgery.[138] Organised criminal groups, then, seek to maximise long-term, rather than short-term, profit.

The study of organised crime has been associated with an economic analysis of criminal organisations.[139] Under this analysis, selling of illegal goods and services is the primary purpose of organised crime, and organised criminal groups are regarded as rational entities which attempt to maximise profits by responding to demand for such illegal goods and services.[140] In this sense, the activities of organised criminal groups are comparable to legal corporate entities, except that organised criminal groups operate in illegal markets.[141] In relation to trafficking of human beings, some commentators utilise this economic analysis to understand the act. Salt and Stein, for instance, propose a model which divides trafficking into the three stages of mobilisation (recruitment), en route, and integration.[142] Linking trafficking and organised crime, Schloenhardt illustrates that trafficking is a major source of income for organised criminal groups.[143]

One advantage of using this economic analysis of organised crime and trafficking is that it allows one to understand the dynamics of supply and demand in the trafficking market.[144] As noted previously, between 600,000 to 800,000 people are trafficked globally each year.[145] This demonstrates that the supply of

136 Guymon, C.D, 'International Legal Mechanisms for Combating Transnational Organized Crime: The Need for a Multilateral Convention,' 18 *Berkeley Journal of International Law* 53 (2000), pp. 60 and 61.

137 The profiles of traffickers are also explored in Chapter 2.

138 O'Neil Richard, *supra*, p. 1.

139 Schloenhardt, *supra*. The author provides a detailed account of the economic analysis of crime (including organised crime) conducted by different commentators.

140 *Ibid.*, pp. 204 and 205.

141 *Ibid.*, p. 206.

142 Salt, J, and J. Stein, 'Migration as a Business: The Case of Trafficking' 35 (4) *International Migration* 467 (1997).

143 Schloenhardt, *supra*, pp. 212 and 213. He argues that illegal markets are created by strict border control and immigration laws and policies. See also Williams, P, 'Human Commodity Trafficking: An Overview,' in *Illegal Migration and Commercial Sex*, *supra*, p. 1

144 Morrison, J, and B. Crosland, *Trafficking and Smuggling of Refugees: The End Game in European Asylum Policy? (New Issues in Refugee Research, Working Paper No. 39)* (Geneva: UNHCR)(2001), p. 7; and Twomey, *supra*, p. 17.

145 Trafficking Report 2005, *supra*.

trafficked people is abundant. There is also a high demand in States of destinations for trafficked people in domestic work, manufacturing, construction and the sex industry, and traffickers keep transporting a large number of people to meet this.[146] Another advantage of using an economic analysis is that it provides a better basis for understanding the "ordered system of social networks and institutions" under which trafficking is conducted in modern times.[147] In other words, it can promote better understanding of *modus operandi* by organised criminal groups.

However, the linkage between trafficking and organised crime itself does not provide a full picture of trafficking, for the reason that it is also carried out by those other than organised criminal groups. As will be shown in Chapter 2, families, relatives and friends facilitate trafficking in Thailand. Although this is done mainly due to economic reasons such as poverty, the selling of offspring is said to be an established part of the culture there. Further, criminals, organised or otherwise, are not the sole facilitators of trafficking. Legitimate entities such as private corporations (e.g. construction, textile, and garments), job recruitment agencies, and overseas marriage consultant agencies, have become part of trafficking in one way or another.[148] Moreover, it has recently been discovered that the members of national armed forces or international peacekeeping missions also participate in trafficking.[149] Trafficking conducted by these individuals or organisations can be as sophisticated as organised criminal groups. One question raised here is whether or not organised criminal groups should receive heavier penalties than family, friends, or employees of the international organisations. Obviously this is a question which is rather difficult to answer, as it involves moral choices. It suffices to state, however, that focusing too much on organised crime may run a risk of ignoring other actors.

1.4.5 Trafficking and Human Rights

It has widely been accepted in modern times that trafficking entails human rights dimensions as noted earlier. The focuses of actors are different, reflecting their

146 Taylor, I, and R. Jamison, 'Sex Trafficking and the Mainstream of Market Culture,' 32 *Crime, Law & Social Change* 257(1999), pp. 260-263.

147 Salt and Stein, *supra*, p. 484.

148 Ruggiero, V, 'Trafficking in Human Beings: Slaves in Contemporary Europe,' 25 *International Journal of Sociology of Law* 231 (1997), pp. 236-238.

149 On this, UNICRI, *supra*; Human Rights Watch (2002), *supra*; *Written Statements Submitted by the Human Rights Advocates International*, E/CN/4/2002/NGO/43 and E/CN.4/2003/NGO/40; Talleyrand, I, 'Military Prostitution: How the Authorities Worldwide Aid and Abet International Trafficking in Women,' 27 *Syracuse Journal of International Law and Commerce* 151 (2000); and Rawski, F, 'To Waive or not to Waive: Immunity and Accountability in U.N. Peacekeeping Operations,' 11 *Connecticut Journal of International Law* 103 (2002).

views. As shown above, individuals and organisations dealing with women's issues address prostitution and other such relevant matters as discrimination and violence against women. Those concerned with children's rights focus on, among other things, child labour and prostitution resulting from trafficking.[150] Moreover, those involved in the protection of asylum seekers and refugees pay particular attention to counter measures such as immigration control and their impact on the human rights of those trafficked who may qualify as refugees.[151]

In addressing trafficking in human rights terms, many rely on the existing international human rights instruments.[152] There is a wide range of instruments both at regional and international levels which can be applicable to trafficking of human beings. At a regional level, there are three instruments which are pertinent to trafficking. The European Union (EU) recently adopted the *Charter of Fundamental Rights of the European Union* 2000, Article 5(3) of which provides for the prohibition of trafficking of human beings.[153] The *Convention on Action against Trafficking in Human Beings* was also adopted by the Council of Europe in 2005.[154] In the Americas, Article 6(1) of the *American Convention on Human Rights* 1969 (ACHR) speaks of trafficking in women,[155] and the Organisation of American States (OAS) adopted the *Inter-American Convention on International Traffic in Minors* 1994.[156] Moreover, the *Convention on Preventing and Combating Trafficking in Women and Children for Prostitution* 2002 was adopted by States belonging to the South Asian Association for Regional Cooperation (SAARC).[157]

---

150 Somerset, C, *What the Professionals Know: The Trafficking of Children into and through the United Kingdom for Sexual Purposes* (London: ECPAT UK)(2001); ILO, *Specialised Training Manual on Psychological Counselling for Trafficked Youth: Handling the Trauma for Sexual Exploitation* (2002); ILO, *Creating a Healing Environment: Psychosocial Rehabilitation and Occupational Integration of Child Survivors of Trafficking and Other Worst Forms of Child Labour* (2002); and ILO, *Promotion of Gender Equality in Action Against Child Labour and Trafficking: A Practical Guide for Organisations* (2003).

151 Morrison and Crosland, *supra*; Twomey, *supra*; and UNHCR and IOM, *supra*.

152 Toepfer and Wells, *supra*; Farrior, *supra*; Chiang, *supra*; Chuang, *supra*; GAATW (2001), *supra*; and Gallagher, *supra*.

153 Article 5(3) OJ C 364/1 (18/12/00).

154 ETS No. 197.

155 1144 UNTS 123.

156 Organisation of American States at http://www.oas.org/juridico/english/Treaties/b-57.html.

157 SAARC Convention on Preventing and Combating Trafficking in Women and Children for Prostitution. Member States are Bangladesh, Bhutan, India, Maldives, Nepal, Pakistan and Sri Lanka.

There are also relevant human rights instruments at international level. While Article 6 of the *Convention on the Elimination of All Forms of Discrimination Against Women* 1979 (CEDAW), urges States to "suppress all forms of traffic in women and exploitation of prostitution of women,"[158] Article 35 of the *Convention on the Rights of the Child* 1989 (CRC) calls for prevention of the "abduction of, sale of or traffic in children for any purpose or in any form."[159] Article 35 of the CRC was strengthened, when the *Optional Protocol on Sales of Children, Child Prostitution and Child Pornography* 2000[160] was adopted.

Even without specific reference to trafficking, other human rights instruments touch upon some of its aspects. The *International Covenant on Civil and Political Rights* 1966 (ICCPR), for instance, has a provision on the prohibition of slavery, servitude and forced labour.[161] Similar provisions can also be seen in the *International Convention on Rights of All Migrant Workers and Members of Their Families* 1990 (Migrant Workers' Convention).[162] In addition, Article 10(3) of the *International Covenant on Economic, Social and Cultural Rights* 1966 (ICESCR) calls for the adoption of special measures to protect children from economic and social exploitation.[163] The regional instruments, such as the *European Convention for the Protection of Human Rights and Fundamental Freedoms* 1950 (ECHR),[164] the ACHR,[165] and the *African Charter of Human and Peoples' Rights* 1986 (African Charter)[166] are also pertinent.

Furthermore, the Trafficking Protocol touches upon protection of the human rights of victims. The need to protect the "internationally recognised human rights" of those trafficked is spelt out under the Preamble of the Protocol[167] and Article 2 clearly states that protection of victims of trafficking "with full respect for their human rights" is one of the purposes of the Protocol. Moreover, provisions for protection of victims exist under the Trafficking Protocol.[168] All of this is significant, as this clearly illustrates recognition by the international community that trafficking is also a human rights issue.

---

158 1249 UNTS 13.

159 A/RES/44/25.

160 A/RES/54/253.

161 Article 8, 999 UNTS 171.

162 Article 11, 30 ILM 152.

163 Article 10(3), 993 UNTS 3.

164 Article 4 (prohibition on slavery), ETS No.5.

165 Article 6 (prohibition on slavery), *supra*.

166 Article 5 (prohibition on all forms of exploitation), OAU Doc. CAB/LEG/67/Rev.5.

167 Trafficking Protocol, *supra*.

168 Articles 6-8, *ibid*. See Chapter 5 for detail.

All of this suggests that a human rights framework to deal with trafficking is also necessary to supplement global action against the practice. What exactly is a human rights framework then? There are two dimensions to the answer to this question. At one level, it is a framework of analysis. In this sense, applying a human rights framework means exploring and identifying relevant human rights norms and principles in relation to trafficking of human being. These include, but are not limited to, the rights to life, work, health as well as prohibition of torture and slavery. At another level, a human rights framework is a framework of action. It simultaneously attempts to articulate legal obligations imposed upon States, such as obligations to prohibit trafficking, prosecute traffickers, protect victims, and address the causes and consequences of the practice. A human rights framework therefore can put more pressure on States to address the human rights issues pertinent to the phenomenon.

It should be noted from the outset that this book primarily focuses on articulation of the existing human rights norms, principles and obligations established under international human rights law and their application to trafficking of human beings. A question may be asked, then, whether or not there is a value in simply repeating those established human rights principles and obligations. It is submitted that a human rights framework in relation to the practice is still important for several reasons. First, it can facilitate the understanding of the problems experienced by those trafficked. They may be seen as victims of human rights abuses rather than criminals who violate national immigration laws and regulations, and therefore a victim-centred approach may be promoted. Such an approach is important. Victimisation may lead to deprivation of a sense of self-control and autonomy, and victims can also feel more and more isolated from their family, society and the world around them. The victim-centred approach could rectify this situation by empowering them,[169] because their needs become a central issue. There is no precise answer as to what can to be done in this regard, but some examples will be explored in detail later in the book.

Second, a human rights framework addresses not only the process of trafficking itself, but also wider issues such as the causes and consequences. In other words, it has the potential of promoting a holistic response to the act. The causes of trafficking such as poverty, persecution, and humanitarian crises all raise human rights concerns. Torture, inhuman or degrading treatments are relevant features of the process of trafficking. Moreover, many people suffer from human rights violations arising from slavery and forced labour, discrimination as well as law enforcement practices in States of destination. All of these issues must be addressed adequately in order for those concerned to seek effective suppression and prevention. A criminal justice approach to the practice (immigra-

169 Roth-Arriaza, N, 'Punishment, Redress, and Pardon: Theoretical and Psychological Approaches,' in Roth-Arriaza (ed.), *Impunity and Human Rights in International Law and Practice* (Oxford: Oxford University Press)(1995), p. 19

tion and crime control), which is the main response at the national level, is not necessarily best equipped to do so. A human rights framework, however, makes us realise the importance of adopting a holistic approach, and allows us to seek solutions accordingly.

A human rights framework is also beneficial in relation to the smuggling of human beings. While the human rights aspects of trafficking have widely been raised, little attention has been paid to the smuggling of human beings in this respect. The Smuggling Protocol does speak of protection of smuggled migrants, in referring to the right to life and prohibition of torture.[170] It also requires States not to hold people criminally liable for the fact of having been smuggled.[171] However, protection measures are likely to be limited, as the Smuggling Protocol recognises the right of States to prosecute people for violating national immigration and other laws.[172] While the distinction between trafficking and smuggling has important implications for law enforcement, it may distract attention from the broader context of abuse and exploitation.[173] A human rights framework, then, provides a common tool of analysis and action in relation to these two acts.

However, enforcement of human rights norms and principles has generally been problematic. For example, each Treaty Monitoring mechanisms such as the Human Rights Committee and the Committee against Torture faces a backlog of over 100 overdue reports submitted by State parties.[174] A lack of adequate recourses also leads to further delays in considering State reports and individual communications.[175] In addition, Opinions, General Comments and Recommendations issued by these bodies are not legally binding, and therefore States do not necessarily have to follow them. In relation to Special Rapporteurs, Working Groups and others established by the Human Rights Commission, they experience "all the disadvantages of reporting to a political body that only meets in ordinary session once a year," and a lack of political will or co-ordination with other UN system has made it difficult for them to function effectively.[176] All of this illustrates the weaknesses in enforcing human rights norms and principles.

---

170 Article 16, *supra*

171 Article 5, *ibid.*

172 Article 6(4). On this point, see Gallagher, *supra*, p. 999.

173 Skeldon, R, *Irregular Migration in the Greater Mekong Sub-Region : Policy Dimension of a Growing Issue* (Labour Migration and Trafficking within the Greater Mekong Sub-Region: Proceedings of Mekong Sub-Regional Expert Meeting and Explanatory Policy Paper)(Bangkok: ILO)(2001), Annex, p. 32.

174 Lattimer, M, 'Enforcing Human Rights through International Criminal Law,' in Lattimer and Sands (eds.), *Justice for Crimes against Humanity* (Oxford: Hart Publishing)(2003), p. 388.

175 *Ibid.*

176 *Ibid.*

This does not mean, however, that a human rights framework to trafficking is without value. Trafficking of human beings can be found at the intersection of different branches of international law, including international human rights law, international criminal law, and an emerging area of law known as transnational criminal law,[177] and some weaknesses related to international human rights law may be compensated by the other two. For instance, a lack of political will on the part of States to observe and implement human rights obligations related to trafficking may be alleviated by international criminal law under which the practice can be regarded as an international crime. This can put additional pressure on States to prohibit the practice, punish traffickers, and protect victims. If they do not, then the direct control of trafficking before an international tribunal becomes possible. This may appear as embarrassment for States as it not only exposes their inability or unwillingness to deal with the practice, but also affects their State sovereignty.[178]

What is evident after tracing the history of trafficking is that our understanding of the phenomenon evolved over time, and a wide variety of views have been adopted by different actors. Some correspond to the changing nature of the act or perhaps to changing societal priorities. The link with organised crime and a wide variety of subsequent exploitation demonstrate the cases in point. Others are subjective in that personal or organisational values are reflected in other views. The views of actors concerned with the protection of women, children and refugees are illustrative of this.

All of this suggests that there is no single way to understand the practice. While the definition of trafficking under the Trafficking Protocol entails some conceptual difficulties, it seems reasonable to state that its scope is wide enough to accommodate different viewpoints, and therefore offers useful guidance to understand and respond to the practice. Many actors are also in agreement that trafficking is a human rights issue. An important question remains, however, as to whether or not the Trafficking Protocol may be used to promote a human rights framework to address the practice, and this question will be dealt with later in this book.

1.5 Conclusion

This Chapter has illustrated that although there is a general consensus at the very minimum that trafficking entails human rights dimensions, a wide variety of views related to the practice exist. Some views, such as those embodying a gender focus, are subjective, in that personal or organisational ideals and values are reflected. Others are objective as they reflect the changing nature of the act over the course of time. The involvement of organised criminal groups is perhaps a good example.

177 The concept of transnational criminal law will be fully explored in Chapter 5.

178 See Chapter 5 for detail.

All of this highlights the fact that trafficking is highly complex. This means that a response which addresses multi-faceted problems associated with the practice is required. This will be the focus of attention of the next two Chapters. What will become evident is that a wide variety of views lead to different responses, some of which are even in conflict with each other. This in turn suggests that a framework which unifies these responses at the national, regional and international levels is necessary in order to promote effective global action against trafficking. It will be argued throughout this book that a human rights framework has the potential for this, as it seeks to promote a holistic approach to the phenomenon.

Chapter 2

National Case Studies on Trafficking of Human Beings in Thailand, Poland, and the United Kingdom

2.1 Introduction

In this Chapter, national case studies on trafficking of human beings in Thailand, Poland and the United Kingdom are presented. These jurisdictions have been selected primarily because of their status as typical States of origin, transit and destination respectively for trafficked people. One qualification, however, is that categorisation as a State of origin, transit, or destination is not definitive. Thailand and Poland simultaneously are States of origin, transit and destination, whereas it has recently been discovered that the United Kingdom serves as a transit State. Despite this qualification, a comparative analysis of these major States of origin, transit and destination provides insights into the nature of the phenomenon at various points of the process and responses to trafficking at national level.

The Chapter begins by illustrating the scale of trafficking of human beings in Thailand, Poland, and the United Kingdom, with particular reference to the major causes of the phenomenon and the profiles of traffickers. This is followed by a detailed analysis of national laws and polices and their enforcement. The Chapter also contains an analysis of victim protection measures. This is relevant as victim protection is one way of implementing a human rights framework to address the practice at the national level. Finally, the role played by key NGOs is examined.

2.2 The Scale of Trafficking in Thailand, Poland, and the United Kingdom

2.2.1 Statistical Overview

Thailand is a major State of origin. A large number of people are trafficked from Thailand annually. According to the Japanese Immigration Bureau, 14,334 Thai nationals were residing in Japan illegally as of January 2004.[1] Thai male immigrants normally work in factories, food stores, farms and restaurants, while Thai female immigrants work as prostitutes, hostesses or waitresses at bars in

1 Ministry of Justice of Japan, *Immigration Control 2004*, p. 50.

Japan.[2] Not every illegal migrant, however, is trafficked. Some may be smuggled instead of being trafficked, and others may travel independently. Nevertheless, the statistical information on illegal migrants is still an important indicator of the scale of trafficking, as traffickers facilitate illegal migration. Thai nationals are also trafficked into other States such as Taiwan, Germany, and the United States.[3] Thailand also serves as a transit State. Many Chinese nationals are trafficked into Malaysia, Myanmar, and Vietnam via Thailand for commercial sexual exploitation.[4] Finally, many people choose Thailand as a final destination. Between 200,000 to 300,000 foreign women are trafficked into Thailand annually for prostitution,[5] most commonly from Cambodia, Laos and Myanmar on account of the geographical proximity.[6] Further, the evidence suggests that Thai people are trafficked internally for a wide variety of purposes. Many people in the northern part of Thailand, especially women, are known to be trafficked to large cities such as Bangkok for prostitution and sexual exploitation.[7]

Similar to Thailand, Poland is also a State of origin, transit and destination. It has been reported that at least 300,000 Polish nationals work abroad illegally each year.[8] Many foreign nationals are also trafficked through Poland.

---

2 Phongpaichit, P, S. Piriyarangsan, and T. Nualnoi, *Guns, Girls, Gambling Ganja: Thailand's Illegal Economy and Public Policy* (Chiang Mai: Silkworm Books)(1998), p. 163.

3 Phongpaichit , P, 'Trafficking in People in Thailand,' in Williams (ed.), *Illegal Immigration, supra*, pp. 81-89.

4 UNICEF, *Children on the Edge: Protecting Children from Sexual Exploitation and Trafficking in East Asia and the Pacific* (Bangkok: UNICEF East Asia and Pacific)(2001), p. 14.

5 Senta, K, *Trafficking of Human Beings in Asia-Pacific Region* (Workshop of the UN Crime Prevention Network on Trafficking in Human Beings, Especially Women and Children)(May 2003), p. 5.

6 Derks, A, *Combating Trafficking in South-East Asia: A Review of Policy and Programme Responses* (IOM Migration Research Series No. 2)(Geneva: IOM)(2000), p. 17.

7 U.S. Department of States, *Country Reports on Human Rights Practice 2003: Thailand* (2004), at http://www.state.gov/g/drl/rls/hrrpt/2003/27790.htm (hereinafter Human Rights in Thailand 2003); and Beesey, A, 'Selling Sex on the Boundaries: The Crossroads of Sexual Desire and Economic Needs,' Paper Presented at the International Conference on Transborder Issues in the Greater Mekong Sub-region (June30- July 2, 2005), pp. 13 and 14.

8 Chancellery of the Prime Minister of the Republic of Poland and Government Plenipotentiary for Poland's Accession Negotiations to the European Union, *Enlargement of the European Union to the East: Consequences for Prosperity and Employment in Europe: Opinion on the Friedrich Ebert Foundation Report "Die Osterweiterung der Europäischen Union. Konsequenzen für Wohlstand und Beschäftigung in Europa"* (Warsaw: Chancellery of the Prime Minister of the Republic of

While most of them reach Germany due to its proximity to Poland, others move on to the Netherlands, United Kingdom, Belgium, and even the United States and Canada.[9] Moreover, Poland serves a destination for some. People are trafficked not only from Central, Eastern and Southern Europe such as Ukraine, the Czech Republic, and Bulgaria, but also from Asia, Africa and the Middle East, including Afghanistan, Algeria, Iraq and Sri Lanka.[10] According to the National Labour Bureau of Poland, approximately 200,000 foreigners enter illegally into Poland for employment each year.[11]

The United Kingdom is a typical State of destination for trafficked people. They are trafficked not only from Eastern Europe, but also from Asia (Thailand and China) and West Africa (Nigeria, Liberia and Sierra Leone).[12] It has been reported that up to 1,400 foreign women per year are trafficked for the purpose of sexual exploitation in the United Kingdom.[13] The Police estimate that seventy five percent of prostitutes working in Central London are from Eastern Europe,[14] although these Eastern European prostitutes can also be found in cities such as Birmingham, Cardiff, Glasgow, Leeds, and Manchester.[15] Not only women, but also children are trafficked or smuggled into the United Kingdom. Currently 10,000 African children are said to live with strangers in the United Kingdom.[16] These children have been trafficked not only for sexual exploitation, but also for credit card fraud, drug trafficking, and domestic service.[17] Further, the United Kingdom has increasingly been used as a State of transit. While immigration controls are strict on direct flights from regions such as Africa, they are more relaxed on flights from the United Kingdom, as many British nationals travel to

---

Poland)(2000), p. 75. According to this report, many polish nationals work illegally in agricultural sectors in Germany.

9 Okolski, M, 'Migrant Trafficking and Human Smuggling in Poland,' in Laczko and Thompson (eds.), *Migrant Trafficking and Human Smuggling, supra*, p. 259.

10 *Ibid.* pp. 256-258.

11 OECD, *Trends in International Migration* (Paris: OECD)(2002), p. 227.

12 Trafficking Report 2003, *supra*, p. 157.

13 Kelly, L, and L. Regan, *Stopping Traffic: Exploring the Extent of, and Responses to, Trafficking in Women for Sexual Exploitation in the UK* (London: Home Office)(2000), p. 22. It is important to note, however, that many foreign women are not coerced into prostitution, according to the testimony of a former prostitute in Soho. In other words, many women are also smuggled into UK and become prostitutes afterwards. See *The Guardian*, 'Foreign Bodies' (20/2/01).

14 UNICEF UK, *supra*, p. 12.

15 *The Independent*, 'Police Ignores Vice Trade from Eastern Europe' (23/1/02).

16 UNICEF UK, *supra*, p. 13.

17 Somerset, *supra*, p. 22.

other Western European States on holiday or for other purposes.[18] This makes the United Kingdom an attractive transit point for traffickers to utilise.

2.2.2 *Major Causes of Trafficking*

There are a wide variety of reasons why people resort to traffickers. Primarily, though not exclusively, the poor economic condition in States of origin is a key factor that promotes trafficking. Thai people in rural areas are often forced, through a lack of opportunities of employment, to move into larger cities.[19] This became even more of an issue with declining economic conditions in rural areas of Thailand following the outbreak of an economic crisis in Asia in 1997. In that year, the number of people unemployed in rural areas amounted to 0.22 million.[20] One year later this had increased to 0.87 million.[21] In addition, generally unstable economic conditions in Thailand have also contributed to the movement of Thai nationals abroad.[22] As for foreign nationals trafficked into Thailand, even poorer economic conditions in their States of origin and the relative economic wealth of Thailand have made Thailand an attractive destination.[23]

As for Poland, the break-up of the Soviet Union in 1991 had a negative impact on its national economy. The economic reforms implemented by post-Soviet States resulted, *inter alia*, in greater unemployment as governments no longer played a major role in providing jobs for their citizens.[24] This situation has been one of the main reasons why the Polish wanted to move to Western Europe to earn a living.[25] For the same reason, people from Central or Eastern European States (such as Ukraine and the Russian Federation) are trafficked through Poland, whereas those from other regions such as Asia, Africa, and Middle East choose Poland as a destination because of relatively poor economic

18 Kelly and Regan, *supra*, p. 19.

19 Levan, P. D, 'Curtailing Thailand's Child Prostitution Through an International Conscience,' 9(3) *American University Journal of International Law and Policy* 872 (1994), pp. 872 and 873.

20 Chalamwong, Y, 'Thailand,' *Migration and The Labour Market in Asia: Recent Trends and Policies* (Paris: OECD)(2002), p. 291.

21 *Ibid.*

22 Phongpaichit (1999), *supra,* p. 97.

23 Derks, *supra*, p. 17.

24 *Report of the Special Rapporteur on Violence against Women: Mission of the Special Rapporteur to Poland (24 May to 1 June 1996)*, E/CN.4/1997/47/Add.1, paras.33-41 (hereinafter Special Rapporteur on Women in Poland).

25 Limanowska, B, 'Trafficking in Women - Report from Poland,' in Klap, Kerk, and Smith (eds.), *Combating Traffic in Persons*: *SIM Special No. 17* (Utrecht: Netherlands Institute of Human Rights)(1995), p. 61.

prospects in their States of origin.[26] As for the United Kingdom, many wish to go there because it is an economically developed State.[27]

Another cause is a high demand for trafficked people. This is particularly evident in the sex industry in all three States. The origin of the sex industry in Thailand can be traced back to World War II, when women from Southeast and East Asia were "forced to serve as comfort women for the Japanese military."[28] The sex industry in Thailand was further expanded by the presence of the United States armed forces during the Indochinese War. During that period, the governments of the United States and Thailand signed a treaty which allowed American soldiers stationed in Vietnam to visit Thailand on "rest and recreation leave."[29] This treaty was said to be a factor which promoted prostitution in Thailand.[30] The demand for trafficked people in the sex and other industries (such

---

26 Siron, N, and P. Van Baeveghem, *Trafficking in Migrants through Poland: Multidisciplinary Research into the Phenomenon of Transit Migration in the Candidate Member States of the EU, with a View to the Combat of Traffic in Persons* (Antwerp: Maklu)(1999), p. 62.

27 Morrison, J, *The Cost of Survival: The Trafficking of Refugees to the UK* (London: Refugee Council)(1998), p. 24. The author, however, cautions that many are also trafficked into the United Kingdom for other reasons, such as ties with family and friends. It is also important to recognise that traffickers chose the United Kingdom as a destination, and those trafficked do not necessarily have a say in choosing their destinations in many cases. On this latter point, see Koser, K, 'Negotiating Entry into 'Fortress Europe': the Migration Strategies of 'Spontaneous' Asylum Seekers,' in Muus (ed.), *Exclusion and Inclusion of Refugees in Contemporary Europe* (Utrecht: ERCOMER)(1997).

28 Raghu, M, 'Sex Trafficking of Thai Women and the United States Asylum Law Response,' 12 *Georgetown Immigration Law Journal* 145 (1997), p. 153.

29 Levan, *supra*, p. 880.

30 *Ibid.* The sex industry was further expanded in the 1970s when the government, with the co-operation of such institutions as the World Bank, started promoting tourism for economic gain. See also Healy, M. A, 'Prosecuting Child Sex Tourists at Home: Do Laws in Sweden, Australia and the United States Safeguard the Rights of Children as Mandated by International Law?,' 18 *Fordham International Law Journal* 1852 (1995), p. 1865; and Li, V. F, 'Child Sex Tourism to Thailand: The Role of the United States as a Consumer Country,' 4 *Pacific Rim Law & Policy Journal* 505 (1995), p. 508. For further information on sex trafficking in Thailand, see Skrobanek, S, N. Boonpakdee and C. Jantateero, *Traffic in Women: Human Realities of the International Sex Trade* (London: Zed Books Ltd)(1997); Seabrook, J, *Travels in the Skin Trade: Tourism and the Sex Industry* (London: Pluto Press)(2001); and Rho-Ng, E, 'The Conscription of Asian Sex Slaves: Causes and Effects of U.S. Military Sex Colonialism in Thailand and the Call to Expand U.S. Asylum Law,' 7 *Asian Law Journal* 103 (2000).

as farms, construction and factories) is also high in Poland[31] and the United Kingdom.[32]

It is also maintained that trafficking is culturally constructed. In Thailand, for instance, selling of women and children for prostitution to support their family has been tolerated and practised for a long time as part of Thai custom.[33] While parents may do so on their own initiative, it has also been reported that children make their own decision to leave, based on a desire to support their family.[34] Migration for employment abroad has also been an established practice in Poland since the Nineteenth Century; in addition to migration for employment in commercial sectors, trafficking of women for prostitution has also existed for a long time in Poland.[35]

In addition, discrimination on various grounds is a deep-rooted cause of trafficking. It has been noted that a general failure to protect the rights of women is a factor triggering their movement.[36] Both in Thailand and Poland, a lack of employment and educational opportunities for women have made them susceptible to exploitation by traffickers.[37] In a similar vein, discrimination based on ethnic or racial background has contributed to the growth of trafficking. The hill tribe people of Thailand are not ethnic Thai and are not entitled to Thai citi-

31 According to the police, at least 15,000 foreign women are trafficked to Poland for sexual exploitation. The sex industry is particularly concentrated in Zielona Province, which shares its border with Germany. See UNODC, 'Trafficking Project' at http://www.unodc.org/unodc/en/trafficking_projects_poland.html.

32 See Anti-Slavery International, *The Migration-Trafficking Nexus: Combating Trafficking through the Protection of Migrants' Human Rights* (London: Anti-Slavery International)(2003), p. 21; and Scambler, G, and A. Scambler (eds.), *Rethinking of Prostitution: Purchasing Sex in the 1990s* (London: Routledge)(1997).

33 Levan, *supra*, pp. 874-879. Another commentator notes that "cultural values expect girls - from a very young age to help support their parents and family. In Thailand, this is often referred to as a daughter's responsibility to pay back the breast milk money." Tumlin, K. C, *Trafficking in Children and Women: A Regional Overview* (Asia Regional High-level Meeting on Child Labour, Jakarta, Indonesia, 8-10 March 2000) (Bangkok: Chulalongkorn University)(2000), p. 13.

34 ILO-IPEC, *Thailand-Laos People's Democratic Republic and Thailand-Myanmar Border Areas: Trafficking in Children into the Worst Forms of Child Labour, Rapid Assessment* (2000), p. 21.

35 Special Rapporteur on Women in Poland (1997), *supra*, para. 42.

36 Special Rapporteur on Women (2000), *supra*, para. 54.

37 Special Rapporteur on Women in Poland (1997), *supra*, para. 39; Committee on Economic, Social and Cultural Rights: *Summary Record of the 34th meeting : Poland,* E/C.12/2002/SR.34, para. 31; and *Concluding Observations of the Committee on the Elimination of Discrimination Against Women: Thailand*, A/54/38 (1999), para. 236.

zenship.[38] They are treated as 'second-class citizens' and are economically disadvantaged.[39] This has increased the possibility that they turn to traffickers.[40]

Moreover, many people resort to traffickers to escape from humanitarian crises. In Myanmar, for instance, there are approximately 633,000 internally displaced people due to military conflicts, and many have sought refuge in Thailand.[41] As for Poland, people from Romania have been forced into or through Poland due to political, ethnic or other forms of persecution by the Romanian government.[42] People from Afghanistan, Armenia, and Iraq are also reported to have escaped from political persecution by their States and reached Poland.[43] Finally, many of these people and others are trafficked into the United Kingdom for the same reason and seek asylum.[44]

In the case of States of destination, restrictive immigration laws and policies and strict border controls are also factors behind people relying on traffickers. This is particularly evident in Western Europe.[45] The visa requirements, carrier sanctions, and other measures to stop the flow of illegal migrants have been implemented in Western Europe, and this has made it difficult for would-be

---

38 Raghu, *supra*, p. 146.

39 *Ibid.* See further *Regional Seminar on Minority Rights: Cultural Diversity and Development in Southeast Asia*, E/CN.4/Sub.2/AC.5/2003/WP.14.

40 *Ibid.* See further, *Inclusion of Minorities in Public Life in Laos, Thailand and Vietnam*, E/CN.4/Sub.2/AC.5/2003/WP.11, p. 24, which illustrates the negative perceptions held by Thai nationals against hill-tribe people.

41 *Written Statement Submitted by Asian Legal Resource Centre (ALRC)*, E/CN.4/2003/NGO/151, paras. 4 and 6. See also *Written Statement Submitted by Society for Threatened Peoples*, E/CN.4/2003/NGO/256, which reports on sexual violence against Myanmarese nationals committed by the military personnel; and *Written Statement Submitted by Minority Rights Group International*, E/CN.4/2003/NGO/157.

42 Siron and Van Baeveghem, *supra*, p. 25.

43 Okolski, *supra*, pp. 300-313.

44 See, Morrison (1998), *supra*, pp. 21-23.

45 See in general, Weijers, M, 'Keep Your Women Home: European Union Policies on Trafficking in Women,' in Rossilli (ed.), *Gender Policies in the European Union* (New York: P. Lang)(2000); and Albrecht, H. J, 'Fortress Europe? – Controlling Illegal Immigration,' 10 *European Journal of Crime, Criminal Law and Criminal Justice* 1 (2002).

migrants to migrate legally.[46] This has supported illegal markets and opened up economic opportunities for traffickers.[47]

2.2.3 *Profile of Traffickers*

Different types of people are known to facilitate the trafficking process. There are cases where family members, relatives, and/or friends have been involved. Some parents in Thailand sell their sons and daughters in order to sustain themselves economically as noted above, and sometimes facilitate migration abroad for the same reason.[48] The involvement of acquaintances and relatives has also been reported in Poland.[49] In addition, individual agents and brokers facilitate trafficking. In Thailand, for example, agents/brokers not only from Thailand, but also Japan, Singapore and Malaysia, facilitate recruitment, arrange travel plans, and contact overseas agents/brokers.[50] These overseas agents, in turn, arrange transport and jobs in destination States.[51] Moreover, there are small groups of criminals who engage in trafficking. Such groups are said to be common in Poland.[52] They live or work in Western Europe, and travel to Central and Eastern Europe to collect women for sexual exploitation.[53]

Furthermore, the involvement of organised criminal groups in trafficking has increasingly been evident in Thailand, Poland, and the United Kingdom. Many of them are highly structured, large in size and have many members and associates all around the world.[54] All of this makes it easier for them to stage large-scale operations, compared to individual criminals or small group of criminals. In Thailand, Japanese organised criminal groups known as *Yakuza* traffic Thai and other foreign women into Japan for prostitution and sexual exploitation.[55] The involvement of organised criminal groups from Germany and the

46 Obokata, T, 'Trafficking and Smuggling of Human Beings in Europe: Protection of Individual Rights or States' Interests?,' *Web Journal of Current Legal Issues* (Issue 5, 2001), at http://webjcli.nc.ncl.ac.uk. See also, Morrison and Crosland, *supra*. They give a detailed account of Western European immigration laws and policies.

47 Schloenhardt, *supra*, p. 212; and Buchowska, S, 'Breaking the Vicious Circle,' *GAATW Newsletter*, Issue 14 (2000).

48 Human Rights Watch, *Owed Justice: Thai Women Trafficked into Debt Bondage in Japan* (2001) at http://www.hrw.org/reports/2000/japan/3-context.htm (hereinafter Human Rights Watch (2001)).

49 Siron and Van Baeveghem, *supra*, p. 29.

50 Human Rights Watch (2001), *supra*.

51 *Ibid.*

52 Siron and Van Baeveghem, *supra*, p. 31.

53 *Ibid.*

54 NCIS (2003), *supra*, p. 16

55 Human Rights Watch (2001), *supra*.

United States as well as Hong Kong has been reported in Thailand.[56] In Poland, Russian Mafia groups actively engage in trafficking. They are generally organised by region or ethnic lines, and many of them are said to be former employees of the KGB, the intelligence organisation of the former Soviet Union.[57] Finally, in the United Kingdom, trafficking of foreign nationals into its territory has been carried out by Albanian criminal groups,[58] the Hong Kong *Triads*[59] and the Chinese *Snakeheads*,[60] amongst others.

All of this shows that trafficking of human beings is widespread in Thailand, Poland, and the United Kingdom. There are different reasons why people are trafficked, and many are exploited subsequently for a wide variety of purposes by different individuals and groups. This means that effective laws and policies which address the multitude of problems are necessary. Such laws and policies would include measures not only for the prosecution and punishment of offenders and the protection of victims, but also for tackling the root causes and reduction of the demand for trafficked people. The remaining part of the Chapter explores the extent to which Thailand, Poland and the United Kingdom are successful in addressing the problems related to trafficking.

2.3 National Case Study: Thailand[61]

2.3.1 National Laws and Policies

In Thailand, there are several laws pertinent to trafficking of human beings. The first law on the practice, the *Traffic in Women and Girls Act*, was enacted in Thailand as early as 1928 (1928 Act).[62] Section 4 of the 1928 Act provided that:

> Whoever brings or causes another person to bring any woman or girl child into Siam for commercial sexual intercourse; takes or causes another person to take any women out of Siam for commercial sexual intercourse; illegally receives or sells any woman or girl child with the knowledge that the woman

56 Hodgson, D, 'Sex Tourism and Child Prostitution in Asia: Legal Responses and Strategies,' 19 *Melbourne University Law Review* 512 (1994), p. 519.

57 Siron and Van Baeveghem, *supra*, p. 33. See also O'Neill Richard, *supra*, p. 60

58 NCIS, *UK Threat Assessment 2000*, p. 40.

59 *Ibid.*, p. 42.

60 *The Independent*, 'Trucker Jailed for Suffocation of 58 Illegal Immigrants' (6/4/01).

61 Thailand has singed the Organised Crime Convention (13/12/00), the Trafficking Protocol (18/12/01), and the Smuggling Protocol (18/12/01), but has not ratified these instruments as of September 2005. No reservation or declaration has been entered. See Signatories to the UN Convention against Transnational Crime and its Protocols at http://www.unodc.org/unodc/en/crime_cicp_signatures.html.

62 Roujanavong, W, 'Thailand: The Situation of Trafficking in Women,' *Proceedings of the 1997 Regional Conference on Trafficking in Women and Children (Bangkok)* (1999), p. 329.

> or girl child was brought into Siam for such purpose shall be liable to be punished with imprisonment not exceeding seven years or fine not exceeding one thousand baht or both.[63]

The wording of this provision reflects the earlier prevailing view on trafficking, in that the 1928 Act was mainly concerned with the suppression of the trafficking of women and girls for prostitution and sexual exploitation. The 1928 Act was enacted mainly in response to the increased number of foreign nationals, especially Chinese, working in Thai brothels.[64] Thailand then was the primarily a State of destination. This corresponds to a report published by the Commission of Enquiry into Traffic in Women and Children in the East of the League of Nations in 1933, which portrayed Thailand as a major destination for trafficked people.[65]

While the adoption of the law specifically related to trafficking shows the willingness of Thailand to tackle the phenomenon, the 1928 Act was considered to have some problems. For instance, the penalty for traffickers was not heavy, as many were freed by paying 1,000 baht.[66] In addition, while bringing women and girls into and/or taking them outside of Thailand for prostitution and sexual exploitation were criminalised, domestic prostitution was not. Under the *Contagious Disease Act* of 1908, prostitutes and brothels were allowed to conduct their business as long as they registered and paid an appropriate tax to the State.[67] Although law enforcement agencies such as the police were able to monitor activities of prostitutes and brothels to some extent, they could not stop the expansion of prostitution, because a high number of prostitutes and brothels did not register.[68]

The weakness of the 1928 Act led to the enactment of the *Prostitution Prevention and Suppression Act* in 1960 (1960 Act) which made all forms of prostitution illegal.[69] Nevertheless, the 1960 Act was no more effective, mainly because women and girls were punished more severely than the owners of brothels or others engaging in the business. If a woman was arrested for prostitution, she potentially faced imprisonment for 3 to 6 months and/or a fine of 1,000-2,000 baht. Additionally, she could be kept in a closed rehabilitation centre for a fur-

63 *Ibid.* 1000 Baht is currently worth $25.

64 Skrobanek, S, 'Laws Relating to Traffic in Women - Case of Thailand,' *Combating Traffic… supra*, p. 55 (hereinafter Skrobanek (1995)).

65 *Ibid.*, p. 53.

66 *Ibid.*, p. 55. It is fair to state that the value of currency in 1928 was substantially different from the present value, and 1,000 baht might have been considered expensive in Thai standard.

67 *Ibid*, p. 54.

68 *Ibid.*

69 Roujanavong, *supra*, p. 350.

ther 2 years. The maximum punishment for a procurer of prostitutes, however, was only 3 months' imprisonment and a fine not more than 1,000 baht with no rehabilitation requirement. Therefore, the punishments did not exactly deter the procurers and owners of brothels from engaging in the business, given the amount of profits they could make. Moreover, many of those who were involved in trafficking and prostitution were also able to bribe the authorities in many cases.[70] As a result, the business of prostitution and trafficking for this purpose continued to flourish in Thailand.

Another relevant law which was enacted around this time was the *Immigration Act*[71] of 1959. Amongst others, this Act applies to foreign nationals who are trafficked or smuggled into Thailand; those entering the Kingdom without legal permits are treated as illegal immigrants and may face a maximum sentence of 2 years' imprisonment and/or a fine of 20,000 baht.[72] The immigration officers are also authorised to reject entry of those who are suspected of coming to Thailand to sell labour, become prostitutes, traffic women and/or children, or deal in narcotics.[73] Detainees are held in the Immigration Detention Centre and are then expelled from the Kingdom.[74]

Although regulating the flow of illegal migrants is part of the framework to suppress trafficking, there are a number of problems with the 1959 Act from the viewpoint of those trafficked. They are treated not as victims but rather face punishments as offenders of immigration law.[75] If they cannot pay the fine specified, then they face imprisonment. After they are released from prison, they are immediately sent to the Immigration Detention Centre for deportation. The amount of time spent in this Detention Centre can be long, if one's State of origin is far from Thailand and he/she does not have enough money to cover the cost of transportation.[76] The Immigration Bureau has a very limited budget and is unable to bear the cost of repatriation in most cases.[77]

Having reflected on these problems in national law, the government has made some changes. In 1996, the 1960 Act was replaced by the *Prostitution Prevention and Suppression Act* (1996 Act).[78] Unlike the previous Act, the 1996 Act treats prostitutes more as victims and concentrates on punishing the procurers, owners of brothels and others involved in the business of trafficking for the

70 Skrobanek (1995), *supra*, p. 54.

71 B.E. 2522 (1959), Roujanavong, *supra*, p. 353.

72 Sections 11 and 62, *ibid.*

73 Section 12, *ibid.*

74 Derks, *supra*, p. 33.

75 Roujanavong, *supra*, p. 353.

76 *Ibid.*

77 *Ibid.*

78 B.E. 2539.

purpose of prostitution and sexual exploitation. Depending on the degree of involvement in the business (soliciting, congregating others in brothels, advertising, owning brothels, having sexual intercourse in brothels and trafficking), penalties ranging from 1 to 20 years' imprisonment, or fines between 1,000 and 400,000 baht can be imposed.[79] Moreover, if anyone harms prostitutes physically and causes their death, he/she could face life imprisonment (bodily injuries) and the death penalty (causing death).[80]

In addition, some improvements were also made to the 1928 Act. In 1997, the Government passed the *Measures in Prevention and Suppression of Trafficking in Women and Children Act* (1997 Act).[81] Section 5 of the Act reads as follows:

> In committing an offence concerning the trafficking in women and children, buying, selling, vending, bringing from or sending to, receiving, detaining or confining any woman or child, or arranging for any women or child to act or receive any act, for sexual gratification of another person, for an indecent sexual purpose, or for gaining any illegal benefit for his/herself or another person, with or without the consent of the woman or child, which is an offence under the Penal Code, the law on prostitution prevention and suppression, the law on safety and welfare of children and youths, or this Act, the official is authorized to enforce power under this act. [82]

A comparative analysis of this provision with Section 4 of the 1928 Act reveals some insights into the Thai government's shift on policy towards trafficking in recent times. To begin with, those cases involving trafficking of women and children for purposes other than prostitution can also be dealt with under this Act, as the above-mentioned provision is not confined to prostitution. It is also worth noting that under the 1997 Act, trafficking is no longer restricted to circumstances involving crossing of borders. Section 4 of the 1928 Act regulated trafficking of foreign nationals into Thailand and of both Thai and foreign nationals abroad.[83] Section 5 of the 1997 Act, however, does not confine the Act's remit to international movements. This is important because the 1997 Act can also be applied to cases where women and children, including the hill tribe people from rural areas, are trafficked internally. Moreover, the penalties imposed for trafficking or related offences were raised. Whoever conspires to commit, or actually

79 Sections 5 through 11, *ibid.*

80 Section 12. *ibid.*

81 B.E. 2540.

82 *Ibid.*

83 1928 Act, *supra.*

commits sales/trafficking of women and children, may receive anything up to life-imprisonment or death penalty, depending on the severity of the offence.[84]

Further, the 1997 Act treats those trafficked as victims, instead of criminals. This is illustrated by Section 11 which reads:

> The official shall use his/her judgement in giving appropriate assistance to the woman and child, who is the victim of the offence as specified in Section 5, in providing food, shelter, and repatriation to her/his original country or residence.
>
> In providing assistance according to the first paragraph, the official may arrange for the woman or child to be in the care of a "primary shelter" provided by the law on prostitution prevention and suppression, a "primary shelter for children" provided by the law on child and juvenile safety and welfare, or other governmental or non-governmental welfare institution.[85]

This is an important development as the law seems to reflect the need to incorporate a human rights framework.

Finally, in 2003, the Thai Cabinet approved the *National Policy and Plan of Prevention, Suppression and Combating Domestic and Transnational Trafficking in Women and Children*.[86] This is a six-year plan directed towards prevention/suppression of trafficking and protection of victims. Some measures have already been taken in accordance with this Plan. For instance, in the area of prevention and suppression, new legislation is under consideration by Thai Parliament. This legislation is expected to cover trafficking of men for purposes other than prostitution and sexual exploitation.[87] This is a welcome change because it fills the gap created by the previous 1997 Act, and the scope of application will be in line with the Trafficking Protocol.

However, not much is being done to address the root causes of trafficking in Thailand. The government claims that it has been providing more social, vocational and educational services to women and children who are at risk of being

---

84 Under Section 5, the punishment stipulated under the law on prostitution is applicable. Under Section 283 of the *Penal Code of Thailand* 1956 as amended, if someone traffics a boy or a girl under fifteen years of age for sexual exploitation, he/she could face life imprisonment or death penalty. *Penal Code Amendment Act* (No. 14)(B.E. 2540, 1997).

85 *Ibid.*

86 Bureau of Anti-Trafficking in Women and Children, Ministry of Social Development and Human Security, *Combating Trafficking in Women and Children* (September 2004), p. 2.

87 Interview with Ms. Pisawat Sconthaparn, Attorney at Law, Professor, and the Director of the Mekong Region Law Centre (28/6/05).

victimised by traffickers so that they can engage in other gainful activities,[88] and such efforts of the government have been recognised at different levels.[89] Nevertheless, the demand for trafficking people remains high, particularly in the sex industry. The government is said to tolerate this industry because of the large amount of profit it generates.[90] The problem is exacerbated by the fact that thousands of foreign tourists go to Thailand and engage in sexual activities. The Coalition against Trafficking in Women (Asia & Pacific) reports that as many as 500,000 foreign tourists engage in sexual activities annually.[91] Thailand therefore should reduce the flow of foreign sex tourists by adopting an additional legal measure to punish sex tourists who have often only been fined and then deported without severe punishment in the past.[92] In addition, Thailand should also consider other legal measures which include, but are not limited to, economic developments and reforms, and provisions of educational and vocational training for those at risk of becoming victims of trafficking, and elimination of discrimination against women and different racial groups residing in Thailand. These are necessary in order to adopt a holistic approach to the practice.

2.3.2 *Enforcement*

2.3.2.1 Relevant Agencies and Statistical Information

In Thailand, the key agency dealing with the suppression of trafficking and smuggling of human beings is the Royal Thai Police, which also oversees the Immigration Bureau.[93] Within the Royal Thai Police, the Centre for Protection of Children, Juveniles and Women is designated as the lead department to enforce laws on the practice.[94] Some statistical figures on law enforcement activities in Thailand are available. In July 2005, for instance 6,500 Hmong people from Laos, who have been assisted by traffickers, were arrested and detained in Phetchabun Province in northern Thailand.[95] A series of raids against illegal

---

88 Bureau of Anti-Trafficking, *supra*.

89 Interview with Ms. Sconthaparn, *supra*; and Interview with Ms. Anna Engblom, Programme Officer of the ILO Bangkok (27/6/05).

90 See in particular, Li, *supra*.

91 Coalition against Trafficking in Women (Asia & Pacific) at http://www.catw-ap.org/.

92 Li, *supra*, p514.

93 Asia Regional Cooperation to Prevent People Trafficking (ARCPPT), *The Role of Victim Support Agencies in the Criminal Justice Response to Human Trafficking: Lessons from Thailand, Cambodia, Lao PDR and Myanmar* (Bangkok: ARCPPT)(2004), p. 7.

94 *Ibid.*

95 *The Nation*, 'Traffickers Blamed for Hmong influx' (7/7/05).

migrants have also taken place in Bangkok,[96] Mae Hong Son (border area),[97] and Chiang Mai (northern Thailand).[98] In relation to traffickers, there were 607 arrests, resulting in 66 prosecutions and 12 convictions in 2004.[99] What is evident in looking at these figures is that much emphasis is placed upon controlling the flow of illegal migrants, while only a small number of prosecutions are brought against traffickers.

2.3.2.2 Analysis of Law Enforcement

An analysis reveals that laws relating to trafficking are not properly enforced in reality in Thailand. There are a number of reasons for this. For instance, the application of laws on trafficking has been selective. This is partly due to a lack of adequate knowledge of trafficking on the part of law enforcement agencies.[100] Many police officers in different provinces of Thailand are not aware that laws concerning human trafficking exist[101] and instead utilise the Prostitution Act.[102] Another related problem, as reported by one NGO, is that the Prostitution Act is used to prosecute prostitutes rather than traffickers.[103] One way to address this lack of knowledge and training is to create a specialised and permanent unit within the police which would disseminate information and conduct training. Such a unit, however, does not exist in Thailand at this current moment.[104]

Another reason for ineffective law enforcement is a lack of evidence. It prevents agencies from effectively prosecuting and punishing traffickers. A key source of information are the victims themselves; however, they are often not willing to co-operate with law enforcement authorities due to a fear of reprisal by traffickers, or, in the case of illegal immigrants, of enforcement actions against them.[105] One way to improve this problem is to provide protection for witnesses from enforcement action and from traffickers. This is important not only from a

96 *The Nation*, 'Laotian Slaves Freed after Raid on Factory' (16/9/04).

97 *The Nation*, '50 Burmese Migrants Held in Illegal Alien Sweep' (5/6/05).

98 *The Nation*, 'Illegal Burmese Rounded Up in Raids' (17/6/05).

99 Trafficking Report 2005, *supra,* p. 213.

100 U.S. Department of State, *Trafficking in Persons Report 2004*, p. 109 (hereinafter Trafficking Report 2004); Trafficking Report 2005, *supra*, p. 213; and Interview with Ms. Sconthaparn, *supra*.

101 Human Rights Watch (2001), *supra*.

102 Pearson, E, *Human Traffic, Human Rights: Redefining Victim Protection* (London: Anti-Slavery International)(2002), p. 174. The research and report on Thailand was conducted and written by Thai-based NGO *Foundation for Women*.

103 *Ibid.*, pp. 174 and 175.

104 Interview with Nina Vallins, Information Officer, Asia Regional Cooperation to Prevent People Trafficking (28/6/05).

105 Pearson, *supra,* p. 175; and Interview with Ms. Sconthaparn, *supra*.

criminal justice perspective, but also from a human rights perspective as will be shown throughout this book.

In addition, corruption among law enforcement agencies is also an endemic problem in Thailand. Those involved in prostitution bribe law enforcement officials and are able to evade law enforcement in return.[106] In Mae Sai, Northern Thailand, for instance, the brothels pay a certain amount of money to the police each month for each girl.[107] In July 2003, 50 police officers of the Bangkok Metropolitan Police were also removed from active duty because of allegations that they have taken bribes from traffickers.[108] Even worse, some law enforcement officers actively participate in trafficking. In Northern Thailand, police and border patrol officers often escort women and girls trafficked from Myanmar to brothels in such cities as Chiang Mai, at a cost of 2,000 baht per journey.[109] Unfortunately, not much has done to address the problem of corruption in Thailand.[110]

There are several factors which promote corruption among government offices, including law enforcement agencies. In addition to low salaries, which serve as an incentive for law enforcement officers to take bribes,[111] one important factor facilitating corruption is disregard for the rule of law. It has been argued that this applies to Thailand. Although Thailand is a democratic, constitutional monarchy, its political life has always been influenced by the military which has control over many political institutions.[112] The presence of the military in politics often resulted in the "acquisition of power through force instead of recognised constitutional principles and the rule of law."[113] This "culture that disregards the rule of law fosters corruption in the form of bribery and non-enforcement of the law."[114]

States which are undergoing rapid economic, political and social transformations are also susceptible to corruption. This has been particularly relevant for Eastern and Central European States after the break up of the Soviet Union. Opportunities created by the distribution of private property are said to increase "the appeal of obtaining illegal advantages" not only among business people,

106 *Written Statement Submitted by Human Rights Advocates International*, E/CN.4/1998/NGO/48.

107 Brown, L, *Sex Slaves: Trafficking of Women in Asia* (London: Virago)(2001), p. 203.

108 Human Rights in Thailand (2003), *supra*.

109 Brown, *supra*, p. 203.

110 Trafficking Report 2005, *supra*, p. 213.

111 Brown, *supra,* p. 201.

112 Raghu, *supra*, p. 148.

113 *Ibid.* p. 149.

114 *Ibid.*

but also among public officials.[115] The governments, on their part, lack expertise and mechanisms to effectively oversee activities conducted by both public and private sectors in many cases.[116] As will be shown below, many of these factors apply to Poland.

Another equally important factor is the influence of organised criminal groups. Corruption and organised crime have a close nexus, as organised criminal groups use bribery as a way to advance their illegal business.[117] If someone is arrested for trafficking or smuggling, his/her colleagues will use whatever means necessary (e.g. money and violence) to influence the law enforcement agencies as well as victims who are potential witnesses to the crime.[118] The link between corruption and organised crime is important, as it shows that corruption exists not only in developing States, but also in developed ones.

Finally, the situations facing illegal immigrants in Thailand raise serious human rights concerns. Given that most of those trafficked into Thailand are illegal immigrants, law enforcement authorities mainly apply immigration law to deport them without seeking to identify and prosecute traffickers.[119] According to Human Rights Watch, the Thai government expels approximately 10,000 Myanmarese people each month even when they have a risk of being persecuted by their governments upon return.[120] Such a practice violates international human rights norms and principles. It has also been reported that because of their illegal status and a fear of law enforcement, illegal migrants working in Thailand are unwilling to seek medical help.[121] This increases the risk of the spread of disease such as HIV/AIDS. Further, the extra-judicial killing of Myanmarese nationals and a failure of the government to take steps to investigate the incident have also been reported by an NGO.[122]

---

115 UNICRI, *International Cooperation in Combating Transnational Crime: New Challenges in the Twenty First Century: Background Paper for the Workshop on Combating Corruption*, A/CONF.187/9 (1999), para, 10.

116 Center for the Study of Democracy (CSD), *Coalition Building in Transition Countries* (Sofia, Bulgaria: CSD)(2001), p. 4.

117 Savona, E. U, *Corruption and Organised Crime in States in Transition: Joint Project between the Commission of the European Communities and the Council of Europe, Final Recommendation and Guidelines for Action* (Strasbourg: Council of Europe)(1998), p. 5.

118 Roujanavong, *supra*, p. 356.

119 Pearson, *supra*, p. 178; ARCPPT, *supra*, p. 7; and Trafficking Report 2005, *supra*, p. 212.

120 Human Rights Watch, *Out of Sight, Out of Mind: Thai Policy towards Burmese Refugees* (February 2004), pp. 6 and 7.

121 *The Nation*, 'Mae Sot: Burmese Health Dilemma' (8/6/04).

122 *Written Statement Submitted by the Asian Legal Resource Centre*, E/CN.4/2003/NGO/149.

2.3.3 *Victim Protection Measures*

In Thailand, the effort of the government to provide assistance to victims has intensified in the past several years. This may be seen in several measures facilitated by the authorities. In June 1999, the government signed a *Memorandum of Understanding on Common Guidelines of Practices among Concerned Agencies for Operation in Case Women and Children are Victims of Trafficking* jointly with the police, Public Welfare Department, Thai Co-ordinator on Foreign Children and an NGO called the Global Alliance against Trafficking in Women and Children (GAATW), [123] which was renewed in 2003.[124] There are several features of these MoUs which are worth mentioning. For instance, foreign women and children who are trafficked are to be considered victims, rather than criminals, and the MoUs call for provision of assistance.[125] Relevant agencies, such as the police and the Ministry of Social Development and Human Security, are instructed to provide assistance on identifying victims, shelter, medical examinations, vocational training and preparation for legal proceedings against traffickers.[126] All of this shows recognition by the government that similar, if not the same, types of assistance should be given to foreign women and children.

The value of these MoUs, however, can be called into question. In addition to a lack of knowledge on trafficking, many law enforcement officers are not even aware of the existence of the MoUs.[127] As a result, they are often unable to identify victims and concentrate instead on enforcing laws on immigration and prostitution.[128] In addition, the MoUs are not legally binding, and therefore accountability for non-compliance cannot be addressed effectively. As pointed out by one NGO, there is a need for legislation obliging those concerned to provide adequate assistance to victims.[129]

The government also provides shelters for the victims of trafficking of human beings. Currently there are 97 shelters for abused women and children in Thailand and 6 of them are used specifically for victims of trafficking.[130] The Bureau of Anti-Trafficking within the Ministry of Social Development and Human Security, which was established in 2003, oversees these shelters along

123 B.E. 2542 (1999).

124 ARCPPT, *supra*, pp. 42-48.

125 MoUs, *supra*.

126 *Ibid.*

127 Pearson, *supra*, p. 176; and ARCPPT, *supra*, p. 9.

128 *Ibid.*

129 *Ibid.*, p. 179.

130 These are located in Nonthaburi Province (2), Nakhon Ratchasima Province (1), Pitsanulokhe Province (1), Chiang Mai Province (1), and Surat Thani Province (1). Interview with Ms. Swaree Jaiharn, Director of the Division of Resolution on Women and Child Problems, and Ms. Pusa Srivilas, Social Worker of the Bureau of Anti-Trafficking (4/7/05).

with 60 others, and as of July 2005, approximately 200 victims of trafficking are housed in these shelters.[131] Once identified as victims and sent to shelters, these people are exempt from immigration law and can receive medical and psychological treatment as well as vocational and other types of training.[132] However, these shelters are to be used on the temporary basis, with an ultimate aim of repatriating these victims to their own States. One of the main activities of the Bureau of Anti-Trafficking then is family tracing in their States of origin so that these victims can be repatriated.[133]

Although the willingness of the government to assist victims should be recognised, a difficulty arises in deciding who is and is not a victim. The government of Thailand has not ratified the Trafficking Protocol as yet, and it has been noted that the definition of trafficking under the current legislation is not sufficient at this point.[134] Further, many of those trafficked do not regard themselves as victims or do not want to be identified as such.[135] One consequence is that those who are not recognised as victims may be deported instead of receiving protection in the shelters.[136] Another difficulty in relation to these shelters is the amount of time one may spend. Some have to spend more than a few years in those shelters because tracing of their families in States of origin take time and sometimes is difficult due to a lack of co-operation from those States.[137] This is complicated by the fact that some escape from their States of origin due to persecution and other humanitarian crises, and do not necessarily want to contact the authorities of their own States.[138] This prevents Thai authorities from conducting family tracing efficiently, and therefore those individuals have no choice but to remain in these shelters for a long period of time.

Another measure taken by the government is the provision of vocational training for prostitutes. This is either done through services created by the *Prostitution Prevention and Suppression Act 1996* or the Department of Public Welfare.[139] In addition to prostitutes already working in Thailand, these services are open to Thai nationals returned from States of transit and/or destination. Since the adoption of this law, four reception homes and four welfare protection and vocational training centres have been established.[140] Nevertheless, this measure

131 *Ibid.*

132 *Ibid.*

133 *Ibid.*

134 Interview with Ms. Sconthaparn, *supra.*

135 *Ibid.*

136 Interview with Ms. Engblom, *supra.*

137 Interviews with Ms. Sconthaparn, Ms. Jaiharn and Ms. Srivilas, *supra.*

138 *Ibid.*

139 Human Rights Watch (2001), *supra.*

140 *Ibid.*

has also been criticised on several grounds. First, the existence of gender discrimination in these centres is evident. Although men receive high quality training and education in such areas as electronics and computers, women are only trained for low paid jobs - for example, cooking and hairdressing.[141] This is so because women in general are looked down upon, and government officials do not regard them as having the potential to excel.[142] Second, some victims of trafficking are unable to benefit from vocational and other training, as the government does not permit repatriation of trafficked victims without Thai nationality. This is applicable to hill tribe people[143] as well as those who were granted limited rights to remain on humanitarian grounds.[144]

In addition, a certain degree of witness protection is available to victims of trafficking. *Witness Protection Act*[145] came into force in 2004, and the Witness Protection Bureau within the Ministry of Justice started its operation in the same year.[146] Under this act, certain protection measures can be taken to protect the victims of trafficking. They include provision of accommodation, expenses for daily life for 1 year, new identity, vocational training and education, and bodyguards.[147] Witnesses' close family members such as husbands and children can also receive special protection.[148] In addition, those who interfere with protection of witness can face imprisonment of 1 to 3 years and/or a fine of 20,000-

141 *Ibid.*

142 *Ibid.*, quoting Naiyana Spapung, a former director of an NGO called Friends of Women in Asia.

143 The government decided to grant "alien status," which entailed permanent residency, to the adult hill tribe people and Thai citizenship to their children born between 14 December 1972 and 25 February 1992 on August 2000. On August 2001, the government decided to grant citizenship to all children whose parents have alien status. *UN Inter-Agency Project Newsletter*, 'Searching for Identity,' Issue 5 (2001), pp. 1 and 4. It has been noted, however, that the government's practice of granting citizenship is discriminatory towards hill-tribe people. Inclusion of Minorities, *supra,* p. 25, and Regional Seminar on Minority Rights, *supra*, p. 5.

144 Thailand is not a signatory to the Convention Relating to the Status of Refugees 1951, and therefore is not obliged to provide protection. The government has granted the limited right to remain in designated refugee camps in its territory to more than 100,000 refugees, although they do not have a right to return once they leave Thailand. Human Rights Watch (2001), *supra.*

145 BE 2546 (2003).

146 *Written Statement of the Asian Legal Resource Centre*, E/CN.4/2005/NGO/46, para, 2.

147 Section 10 of the *Witness Protection Act, supra.*

148 Section 11, *ibid.*

60,000 Baht.[149] While enactment of this law is an important step forward, the extent to which this law covers foreign victims is not clear.

2.3.4 NGOs Working on Trafficking in Thailand

In Thailand, there are several prominent organisations which deal with trafficking of human beings directly or indirectly. One example is an organisation called Development and Education Programme for Daughters and Communities Centre (DEPDC) which works on prevention and protection. The main aim of this organisation is to prevent children, both girls and boys, from being subjected to sexual and labour exploitation.[150] The organisation has implemented different programmes to achieve this goal, ranging from free education for disadvantaged children, to sex and health counselling.[151] In addition, the organisation also provides temporary accommodation for those who are trafficked from States such as Myanmar, Laos and China under a scheme called Halfway Home.[152] Each year, approximately 1,200 people benefit from this service.[153]

Another key organisation based in Thailand is the GAATW. Formed in 1994, it is a human rights organisation composed of more than 68 members (organisations) and specialises in research and advocacy.[154] The main objective of this organisation is to promote a human rights approach to address issues surrounding trafficking of human beings.[155] To this end, one of the important initiatives taken was the adoption of the "Human Rights Standards for the Treatment of Trafficked Persons" together with the International Human Rights Law Group and the Foundation Against Trafficking in Women.[156] In the area of research, the GAATW, conducted a project on Mobility and Health in Thailand between 2003-2004. The study examined the experience of women migrant workers from Myanmar, Cambodia and Laos in domestic work, sex work and factory work.[157] The study discovered, among other issues, that instead of forcibly transported into Thailand, many women actually have chosen to migrate in order to live in a new country and earn more money, and that many have experienced various health problems due to harsh working conditions.[158]

149 Sections 21-23, *ibid.*

150 DEPDC, at http://www.depdc.org/english/about_us1.htm.

151 *Report of the Special Rapporteur on Sales of Children, Child Prostitution and Child Pornography*, E/CN.4/2004/9, para. 108.

152 Electronic correspondence from Ms. Emma Nicholson of the DEPDC (27/5/02).

153 Electronic correspondence from Ms. Eileen Woliner of the DEPDC (22/9/05).

154 Interview with Ms. Bandana Pattanaik, Co-ordinator of GAATW (15/7/05).

155 *Ibid.*

156 *Human Rights Standards for the Treatment of Trafficked Persons* (1999).

157 *GAATW Newsletter*, Issue 23 (June 2005), p. 63.

158 *Ibid.*

2.4 National Case Study: Poland[159]

2.4.1 *National Laws and Policies*

Similar to Thailand, trafficking of human beings is dealt with by criminal and immigration laws in Poland. The key legislation in this regard is the *Polish Penal Code* 1997.[160] There are several provisions which are relevant to trafficking. Article 204 of the Code, for instance, reads as follows:

> § 1. Who, with the purpose of obtaining a material benefit, incites a person to prostitution or facilitates prostitution of a person is subject to a sentence of imprisonment for a period of time of up to 3 years.
>
> § 2. The sentence specified in § 1 is applicable to the perpetrator who is profiting by another person's prostitution.
>
> § 3. If the person referred to in § 1 or 2 is a minor, the perpetrator is subject to a sentence of imprisonment for a period of time from 1 to 10 years.
>
> § 4. The sentence specified in § 3 is applicable to the perpetrator who entices or abducts a person into prostitution abroad.

Article 253 of the Code further states:

> § 1. Who traffics in persons, even with their consent, is subject to a sentence of imprisonment for a period of time not shorter than 3 years.
>
> § 2. Who, with the purpose of obtaining a material benefit, organises adoption of children contrary to the provisions of the Act is subject to a sentence of imprisonment for a period of time from 3 months to 5 years.

Moreover, according to Article 264, § 3:

> Whoever organises for other persons the crossing of the borders of the Polish Republic contrary to the regulations, is liable to the punishment of deprivation of liberty from three months to five years.

159 Poland has signed (12//12/00) and ratified (12/11/01) the Organised Crime Convention. It has also signed (both on 4/10/01) and ratified (both on 26/9/03) the Trafficking and Smuggling Protocols. No reservation or declaration has been entered. See Signatories, *supra.*

160 Dz.U. Nr.88 poz. 553. The Stability Pact Legislationline at http://www.legislationline.org/.

There are several points which should be mentioned. First, the Penal Code makes a distinction between trafficking and smuggling of human beings. Although Article 264 does not include the term "smuggling," the description of the offence is similar to the definition of smuggling under the Smuggling Protocol. To be specific, Article 264, paragraph 3, does not entail elements of coercion, deception, and subsequent exploitation. Second, as for trafficking, the Penal Code can be applied to trafficking for purposes other than prostitution and sexual exploitation. Although a mention of prostitution and sexual exploitation is made under Article 204, Article 253 does not limit the application for those purposes only. A related point to this is that the law is neutral as to gender. In other words, the Penal Code also applies to cases where men and boys are trafficked for purposes other than prostitution and sexual exploitation. Third, penalties imposed for trafficking for prostitution abroad and trafficking in general are different. The penalty is heavier for trafficking in general under Article 253, because trafficking in women for prostitution constitutes a misdemeanour, while trafficking in general is treated as a more serious crime.[161]

There is another Article which is relevant under the Penal Code. That is Article 258, which targets organised criminal groups.[162] Under this Article, "belonging to an organised group/association that intends to commit an offence is illegal" and is punishable with a maximum sentence of 3 years' imprisonment. The penalty can be higher if a group is armed with weapons (5 years' imprisonment). However, if a member voluntarily leaves an organised criminal group and provides information on criminal activities to the authorities, that member will not be prosecuted under Article 259.

In addition to the Penal Code, trafficking also falls within the *Act on Aliens* 1997 as amended in 2003.[163] A point to note is that provisions governing those trafficked are far more extensive than those covering traffickers. For example, those who reside in Poland without visas/entry permits (Article 88.1.1), engage in employment without authorisation (Article 88.1.2), and cross borders illegally (Article 88.1.6) are subject to expulsion. Those who have been issued with a decision for expulsion are sent to State border or sea/airports for immediate removal if they pose threats to national security or refuse to obey the expulsion orders (Articles 90.2, and 95). In addition, some individuals may be detained under the Act. The detention applies to those who do not comply with orders for expulsion. They can be detained for up to 48 hours, during which time the authorities must make appropriate arrangements for their expulsion (Article 101). One can

161 International Helsinki Federation for Human Rights (IHF), *A Form of Slavery: Trafficking in Women in OSCE Member States* (Vienna: IHF)(2000), p. 44; and Siron and Van Baeveghem, *supra*, p. 199.

162 Niesner, E, and C. Jones-Pauly, *Trafficking in Women in Europe: Prosecution and Victim Protection in a European Context* (Bielefeld: Klein Verlag)(2001), p. 99.

163 Journal of Laws of 2003, No. 128, it 1175.

also be detained for up to 90 days while he/she awaits expulsion (Article 106). As for traffickers, the only relevant penal provision is Article 147 which prohibits one from taking identity and travel documents from aliens.

2.4.2 *Enforcement*

2.4.2.1 Relevant Agencies and Statistical Information

In Poland, there are two main law enforcement agencies which address trafficking. The first is the Border Guard, whose functions are stipulated in, amongst others, *Act on Aliens*. The second agency is the police. The central authority comes in part from the Co-ordination Bureau of Criminal Justice, within which a special unit for dealing with trafficking of human beings was recently established.[164] The unit is responsible for gathering evidence in relation to trafficking so as to bring cases before the courts.[165] The Border Guard and the Police are said to co-operate with each other by exchanging information and conducting joint anti-trafficking activities.[166] Further, they also co-operate with NGOs such as the La Strada[167] in the area of information exchange and campaigns.[168]

Some examples on enforcement activities are available. In 1999, the Border Guard and the Police conducted a joint operation which resulted in the breaking-up of a gang of traffickers who were said to have earned 10 million Euro by trafficking around 3,800 immigrants into the European Union.[169] In the same year, the police also conducted crackdowns on highway trafficking and prostitution, which contributed to a twenty percent reduction on this type of trafficking.[170] Between 2001 and 2002, the Police conducted 149 investigations into cases of trafficking, leading to 47 arrests.[171]

Some people involved in trafficking have also been prosecuted. According to the Public Prosecutor's Office, 103 cases under Articles 204(4) and 253, involving 818 victims and 248 traffickers, were brought before courts between

164 Siron and Van Baeveghem, *supra*, p. 254.

165 *Ibid.*, p. 255.

166 Rybicki, R (Ministry of Interior and Administration), *Trafficking in Human Beings: Role of Governments – Polish Perspective* (Holy See, 15-16 May 2002).

167 See below for detail.

168 Rybicki, *supra*. The importance of co-operation with NGOs was also reiterated by Sylweiusz M. Krolack, the Deputy Minister of Justice, in his speech at the European Conference on Human Trafficking, held in September 2002, at which the author was a participant.

169 Siron and Van Baeveghem, *supra*, p. 34.

170 U.S. Department of State, *Country Reports on Human Rights Practice 2000: Poland* at http://www.state.gov/g/drl/rls/hrrpt/2000/eur/879.htm (hereinafter Human Rights in Poland (2000)).

171 Trafficking Report 2003, *supra*, p. 121.

1995 and 1999.[172] In recent times, 190 individuals have been prosecuted under the same Articles between 2000 and 2001.[173] In total, 240 investigations led to the prosecution of 187 cases (483 traffickers/smugglers and 1083 victims) between 1995 and 2001, and 53 cases were terminated.[174] In relation to sentencing, a total of 181 people were found guilty, of which 62 people received between 2 to 5 years' imprisonment while the majority received suspended sentences.[175]

2.4.2.2 Analysis of Law Enforcement

While the tasks undertaken by these law enforcement agencies are important in the prevention and suppression of trafficking of human beings, some problems have been reported in relation to enforcement. For instance, while Article 253 of the Penal Code mentioned above is applicable to trafficking for purposes other than prostitution, it has been reported that the law enforcement agencies rarely apply that provision.[176] A result of this is that prosecution of cases of trafficking carried out for purposes other than prostitution are rare. This indicates that the law enforcement agencies in Poland consider trafficking mostly in terms of prostitution and sexual exploitation.

The law enforcement agencies also suffer from a lack of resources, expertise and training to deal with trafficking. To begin with, the phenomenon is still considered to be a low priority by the law enforcement agencies.[177] One reason for this is that the law enforcement agencies lack adequate knowledge on trafficking and the government has not been able to conduct in-depth research on the matter.[178] Moreover, it has been reported that law enforcement agencies are not sufficiently trained to identify those trafficked as victims.[179] One consequence

172 Rybicki, *supra*.

173 *Ibid.*

174 *Ibid.* These cases were either found to have no perpetrators involved or did not amount to offences under Articles 204 and 253.

175 Karsznicki, K (National Prosecutor's Office) 'Trafficking in Human Beings in Light of Criminal Proceedings Conducted in Poland between 1995-2002," *Report of the International Conference on Combating Trafficking in Human Beings: Prevention through Legal Solutions* (23-24 May 2003), p. 4.

176 Pearson, *supra*, p. 212. The research and report on Poland was conducted and written by an NGO *La Strada Foundation*.

177 Okolski, *supra*, p. 249: and Special Rapporteur on Women in Poland (1997), *supra*, paras. 92 and 93.

178 Mirecki, P (Ministry of Interior and Administration of Poland), 'Trafficking in Human Beings: Situation in Poland,' International Conference, *supra*, p. 16.

179 European Commission, *Comprehensive Monitoring Report on Poland's Preparation for Membership* (2003), p. 54; and Pearson, *supra*, p. 214.

of all of this is that human, financial and material resources are inadequate to effectively combat trafficking.[180]

In addition, border control is also not effective. It has been reported that it does not conduct extensive examinations at some borders and normally allow people to come and go, unless they detect something unusual.[181] The citizens of Szczecin in Poland, for instance, only need their personal identification cards to cross the border to Germany.[182] Moreover, despite the fact that the *Act on Aliens* allows victims to stay for a certain period of time,[183] a priority for border control and management is said to be immediate deportation, and this makes it difficult for concerned law enforcement agencies to collect evidence to be used in a court of law for prosecution and punishment of traffickers.[184]

Corruption is also acknowledged as a problem among law enforcement agencies. Based on research conducted, women's groups in Poland report that many law enforcement officers co-operate with traffickers for their own benefit.[185] For instance, some members of the Border Guard have been charged with abducting two Ukrainians and handing them over to traffickers.[186] An army officer in Poland was also found guilty of co-operating with traffickers on the Polish-Ukrainian Border.[187] It was noted by the European Commission in this connection that there has not been much progress in combating corruption in Poland.[188]

Furthermore, given the widespread nature of trafficking, the rates of arrest and conviction of traffickers are low, and the punishments received are not heavy. There are several reasons for this. First, the law enforcement agencies regard trafficking as transitory in nature and concentrate more on removing illegal immigrants.[189] Second, some judges are threatened with violence or death by organised criminal groups unless cases are dropped.[190] Third, victims do not report to the law enforcement agencies. Prostitution itself is not prohibited in

180 Okolski, *supra*, p. 250. The European Commission also notes that the staffing of the police remains a problem, *ibid.*

181 Special Rapporteur on Women in Poland (1997), *supra*, para. 90.

182 *Ibid.*

183 See below.

184 Karsznicki, *supra*, p. 4; and Trafficking Report 2003, *supra*, p. 121.

185 Special Rapporteur on Women in Poland (1997), *supra*, para. 90.

186 IHF, *Anti-Trafficking Efforts Crippled by Corruption and Lack of Proper Official Response to the Victims' Needs* (3/2/02), at http://www.ihf-hr.org/viewbinary/viewhtml.php?doc_id=1111.

187 Okolski, *supra*, p. 290.

188 European Commission, *supra*, p. 16.

189 Okolski, *supra*, p. 249.

190 Special Rapporteur on Women in Poland (1997), *supra*, para. 98.

Poland, and women are reluctant to come forward to the authorities as prostitution is a good source of income.[191] It is also rare for foreign victims to come forward as they are fearful of enforcement action and reprisal by traffickers.[192] This makes it difficult to obtain evidence to prosecute and punish traffickers as noted elsewhere.

2.4.3 Victim Protection Measures

In analysing victim protection measures in Poland, it becomes apparent that they are not sufficient, leading to a conclusion that Poland has not fully adopted a human rights framework. There are several examples which support this conclusion. Article 14 of the *Act on Aliens*, for instance, provides that an alien whose sojourn in Poland is contrary to his previous declaration or whose residence is unwelcome on the grounds of safeguarding public order (e.g. prostitution) can obtain in extraordinary situations (e.g. providing testimony in courts) a temporary visa for a specified period of time.[193] However, temporary residence permits are not given to many in practice. In addition to the fact that deportation of victims takes precedence over their protection as noted above, there are no financial solutions to cover the accommodation for the victim during their stay in Poland.[194]

In addition, social assistance measures for victims of trafficking are not adequate. In theory, Polish nationals who are victims of trafficking are entitled to social welfare.[195] In practice, however, providing social welfare has proven to be difficult because the government lacks resources, and therefore many cannot benefit from it.[196] Foreign victims are in a worse position. Except for refugees and those with legal status, foreign nationals are not entitled to social welfare benefits, and are normally deported in order to reduce the costs of keeping them in detention.[197] As a consequence, many victims are forced to seek assistance from NGOs, which are often unable to provide sufficient assistance due to a lack of financial and other resources.[198]

Moreover, there is much room for improvement in relation to protection of witnesses. The *Code of Criminal Procedure* 1997[199] provides for several measures

191 Niesner and Jones-Pauly, *supra*, p. 103.

192 *Ibid.,* p. 104.

193 *supra.*

194 Karsznicki, *supra*, p. 8 .

195 Niesner and Jones-Pauly, *supra*, p. 106.

196 *Ibid.*

197 Mirecki, *supra*, p. 17; and Pearson, *supra*, p. 217.

198 Pearson, *ibid.*, p. 217.

199 The Stability Pact Legislationline at http://www.legislationline.org/view.php?document=55268.

to protect witnesses. They include examining a case in a closed session (Article 183), protecting personal data of victims (Article 184.1) and withholding their identities during cross-examination (Article 184.4). A witness protection section was also created within the police as a result of the entry into force of this law in 1998.[200] Nevertheless, there are several problems. The same situation with Thailand applies, in that this law does not cover illegal immigrants, as their conduct is governed by the immigration law. It has also been reported that victims often have to serve as witnesses without professional help due to a lack of sufficient financial resources.[201] This is particularly damaging for victims, as they are not entitled to free legal aid.[202] The status of an anonymous witness, which may be granted to victims, is not helpful either, as traffickers can easily identify victims from the statements given by them.[203] Finally, the witness protection scheme does not function properly, due to a lack of experience and proper training.[204]

Poland joined the European Union (EU) in May 2004, and some changes will be made in relation to protection of victims in the near future. Several initiatives have been taken in relation to trafficking at the EU level, and Poland will be obliged to implement them. One example is the Framework Decision on Trafficking in Human Beings which aims to create a common EU approach to trafficking through approximation of national laws and policies.[205] It obliges Member States to adopt a common definition of trafficking, minimum threshold for penalties, and victim protection procedures. Therefore, there are future prospects for victims to be protected.

A question remains, however, as to the effect of the elimination of external borders on the scale of trafficking. On the one hand, trafficking of Polish nationals into EU Member States is likely to be reduced as the principle of the free movement of people will be applied.[206] On the other hand, the elimination of external borders is likely to force traffickers to concentrate on trafficking of non-EU nationals into other EU Member States through Poland. Facilitating entry into new Member States is easy because traffickers actively use bribes and

---

200 European Commission, *1999 Regular Report on Poland's Progress Towards Accession,* p. 74.

201 Niesner and Jones-Pauly, *supra*, p. 106; and Pearson, *supra,* p. 214.

202 Siron and Van Baeveghem, *supra*, p. 263.

203 Niesner and Jones-Pauly, *supra*, p. 109.

204 European Commission (1999), *supra*, p. 74.

205 See Chapter 3. For a critical analysis of this instrument, see Obokata, T, 'EU Council Framework Decision on Combating Trafficking in Human Beings: A Critical Appraisal' 40 *Common Market Law Review* 917 (2003).

206 However, the freedom of movement will not be granted until sometime after the accession. Phuong, C, 'Enlarging 'Fortress Europe': EU Accession, Asylum, and Immigration in Candidate Countries,' 52 *International & Comparative Law Quarterly* 641 (2003), p. 648.

violence as a means to advance their illegal business, and States in transition, including Poland, are particularly vulnerable to such practices. This will put more pressure on the Polish government to control the flow of migrants on borders linking Poland and former Soviet States such as Ukraine and Belarus.

2.4.4 NGOs Working on Trafficking in Poland

Although there are many NGOs in Poland, the number of those working in the field of trafficking is limited. One of the most active NGOs working in Poland is the La Strada Foundation, an organisation which focuses exclusively on trafficking. Established in 1995, this organisation deals mainly with trafficking of women, not only in Poland, but also in other States, such as Ukraine, the Czech Republic, and the Balkans, all of which are deeply affected by the practice.[207] Its activities consist of a combination of prevention, protection of victims, research and advocacy.

In relation to prevention, the organisation provides information and education, among other things, on the risks involved in trafficking, the labour market, and conditions of migrants abroad, to young girls, students, and "dropouts."[208] As for protection, the organisation co-ordinates the provision of legal, economic, social, medical and psychological assistance to victims of trafficking, and provides temporary accommodation and vocational training through a network of governmental and non-governmental organisations which provide these services.[209] In 2000, for instance, the organisation received $ 3,850 from the Ministry of Internal Affairs, which was used to provide food and social workers to assist victims for 4 months. [210] Advocacy activities include dissemination of information to the mass media and political and law enforcement bodies, such as Parliament, the police, and the Prosecutor's Office, and organising seminars and meetings for them.[211]

Another important NGO is the Helsinki Foundation for Human Rights.[212] It was established in 1989 and is a part of the International Helsinki Federation of Human Rights.[213] It conducts a wide variety of activities related to the protection and promotion of human rights, including running a Human Rights School for students, professionals and government officials and training courses

207 La Strada Foundation at http://free.ngo.pl/lastrada/index_en.html.

208 Buchowska, *supra.*

209 *Ibid.*

210 Human Rights in Poland (2000), *supra.*

211 U.S. Department of State, Country Reports on Human Rights Practice 2003: Poland (2004) at http://www.state.gov/g/drl/rls/hrrpt/2003/27858.htm (hereinafter Human Rights in Poland (2003)).

212 Helsinki Foundation for Human Rights at http://www.hfhrpol.waw.pl/En/.

213 IHF at http://www.ihf-hr.org/index.php.

for law enforcement and prison officials.[214] In relation to trafficking of human beings, the Foundation developed the "Guardian Angel" programme together with the La Strada Foundation in 2003. This programme trained social workers to help victims of trafficking with legal issues so that they could be advocates for the victims before the courts, police, and prosecutors.[215] The Helsinki Federation also issues reports and statements on trafficking of human beings, in an attempt to mobilise global action against the phenomenon.[216]

2.5 National Case Study: United Kingdom[217]

2.5.1 National Laws and Policies[218]

In the United Kingdom, several laws are relevant to trafficking. One example is the *Offences Against the Person Act 1861*.[219] The Act covers offences of assault occasioning actual bodily harm, wounding or causing GBH and others which cause danger to life or bodily harm (with or without weapons).[220] These offences are relevant as there are cases where those trafficked are placed under harsh conditions and suffer from bodily injuries. If people end up dying, then the charges of murder or manslaughter may be brought against traffickers.[221]

In addition, common end purposes of trafficking, namely prostitution and sexual exploitation, has been regulated by the *Sexual Offences Act 1956*.[222]

---

214 Helsinki Foundation, *supra*.

215 Human Rights in Poland (2003), *supra*.

216 See for instance, *OSCE Human Dimension Implementation Meeting (October 2003): Interventions and Recommendations by the International Helsinki Federation of Human Rights* (2003); *Statements of the International Helsinki Federation of Human Rights to the OSCE Implementation Meeting on Human Dimension Issues* (2001); and *A Perspective on Women's Human Rights in Poland* (2000).

217 The United Kingdom has signed (14/12/00) and ratified (9/2/06) the Organised Crime Convention. It has also signed (both on 14/12/00) and ratified (both on 9/2/06) the Trafficking and Smuggling Protocols. No declaration or reservation has been entered. Signatories, *supra*.

218 Legislation mentioned in this section applies to England, Wales, Northern Ireland and Scotland unless otherwise stated.

219 24 &25 Vict, c. 100. This Act does not extend to Scotland. Pertinent offences are established at common law.

220 *Ibid.* Section 39 of the *Criminal Justice Act 1988* (c.33) is also relevant. This Section applies to common assault. Originally a common law offence, common assault applies to a case where there is an assault, but no actual injury is caused.

221 Murder and manslaughter are also common law offences. See for instance, *R v Wacker* [2003] QB 1207. Wacker, a Dutch lorry driver, was convicted of manslaughter as he let 58 Chinese nationals die in the sealed container.

222 c. 69. This law does not apply to Scotland. Trafficking related offences are covered by *Criminal Law (Consolidation) (Scotland) Act 1995* (c. 39) instead.

Although the Act does not specifically use the terms "traffic" or "trafficking," it does cover some aspects of the phenomenon. For instance, Sections 2 and 3 stipulate that procuring of women by threats or false representations for unlawful sexual intercourse in any part of the world is an offence. These provisions were adopted mainly to combat the white slave traffic.[223] Sections 17-21 establish offences of abduction of women or girls for unlawful sexual intercourse or marriage. In addition, there are Sections on prostitution which not only criminalise the procuring of, and exercising control over women and girls to become prostitutes in any parts of the world (Sections 22-31), but also prohibit soliciting and owning/managing brothels (including landlords and tenants permitting premises for prostitution)(Sections 32-37).[224] The punishments for these offences range from 3 months' imprisonment and/or a fine of £100 (first time offence for owning brothels) to life imprisonment (permitting a girl under thirteen to use premises for sexual intercourse under Section 25).[225]

Some amendments have been made to the *Sexual Offences Act 1956* over the course of time[226] and the laws on sexual offences have recently been reviewed by the government. A White Paper in relation to new legislation was published by the government in 2000[227] and the *Sexual Offences Act 2003* came into force in May 2004.[228] Of particular importance is the introduction of offence of trafficking for sexual exploitation. Sections 57-60 apply to trafficking people into, within or from the United Kingdom for sexual exploitation, and provide for a maximum penalty of 14 years' imprisonment. This is a welcome change, as the degree of punishment under the Sexual Offences Act 1956 has been criticised as being very lenient.[229]

---

223 Temkin, J, *Rape and Legal Process* (2nd ed) (Oxford: Oxford University Press)(2003), p. 58.

224 It should be noted that procuring of prostitutes or sex workers to perform prostitution is not an offence under Section 22. The phrase procuring "to become prostitute" suggests that those trafficked were not prostitutes before being procured. Tiggey, M, et al., *For Love or Money: Pimps and the Management of Sex Work (Police Research Series Paper No. 134)* (London: Home Office)(2000), p. 6.

225 *Sexual Offences Act 1956,* Second Schedule.

226 See for instance, *Sexual Offences Act 1967*(c. 60); and *Sexual Offences Act 1985* (c. 44).

227 Home Office, *Setting the Boundaries: Reforming the Law on Sex Offences* (London: Home Office)(2000) (hereinafter Setting the Boundaries).

228 c. 42. The Sexual Offences Bill was introduced to Parliament in January 2003. This applies to England and Wales. By virtue of s. 142, trafficking offences also apply to Northern Ireland.

229 For instance, Sections 2, 3, 22 and 24 are rarely enforced partly because they carry a maximum of 2 years' imprisonment. Setting the Boundaries, *supra*, pp. 30 and 106.

In addition to legislation on sexual offences, immigration law is also pertinent. The principle Act is the *Immigration Act 1971*.[230] Some provisions apply to those who are trafficked. Section 24, for instance, stipulates that those who enter the United Kingdom illegally or stay beyond the time allowed by the leave to remain may face a maximum fine of £200 and/or imprisonment not exceeding 6 months. Similarly, under Section 26, those who fail to undergo examination by the immigration officers, fail to produce any information or documents on their possessions, and make false statements or representations, or alter entry clearance, visas, and work permits, can be liable to the same degree of penalties as Section 24. In addition, those trafficked may be deported if they remain beyond the time limit imposed by the leave, or are convicted of offence (for those over the age of 17) in the United Kingdom.[231]

As for traffickers, Section 25 is applicable. The main purpose of this provision was to impose "severe new penalties on people who engage in trafficking in illegal migrants."[232] Under Section 25, those securing unlawful entry can be fined a maximum of £400 or imprisoned up to 7 years (on conviction on indictment), while those harbouring illegal entrants or overstayers are liable for a fine of £400 or imprisonment of up to 6 months.

A subsequent piece of legislation, the *Asylum and Immigration Act 1996*,[233] made some amendments to the previous Act. For instance, an offence of obtaining leave to enter by deception is added under Section 4. Section 5 criminalises the act of facilitating the illegal entry of asylum claimants. This is particularly important, as many asylum seekers and refugees have been trafficked into or through the United Kingdom. Finally, under paragraph 1(2) of Schedule 2 of the Act, those who obtain leave to remain by deception are liable to deportation.

Similarly, the *Immigration and Asylum Act 1999*[234] made some changes to the previous Acts. Section 28 on deception extends not only to obtaining the leave to enter or remain, but also to securing the avoidance, postponement or revocation of enforcement actions against an illegal entrant. By Section 29, the penalty for assisting illegal entry was increased from 7 years to 10 years imprisonment. In addition, a new crime of assisting clandestine entries was also created by the Act.[235] The new law extends the coverage of the earlier laws which focused on movements of people by air and sea (aircraft and ships) to include vehicles (including trailers, semi-trailers, and caravans), detached trailers, rail

230 c. 77.

231 Section 3(5), *ibid.*

232 Maulding, Hansard, Vol. 813, Col. 54.

233 c.49.

234 c.77.

235 Sections 32 through 39, *ibid.*

freights and trains.[236] This provision resulted from the completion of the Channel Tunnel linking the United Kingdom and France.

The UK laws on immigration have also undergone review by the government. The Home Office published a White Paper entitled *Secure Border, Safe Haven: Integration with Diversity in Modern Britain* in February 2002.[237] This White Paper set out a list of proposals for the suppression of trafficking and smuggling. Subsequently, the Nationality, Immigration and Asylum Bill was introduced in Parliament in April 2002, and the *Nationality, Immigration and Asylum Act 2002*[238] came into force in February 2003. A critical point to be made is that the Act only covers trafficking for the purpose of prostitution,[239] contrary to the White Paper which recognised the necessity to deal with a wide variety of exploitation.[240] The government considered at the time that a provision addressing wider exploitation would go beyond the scope of the Act, and therefore the introduction of more comprehensive legislation in the future was suggested.[241] In the meantime, the government envisaged the Act as a temporary solution to deal with exploitation by way of prostitution, which it regarded to be the worst form of exploitation.[242]

Other forms of exploitation were finally addressed in June 2004, when the *Asylum and Immigration (Treatment of Claimants, etc) Act 2004*[243] received Royal Assent. Section 4 creates an offence of trafficking for general exploitation, which carries a maximum of 14 years' imprisonment. This is a welcome change for the obvious reason that traffickers who transport people for purposes other than sexual exploitation will be punished. This is also in line with the Trafficking Protocol.

236 Section 43, *ibid.*

237 Home Office, *Secure Border, Safe Haven: Integration with Diversity in Modern Britain* (London: HMSO)(2002)(hereinafter Secure Border).

238 c. 41.

239 s. 145, *ibid.* This provision, however, does not apply to Scotland by virtue of s. 163. Instead, s. 22 of *Criminal Justice (Scotland) Act 2003* (asp 7), which provides for the same offence of trafficking in prostitution, applies to Scotland. The scope of this provision was expanded when *Sexual Offences Act 2003* came into force, as it addresses trafficking not only for prostitution, but also for other sexual exploitation.

240 Secure Border, *supra.*

241 Lord Filkin, *Hansard*, H.L., Vol. 639, Col. 412.

242 *Ibid.*

243 c. 19.

2.5.2 *Enforcement*

2.5.2.1 Relevant Agencies and Statistical Information

The United Kingdom has several agencies charged with enforcement of those laws which cover trafficking; for instance, the police. In March 2004, for instance, 40 people, (including 9 people being suspected of facilitating illegal entry), were arrested in a series of raid conducted in London and surrounding areas.[244] In March 2005, more than 230 asylum seekers were arrested for not possessing passports, which became an offence under the *Asylum and Immigration (Treatment of Claimants, etc) Act 2004*.[245]

Two other organisations deal with trafficking of human beings; they are the National Criminal Intelligence Service (NCIS) and the National Crime Squad (NCS).[246] In the summer of 2000, the NCS, together with the Home Office and other relevant agencies, put together plans for operations against human trafficking. Initiatives such as *Operation Medway* and *Operation Zephaniah* contributed to the arrests of a number of suspects, not only in the United Kingdom, but also Australia, Germany and Hong Kong.[247] In a more recent example, the NCS has arrested 147 traffickers and smugglers, dismantled 51 criminal organisations and seized £266,000 under the *Proceeds of Crime Act 2002*[248] between April 2004 and March 2005.[249]

In addition, the immigration authority also has an important role to play in relation to trafficking of human beings. The Immigration and Nationality Directorate (IND) of the Home Office is responsible for immigration control in the United Kingdom, and the immigration officers working for the IND are given wider powers than the police in this area of law. The immigration authority has also contributed to the reduction of the instances of trafficking to some extent. For instance, the number of people refused entry at ports increased from 16,740 in 1993 to 38,110 in 2003.[250] The total number of people deported as a result of enforcement action also rose from 6,080 in 1993 to 19,630 in 2003.[251] Immigration officers also work abroad to prevent the flow of illegal immigrants into the United Kingdom. One media source reported recently that 9 immigration

244 *The Guardian*, 'Gangmaster Ring Arrests in Dawn Raids' (26/3/04).

245 *The Guardian*, 'Asylum Seekers Jailed for Having No Passport' (18/3/05).

246 The NCS and the NCIS were replaced by the Serious and Organised Crime Agency (SOCA) in 2006 under the *Serious and Organised Crime and Police Act 2005* (c.15). For more detail, see Home Office, *One Step Ahead: A 21st Century Strategy to Defeat Organised Crime* (London: HMSO)(2004).

247 National Crime Squad (NCS), *Annual Report 2001*, p. 19.

248 c.22.

249 NCS, *Annual Report 2005*, p. 9.

250 Home Office, *Control of Immigration: Statistics, United Kingdom 2003* (London: HMSO)(2004), p. 73 (hereinafter Control of Immigration (2003)).

251 *Ibid.*

officers were working with the Secret Intelligence Service (MI6) in the Balkans to gather information on Turkish and Kosovan gangs who have been trafficking thousands of people.[252] Moreover, 7 immigration officers from the United Kingdom, together with an immigration officer from Denmark, assisted the State Border Service in Bosnia to improve detection capabilities in the past.[253]

Law enforcement against trafficking was consolidated in 2000, when an inter-agency initiative known as *Reflex* was established by the government. This initiative is led by the SOCA, in co-operation with major law enforcement agencies such as the IND and police forces such as the Metropolitan Police, Kent Police and the British Transport Police. One of *Reflex*'s first initiatives was the establishment of the Immigration Crime Team whose primary aim is to target organised criminal groups by disrupting and dismantling them and attacking all aspects of their operation (i.e. fraudulent document production, money laundering, and asset seizure).[254] Since its inception in 2000, *Reflex* has launched 82 operations which have dismantled 17 organised criminal groups, resulting in 69 arrests.[255]

Finally, some traffickers have been convicted. In 2003, 260 people were brought before the Magistrates' Courts for violating Section 25 of the Immigration Act mentioned above.[256] Of these, 65 people were found guilty.[257] As for the Crown Courts, a total of 162 people were charged for violation of Section 25, and 119 people were actually convicted.[258] With regard to sexual offences, a total

252 *The Independent*, 'UK Experts Sent to New Front Line in War on Mafia' (22/1/02).

253 *The Independent*, 'Sex, Drugs and Illegal Migrants: Sarajevo's Export Trade to Britain' (21/1/02).

254 Written Correspondence from Mr. Sean McKenna, Detective Chief Inspector, NCS Immigration Crime Team (11/3/03).

255 Electronic Correspondence from the Home Office and NSC Immigration Crime Team, *National Operational Plan 2003/2004*.

256 Control of Immigration (2003), *supra*, p. 77. The figure can be broken down as follows: 226 (knowingly facilitating the entry of an illegal entrant), 15 (knowingly facilitating the entry of an asylum claimant), 9 (knowingly facilitating leave to remain of persons by means of deception) and 10 (knowingly harbouring an illegal entrants or person who is in breach of the conditions of his leave).

257 *Ibid.* The figure can be broken down as follows: 58 (knowingly facilitating the entry of an illegal entrant), 4(knowingly facilitating the entry of an asylum claimant), 2 (knowingly facilitating leave to remain of persons by means of deception), and 1 (knowingly harbouring an illegal entrant or person who is in breach of the conditions of his leave).

258 *Ibid.* The figure can be broken down as follows: 145 (knowingly facilitating the entry of an illegal entrant), 8 (knowingly facilitating the entry of an asylum claimant) and 9 (knowingly facilitating leave to remain of persons by means of deception). As for conviction: 107 (knowingly facilitating the entry of an illegal entrant), 5 (knowingly

of 5,587 offenders were found guilty or cautioned at all courts in 2002.[259] Some of these were convicted and sentenced for offences of relevance to trafficking. While 41 were found guilty or cautioned for procurement, 6 were convicted for abduction.[260] As for the trafficking and smuggling offences under the NIAA, 572 people were arrested, resulting in 66 conviction in 2004.[261]

2.5.2.2 Analysis of Law Enforcement

Several observations can be made in analysing law enforcement in the United Kingdom. For instance, issues relating to trafficking are not well understood by law enforcement agencies. Anti-Slavery International, an NGO based in London, reports that the immigration authority tends to see those trafficked not as victims, but merely as violators of immigration laws and regulations.[262] Further, many police forces in the United Kingdom still do not believe that trafficking is serious enough to merit attention.[263] Such a mentality is shared by many police forces in the United Kingdom, and dealing with the phenomenon is low in their list of priorities.[264] One consequence of this is that there is little interest in providing adequate resources to deal with trafficking.[265] It is worth noting in this respect that some police forces have disbanded their vice units which deal with the sex industry, including trafficking.[266] The lack of resources also means that officers receive insufficient training on foreign languages, identification of false travel documents and visas, treatment of victims of trafficking, and other issues related to the phenomenon.[267]

Moreover, the treatments of trafficked people raise human rights concerns. The decision to implement enforcement actions are sometimes made by immigration officers who may lack adequate knowledge of refugee laws and of human rights situations in the States of origin.[268] Many illegal immigrants are

---

facilitating the entry of an asylum claimant), and 7 (knowingly facilitating leave to remain of persons by means of deception).

259 Home Office, *Criminal Statistics England and Wales 2002: Statistics Relating to Criminal Proceedings for the Year 2002* (London: Home Office)(2003), p. 45.

260 *Ibid.*

261 Trafficking Report 2005, *supra.*

262 Pearson, *supra*, p. 108.

263 *The Independent*, 'Red Light Squads Axed by Police' (6/5/01).

264 *Ibid.*

265 Kelly and Regan, *supra*, p. 35; and Somerset, *supra*, p. 35.

266 The police forces in Bedfordshire, Thames Valley, Humberside, and Derbyshire no longer have vice squads. *The Independent*, 'Red Light,' *supra.*

267 Lord Wilberforce, Hansard, H.L., Vol. 632, Col. 899.

268 *Report of the Working Group on Arbitrary Detention: Report on the Visit of the Working Group to the United Kingdom on Issue of Immigrants and Asylum Seekers,*

also detained for a long period of time prior to deportation.[269] One reason for this is that many States of origin are said to be unwilling to accept their own nationals, and this is making it difficult to accelerate the deportation procedure.[270] Moreover, instances of racial harassment against refugees, asylum seekers and ethnic minorities have been reported in local communities, and not much has been done to alleviate the situation.[271] Finally, the government primarily treat trafficking as a migration issue and therefore concentrates on deporting the trafficked victims.[272]

2.5.3 Victim Protection Measures

There are several protection measures which are applicable to victims of trafficking in the United Kingdom. One example is the grant of temporary permission to stay. It may be granted on a case-by-case basis if those trafficked are willing to co-operate with law enforcement authorities and to provide evidence.[273] An initial stay of 3 years is granted under "humanitarian protection" or "discretionary leave."[274] After the passage of 3 years, those victims may be able to apply for "indefinite leave to remain," which is equivalent to permanent residency in the United Kingdom.[275]

Since March 2003, the government also has been funding a pilot project called the Poppy Project. This is run by an NGO Eaves Housing for Women and provides shelters and support for up to 25 women who satisfy the following conditions: 1) the woman was working as a prostitute; 2) she has been forcibly exploited; 3) she has come forward to the authorities; and 4) she is willing to co-

E/CN.4/1999/63/Add.3, para. 18.

269 *Concluding Observations of the Human Rights Committee: United Kingdom of Great Britain and Northern Ireland*, CCPR/CO/73/UK and CCPR/CO/73/UKOT (2001), para. 16.

270 Working Group on Arbitrary Detention, *supra*, para. 24. If States of origin refuse to accept, then the government attempts to find a third State, and this can take at least a few months.

271 *Concluding Observation of the Committee on the Elimination of Racial Discrimination: United Kingdom of Great Britain and Northern Ireland*, CERD/C/304/Add.2 (2001), paras. 13-15.

272 Women's Commission for Refugee Women and Children, *The Struggle between Migration Control and Victim Protection: The UK Approach to Human Trafficking* (New York: Women's Commission for Refugee Women and Children)(2005), p. 35.

273 Pearson, *supra*, p. 106.

274 Formerly known as "exceptional leave to remain."

275 Pearson, *supra*, p. 106.

operate with the authorities.[276] As of 2005, a total of 75 victims benefited from the Poppy Project.[277]

Moreover, there are some services provided to witnesses during court hearings. Protection measures are stipulated in different laws. For instance, the *Sexual Offences (Amendment) Act 1976* prohibits publication (written or broadcast) of the identities of complainants of rape under Section 4.[278] In the case of child witnesses and adult complainants in sexual offences cases, provision of a screen in courts to shield them from the accused can be granted. In addition, testimonies over a television link, in private, or over video-recording can be given under the *Youth Justice and Criminal Evidence Act 1999*.[279] Further, several laws prohibit intimidating or harming witnesses. Section 51 of the *Criminal Justice and Public Order Act 1994* provides that intimidation of witnesses is an offence.[280] Similar provisions can also be found in the *Criminal Justice and Police Act 2001*.[281]

In addition, victims of trafficking may also benefit from the Criminal Injury Compensation Scheme, established under the *Criminal Justice Act* 1988.[282] Under this scheme, victims suffering from criminal injuries are entitled to compensation. Criminal injuries include, but are not limited to, rape, assault, kidnapping, and abduction.[283]

The main problem with above measures on protection of victims is that they are applied selectively. For one, only those who are willing co-operate with the authorities can benefit from them. It has been reported in this regard that there are only a few cases of granting humanitarian protection to those who

---

276 Written Correspondence from Ms. Alice Peycke, Information Officer, Poppy Project, Eaves Housing for Women (15/1/04). See also http://www.poppy.ik.com/ (22/05/04).

277 Electronic Correspondence from Ms. Louise Hinchliffe, Information Officer, Poppy Project (16/8/05).

278 c.82. A subsequent piece of legislation, *Sexual Offences (Amendment) Act 1992* (c. 34), expanded the scope of application to include other offences described in *Sexual Offences Act 1956*. See further the *Sexual Offences (Protected Material) Act 1997* (c. 39). Under this Act, the defendants could only view protected materials such as statements related to sexual offences made by victims and their photographs and medical records through their legal representatives under supervised condition.

279 c.23. Relevant provisions are Sections 23, 24, 25, and 27. In relation to children's evidence, see the *Criminal Justice Act 1988, supra*, Sections 32 -34, and the *Criminal Justice Act 1991* (c. 53), Sections 52-55.

280 c. 33.

281 c. 16, Sections 39-41.

282 *supra*. This act was replaced by the *Criminal Injuries Compensation Act 1995* (c. 53).

283 *Ibid.*, Section 109.

have not co-operated with authorities.[284] Such an approach does not reflect the reality that many victims are afraid to come forward due to enforcement actions and reprisals from traffickers as noted elsewhere. In addition, the shelters funded by the Home Office mentioned above can only be utilised by women over 18 years of age who have been trafficked for the purpose of prostitution.[285] This excludes certain categories of people to be protected, such as children and adult men trafficked for all purposes, and women trafficked for purposes other than sexual exploitation. One consequence of course is that law enforcement authorities are not able to obtain valuable information to prosecute and punish traffickers, much like other jurisdictions studied in this Chapter.

2.5.4 NGOs Working on Trafficking in the United Kingdom

In the United Kingdom, the majority of NGOs dealing with trafficking are networking organisations which specialise in international advocacy, similar to the GAATW described earlier. One example is Anti-Slavery International. It was set up in 1893 with the main objective of ending slavery all around the world.[286] Their main tasks include gathering information on the subject, publishing reports, and conducting education and communication campaigns for policy makers and the general public. In 2000, for instance, the organisation launched the "Trafficking Programme" which consisted of extensive research on victim protection for victims of trafficking.[287] The full report was published in June 2002.[288] In a more recent example, the organisation has successfully lobbied the UK government to adopt laws relating to trafficking mentioned above.[289] The organisation also lobbied the Council of Europe to adopt the *Convention on Action against Trafficking in Human Beings* which aims to protect the human rights of victims.

CHANGE is another organisation which has recently worked in the area of trafficking.[290] This is a women's human rights organisation based in London, whose main aim is to promote and protect the human rights of women and to enhance their status all around the world.[291] It is an international advocacy organisation, and as such, it engages in research and other activities in order to raise awareness of women's human rights among different audiences (general

284 Pearson, *supra,* p. 106.

285 Women's Commission for Refugee Women and Children, *supra,* p. 3.

286 Anti-Slavery International at http://www.antislavery.org.

287 *Ibid.*

288 Pearson, *supra.*

289 Anti-Slavery International, *Annual Review 2005*, p. 5.

290 Due to a lack of funding, CHANGE is not implementing any new project on trafficking as of October 2003.

291 Interview with Ms. Marina Tzvetkova, Programme Officer, CHANGE (5/4/02).

public, government, NGOs, etc).[292] It initiated an "Anti-Trafficking Programme" in 2000, the aim of which was to "identify, collect and analyse information on governmental and non-governmental organisations that offer services to women and girls trafficked for the purposes of prostitution, marriage, and/or domestic service."[293] The final version of the directory of these organisations was completed in Spring 2002 and was distributed all over the world for the purposes of awareness-raising, protection of trafficked women and girls, and promotion of changes in national legislation.[294] In addition, the organisation hosted a seminar in March 2003 in order to exchange information and views among those who have been working in the field in the United Kingdom and other European States.[295]

ECPAT UK is also an active NGO in the United Kingdom. It is part of the network of ECPAT International (End Child Prostitution, Child Pornography And Trafficking) based in Bangkok. It is a global network of organisations and individuals "working together for the elimination of child prostitution, child pornography and the trafficking of children for sexual purposes."[296] ECPAT UK consists of a coalition of charity organisations in the United Kingdom, which are Anti-Slavery International, Barnardo's, Jubilee Campaign, NSPCC, Save the Children UK, The Body Shop Foundation, The Children's Society, World Vision UK, and UNICEF UK.[297] It has in the past conducted a tourism campaign involving production and dissemination of information on child sex tourism in order to raise awareness in the United Kingdom.[298] Between 2000-2001, the organisation also conducted research on the trafficking of children in the United Kingdom for sexual exploitation. The research consisted of, *inter alia*, interviews with government officials, NGO representatives, academics and journalists, an examination of the existing laws in the United Kingdom and some case studies of victims.[299] The main finding was that trafficking of children into the United Kingdom is a serious problem, and that although different actors have become more aware of the problems relating to trafficking, the nature and the extent of trafficking in the United Kingdom is not fully understood.[300] In addition, the organisation has campaigned for an amendment to the law on the registration of

292 *Ibid.*

293 Electronic Correspondence from Ms. Marina Tzvetkova, (5/12/01).

294 Electronic Correspondence from Ms. Fiona Luckhoo, ATP Co-ordinator (12/4/02).

295 Electronic Correspondence from Ms. Marina Tzvetkova (8/4/03).

296 ECPAT International, at http://www.ecpat.net/eng/index.asp.

297 ECPAT UK at http://www.ecpat.org.uk/.

298 ECPAT International, *2004 Annual Report*, p. 161.

299 Somerset, *supra*.

300 *Ibid.*

sex offenders. As a result in June 2001, secondary legislation to the *Sex Offenders Act 1997*, under which sex offenders must register their full overseas address when they travel, was introduced by the government.[301]

2.6 Comparative Analysis

2.6.1 National Laws and Policies

In analysing the national laws and policies of three jurisdictions, it becomes apparent that a criminal justice response to trafficking dominates at national level. The practice is regulated, for the most part, through crime and immigration control in each jurisdiction. In this respect, the national laws in Thailand, Poland, and the United Kingdom do not display major disparities. Trafficking is established as a criminal offence in each jurisdiction, and the emphasis is placed upon prosecution and punishment of offenders, both traffickers/smugglers and the trafficked/smuggled. A criminal justice response taken by these States may be a natural response, as it can serve as a deterrent against traffickers from carrying out the practice.

However, a criminal justice response simultaneously leads to the actual facilitation of trafficking. It breeds illegal markets for trafficking as the prohibition gives more incentive to traffickers, such as organised criminal groups. A side-effect of this is that the rule of law is undermined because these criminals use threats and bribes to maintain their business of trafficking. From the viewpoint of those trafficked, a lack of opportunities for legal migration to a State forces them to rely more on traffickers, as stated elsewhere.

Therefore, there is a need to pay more attention to wider issues surrounding the phenomenon. This means that laws and policies which effectively address and alleviate poverty, unemployment, discrimination, and other factors are necessary. In States of origin, labour laws and policies must reflect the principle of non-discrimination so that women and those belonging to racial/ethnic minorities are granted equal access to employment. These States also must implement laws to guarantee equal access to education and vocational training. In States of destination, adoption or amendment of labour and immigration laws and policies which allow migrant workers to work and reside legally would be an advantage. This prevents people from resorting to traffickers and being exploited in forced or cheap labour. In relation to poverty, although States of origin may primarily be responsible for implementing poverty reduction strategies, it will be shown in Chapter 5 that other States, including those of transit and destination, have an obligation to assist them. Supply and demand are inter-linked, and therefore all three jurisdictions share an equal responsibility to tackle wider issues.

---

301 2004 Annual Report, *supra*, p. 161. The Statutory Instrument is *Sex Offenders (Notice Requirements) (Foreign Travel) Regulations 2001*(No. 1846).

2.6.2 *Law Enforcement*

An emphasis on crime/immigration control in national legislation means that law enforcement agencies also promote a criminal justice response to trafficking of human beings. It becomes apparent, however, that these law enforcement agencies are concentrating more on the arrest and deportation of illegal migrants, with a few traffickers being prosecuted and punished in reality. In all jurisdictions, the performance of these agencies has been hampered by a number of obstacles. One of the common problems experienced by all jurisdictions is a lack of adequate human, financial, and material resources. One possible explanation for this is a lack of willingness to deal with trafficking on the part of political bodies at a higher level. Lawmakers in each jurisdiction regard trafficking of human beings to be serious, as shown by the adoption of laws and provisions as well as ongoing debates in Parliaments on the practice. However, governmental agencies charged with enforcing laws do not necessarily regard trafficking as being one of the most serious problems as shown earlier. Had they done so, they would have done more to strengthen law enforcement capabilities by providing human, financial and material resources. At one level, this is caused by a lack of communication between the lawmakers and the governmental bodies. At another level, this can be the result of differences in perceptions of the threats posed by trafficking of human beings.

The growing influence of organised criminal groups is another weak point in law enforcement in three jurisdictions. Many organised criminal groups are highly sophisticated in their operations and they are extremely difficult and dangerous to infiltrate. The lack of resources once again prevents the law enforcement agencies from enhancing their intelligence and law enforcement capabilities against organised criminal groups. Corruption is also a problem partly caused by the influence of organised criminal groups. The widespread nature of transnational or international activities conducted by these groups also suggests that multi-lateral or international law enforcement co-operation is required to suppress them.

2.6.3 *Protection of Victims*

Protection of victims is an important aspect of a human rights framework to trafficking of human beings. However, a comparative analysis shows that it is not sufficiently provided for. The willingness to assist victims is more evident in Thailand. This can be seen, among other things, in Section 11 of the 1997 Law and the MoUs which have been adopted by different agencies. However, victim protection is not sufficient as noted earlier. In Poland and the United Kingdom, although it is true that some protection measures exist, their value can be called into question, as many victims in these States are illegal immigrants, and therefore are more likely to face enforcement actions including deportation.

What is evident, then, is that victims of trafficking receive more or less the same treatment as those smuggled. It was noted in Chapter 1 that the distinction between trafficking and smuggling is likely to result in separate treatment of those trafficked or smuggled, in that the former would receive more protection than the latter. However, an emphasis on their deportation and a tendency to protect only those willing to co-operate seem to illustrate that immigration and crime control has been the priority in these jurisdictions in order to protect the principle of national sovereignty and territorial integrity, and that the protection of human rights remains a secondary concern at the national level.

2.6.4 NGOs

Unlike the governments in Thailand, Poland, and the United Kingdom, there are differences in the way in which NGOs respond to trafficking of human beings in three jurisdictions. Those NGOs in Thailand and Poland, the major States of origin and transit, implement preventive programmes, as many Thai and Polish, as well as foreign nationals are trafficked through or into Thailand and Poland. In a similar vein, NGOs in these two States also conduct activities for the protection of victims. This again is a natural response as Thailand and Poland also serve as States of destination. All of this demonstrates that NGOs in these States have not only been able to recognise the challenges and problems caused by trafficking, but also to adopt measures to address them.

In the United Kingdom, although the need to provide protection has been recognised by some NGOs,[302] an emphasis is placed more upon research and advocacy, mainly because they do not have a mandate to do more. While the Poppy Project is run by an NGO as noted earlier, it is an initiative of the government. ECPAT UK also reports that NGOs in Thailand and Poland are able to do more, as the problems related to trafficking have been more evident for a longer period of time than in the United Kingdom.[303] This suggests that problems of trafficking have only recently been recognised within the NGO community in the United Kingdom. One solution to this problem is to co-operate closely with NGOs which provide direct assistance to women and children as well as refugees and asylum seekers, similar to what La Strada does in Poland.

There are several other observations to be made in relation to NGOs in three jurisdictions. For instance, NGOs seem to have been able to recognise quickly that trafficking is global in nature. Some of these organisations have global networks in relation to trafficking. This alone suggests an acknowledgement by NGOs that a co-ordinated strategy is required at the global level. Under State-to-State relations, the principle of State sovereignty normally makes it difficult for States to actively co-operate. As shown in Chapter 1, this is one of the reasons why earlier treaties on trafficking were ineffective, because prostitution was considered to be a domestic matter. NGOs, however, are not constrained by

302 Interviews with Ms. Tzvetkova, *supra* and with Ms. Elaine Pearson, Trafficking Programme Officer (Anti-Slavery International) (5/4/02).

303 Electronic Correspondence from Ms. Carron Somerset, ECPAT UK. (2/8/02).

this principle and are able to seek co-operation more freely, purely out of human rights or humanitarian concerns.

It is also the case that NGOs described above attempt to promote a human rights framework to the act. Some organisations regard subsequent exploitation, especially prostitution, as a human rights violation,[304] while others consider that the entire process of trafficking (from the beginning to the end of journey) raises human rights concerns.[305] Despite these differences as to which aspect raises human rights concerns, they all view those trafficked as victims, and attempt to protect and restore their human rights.

However, addressing the human rights aspects of trafficking has not been entirely effective in practice for a number of reasons. These NGOs suffer from a lack of adequate human, material and financial resources. La Strada Foundation, for instance, has not been able to provide adequate protection, such as counselling and providing accommodation for victims, for this reason.[306] The lack of funding has also been a problem for DEPDC[307] and GAATW[308] and CHANGE in the United Kingdom.[309] This reflects the difficulty in acquiring co-operation from different sectors of civil society, including the general public. This is perhaps because there is a lack of interest among them to do something about trafficking. Language is another barrier affecting the performance of NGOs. Many of the victims are foreigners in all three jurisdictions, and communicating with them is not an easy task. This obviously makes it difficult for NGOs to provide quality services and activities for them. In addition, for those specialising in research and advocacy, conducting field research in different States can also be difficult, because researchers in many cases are not proficient in local languages.[310] Finally, although NGOs are quick in recognising the need to protect victims human rights, many have not taken a holistic approach to address wider human rights issues such as poverty, humanitarian crisis, torture and inhuman treatment imposed by traffickers.

Further, there seems to be duplication of work among NGOs. Many organisations conduct seminars and conferences as well as research on similar topics related to trafficking around the world. This highlights the necessity to improve co-ordination and communication among NGOs. This is crucial in order to save

---

304 DEPDC, *supra*.

305 GAATW (website), *supra*. The GAATW considers that a woman has a right to choose her profession. Therefore, it does not necessarily regard prostitution as a violation of human rights. See also Anti-Slavery International (website), *supra*.

306 Niesner and Jones-Pauly, *supra*, p. 105.

307 Electronic correspondence from Ms. Nicolson, *supra*.

308 Interview with Ms. Pattanaik, *supra*.

309 Interview with Ms. Tzvetkova, *supra*.

310 Interview with Ms. Pearson, *supra*.

already scarce financial resources available to them. In sum, although the role of NGOs is quite important especially in relation to protection of victims, a wide variety of problems affect their performance. As a result, the protection and promotion of a human rights framework is not as effective as it might otherwise be.

Finally, the majority of the organisations explored are concerned with the protection of women and children who are being exploited sexually. Tackling issues of prostitution and sexual exploitation can be justified because of the fact that women and children are mainly trafficked for these purposes. It can also be added that the majority of the organisations explored are women's organisations or those which have a clear mandate to protect women and children. Nevertheless, the focus on women and children, and on prostitution and sexual exploitation does not accurately address the phenomenon. States have the primary responsibility to protect victims more than any other actors. However, NGOs could, and should, play their part by expanding the scope of their mandates and activities so that people other than women and children trafficked for sexual exploitation can also be protected.

2.7 Conclusion

This Chapter has presented national case studies of trafficking of human beings in Thailand, Poland, and the United Kingdom. The main conclusion reached is that although it is easy to regard trafficking as a human rights issue in theory, it is difficult to address the human rights aspects inherent in the phenomenon in practice at the national level. Each State has measures mainly for protection of their own nationals and foreign nationals who are permitted to stay and live. Nevertheless, illegal migrants are not able to benefit from protection fully, as they are more likely to be detained and deported. In addition, three States do not deal with wider human rights issues including the causes and consequences of the act. NGOs examined are more proactive in addressing the human rights aspects of trafficking. However, such factors as a lack of adequate funding and co-operation from the governments and other sectors serve as obstacles to promoting a human rights framework.

It is obvious that trafficking cannot be suppressed solely by domestic efforts of States and NGOs. The practice is a global phenomenon that has increasingly been facilitated by transnational organised criminal groups. Therefore, even if States and NGOs are able to some extent to address problems domestically, traffickers will continue transporting people, unless the act is simultaneously addressed both regionally and internationally. The role of regional organisations such as the European Union, as well as those at the international level including the United Nations becomes particularly crucial in this respect. The following Chapter examines key IGOs dealing with trafficking of human beings in order to illustrate the extent to which they have been or will be successful in addressing the practice at the regional and international levels.

Chapter 3

The Role of Inter-Governmental Organisations in relation to Trafficking of Human Beings

3.1 Introduction

This Chapter examines the role of IGOs. The trafficking of human beings has gained much attention at the regional and international levels, and every major IGO, including the United Nations, now deals with the phenomenon in one way or another. The focus of activity varies from one organisation to another, depending on the IGO's mandate. The United Nations High Commissioner for Refugees, for instance, deals with trafficking in the context of refugee protection,[1] while the International Labour Organisation pays close attention to the subsequent exploitation which is inherent in the practice.[2] Whatever the differences in focus, one common view held by these IGOs is that trafficking of human beings is a human rights issue.

The main purpose of this Chapter is to review what some of the key IGOs do in relation to trafficking of human beings by providing a comparative analysis of their efforts and an analysis of the extent to which they are successful in the suppression of the phenomenon and the promotion of a human rights framework. The Chapter starts with an examination of the policies and programmes of one key regional organisation, the European Union (EU). While regional organisations around the world such as the Association of South-East Asian Nations (ASEAN),[3] the Organisation for Security and Co-operation in

1 Interview with Ms. Grainne O'Hara, Legal Advisor, Protection Policy and Legal Advice Section at the Department of International Protection, at the UNHCR in Geneva (22/10/03).

2 See below.

3 See *ASEAN Annual Report 2002-2003*, particularly Chapter 4 (Transnational Issues).

Europe (OSCE),[4] the Council of Europe[5] and the Organisation of American States (OAS)[6] deal with trafficking to some extent, the EU has been selected because of relative development of policies and programmes on trafficking

The study of the EU is followed by that of the United Nations Inter-Agency Project on Trafficking of Women and Children in Mekong Sub-region (UNIAP),[7] a project being implemented under the auspices of the United Nations. In addition, the International Organisation for Migration (IOM) and the International Labour Organisation (ILO)[8] are also explored as both of these organisations have been the key players in the fight against trafficking of human beings. A descriptive account of these IGOs will be followed by a comparative analysis.

3.2 European Union (EU)

As with other regions of the world, Europe is heavily affected by trafficking of human beings. According to the European Police Office (Europol), approximately 500,000 people enter into Member States of the EU each year, half of

4 See, among others, *Proposed Action Plan 2000 for Activities to Combat Trafficking in Human Beings (*1999); and *Trafficking in Human Beings: Implications for the OSCE* (1999), *Supplementary Human Dimension Meeting on Trafficking in Human Beings: Final Report* (2000). These and other documents can be found at http://www.osce.org/odihr/democratization/trafficking/.

5 See, Council of Europe, Division of Equality between Women and Men (CDEG), *Action Against Traffic in Human Beings for the Purpose of Sexual Exploitation: The Role of NGOs* (Strasbourg, 29-30 June 1998); *Workshop on "Good" and "Bad" Practices Regarding the Image of Women in Media: The Case of Trafficking in Human Beings for the Purpose of Sexual Exploitation* (Strasbourg, 28-29 September 1998); and *International Seminar "Co-ordinated Action against Trafficking in Human Beings in South-East Europe: Towards a Regional Action Plan"* (Athens, 29 June - 1 July 2000). For more information on the activities of the CDEG and the Council of Europe in general in relation to trafficking, see *Fact Sheet: Trafficking in Human Beings for the Purpose of Sexual Exploitation* (October 2002).

6 *Trafficking in Women and Children: Research Findings and Follow-Up*, CIM/doc.9/02, OEA/Ser.L/II.2.31 (August 2002); and *Resolution on Fighting the Crime of Trafficking in Persons, Especially Women, Adolescents, and Children*, AG/RES. 1948 (XXXIII-O/03)(June 2003).

7 UNIAP at http://www.no-trafficking.org/uniap_frontend/Default.aspx. The Mekong sub-region consists of a border area shared by Cambodia, China (Yunnan and Guangzi Provinces), Laos, Myanmar, Thailand and Vietnam.

8 Detailed information in relation to their work on trafficking is provided in their website http://www.iom.int/en/who/main_service_areas_counter.shtml (IOM) and http://www.ilo.org/public/english/standards/ipec/index.htm (ILO). Although the ILO is a UN affiliated agency, a separate examination will be presented in this Chapter.

whom are assisted by traffickers such as organised criminal groups.[9] The most common movement of people within Europe is said to be East-West migration. Although nationals of Central, Southern, and Eastern European States are trafficked to Western Europe, these States are also used as transit points for people from around the world.

Against this reality, the EU started taking action, particularly after the entry into force of the *Treaty on European Union* (Maastricht Treaty) in November 1993. The Maastricht Treaty established three so-called pillars of the EU: the first being the Community pillar (Titles II, III and IV); the second pillar relating to common foreign and security policy (Title V); and the third pillar on justice and home affairs (Title VI). All of these pillars are pertinent to the trafficking of human beings. The exploitation of labour inherent in trafficking and its impact on the labour markets of Member States are relevant to the first pillar. The transnational nature of trafficking, particularly the involvement of foreign nationals, requires the EU to have policies towards States where those trafficked originate or move through on the way to their ultimate destination, and the second pillar may come into play.

Nevertheless, an analysis of the EU's action against trafficking reveals that policy and programme development tends to concentrate upon promotion of law enforcement and judicial co-operation among Member States under the third pillar. Trafficking amounts to criminal conduct and therefore the EU's reliance on the third pillar for its suppression through punishment of traffickers may be a reasonable response. What follows is an analysis of the EU's actions against trafficking both under the Maastricht Treaty and later the *Treaty of Amsterdam*, which entered into force in May 1999.

3.2.1 Policies and Programmes under Maastricht Treaty

Under the Maastricht Treaty, trafficking of human beings was dealt with in Title VI (Provisions on Co-operation in the Fields of Justice and Home Affairs). In line with this Title, joint positions, joint actions, or conventions were adopted,[10] and several actions in relation to trafficking were implemented. One of the early examples was the *Convention on the Establishment of the European Police Office* (Europol Convention) adopted on the basis of Article K.3[11] of the Maastricht

9 Bruggeman, W, (Deputy Director, Europol), *Illegal Immigration and Trafficking in Human Beings Seen as a Security Problem for Europe*, Paper delivered at the European Conference on Preventing and Combating Trafficking in Human Beings: Global Challenge for the 21st Century (18-20 September 2002).

10 Article K.3.2 (now Article 29). The legal effects of these measures will be discussed below.

11 Now Article 31.

Treaty[12] by the Council of European Union. Europol was envisaged to have an important role to play in relation to trafficking of human beings as stipulated by Article 1(2), which provided that the initial role of Europol was to prevent and combat, among other things, "illegal immigrant smuggling and trade in human beings."[13] In order to achieve this objective, Europol was mandated to enhance effective co-operation between the competent authorities in the Member States.[14]

A slightly different approach from the emphasis on criminal justice came from institutions other than the Council. In 1995, the European Parliament adopted the *Resolution on Trafficking in Human Beings.*[15] The Resolution clearly

12 OJ C 316/2 (27/11/95). Europol's predecessor was known as the European Drug Unit (EDU) which was established in 1993. The mandate of the EDU was extended to deal with trafficking of human beings before the coming into force of the Europol Convention. See for instance, *Joint Action of 10 March 1995 adopted by the Council on the basis of Article K.3 of the Treaty on European Union concerning Europol Drug Unit*, 95/73/JHA, OJ L 62/1 (20/3/95). Article 2(2) of this Joint Action states that the "Unit shall act as non-operational team for the exchange and analysis of information and intelligence" in relation to, among other things, crime involving clandestine immigration network. This Joint Action was replaced by the *Joint Action of 16 December 1996 adopted by the Council on the basis of Article K.3 of the Treaty on European Union extending the mandate given to the European Drugs Unit*, 96/748/JHA, OJ L 342/4 (31/12/96), and the term "traffic in human beings" was added under the EDU's mandate. The EDU ceased to exist on 30 June 1999, and Europol began its activities on 1 July 1999, in accordance with the provisions of the Europol Convention.

13 *Ibid.* Some amendments were made to the original Europol Convention. Of particular relevance was the *Council Decision of 3 December 1998 supplementing the definition of the form of crime 'traffic in human beings in the annex to the Europol Convention,* OJ C 26/21 (30/1/99). Under Article 1, trafficking in human beings was defined as "subjection of a person to the real and illegal sway of other persons by using violence or menaces or by abuse of authority or intrigue, especially with a view to the exploitation of prostitution, forms of sexual exploitation and assault of minors or trade in abandoned children. These forms of exploitation also include the production, sale or distribution of child-pornography material."

14 See in general, Flynn, V, 'Europol – A Watershed in EU Law Enforcement Cooperation?' in Barrett (ed.), *Justice Cooperation in the European Union: The Creation of a European Legal Space* (Dublin: Institute of European Affairs)(1997), pp. 79-113.

15 A4-0326/95, OJ C 32/88 (5/2/96). The resolution defined trafficking as "the illegal action of someone who, directly or indirectly, encourages a citizen from a third country to enter or stay in another country in order to exploit that person by using deceit or any other form of coercion or by abusing that person's vulnerable situation or administrative status." The European Parliament also touched upon trafficking in its *Resolution on Violence against Women,* OJ C 176/73 (14/7/86); *Resolution on the Exploitation of Prostitution and the Trafficking in Human Beings*, A2-52/89, OJ C 120/352 (14/4/89); *Resolution on Trade in Women*, B3-1264, 1283 and 1309/93,

regarded those trafficked as victims and stated that trafficking of human beings constituted a serious violation of human rights. Therefore, the European Parliament went further to call upon Member States to take such measures as ensuring the safety and dignity of victims, issuing temporary residence permits, and providing social and legal assistance as well as witness protection in cases where victims testify at a trial.[16]

The idea that trafficking of human beings is a human rights issue is also shared by the European Commission. The first document on trafficking adopted by the Commission was the *Communication from the Commission to the Council and the European Parliament on Trafficking in Women for the Purpose of Sexual Exploitation,*[17] in which the Commission stated that the focus of attention should be "the devastating effect it (trafficking) has on the victims," recognising that trafficking is a human rights issue. Through this Communication, the Commission stressed the need to develop "an integrated and multidisciplinary policy" and outlined various action plans. For instance, it called for improvements in, among others, data/information collection, co-ordination among different actors, awareness-raising campaigns and training. The Communication also stipulated that the protection of victims, including temporary residence permits, social and other assistance, was necessary, and the Commission suggested that the EU should reach an agreement on this matter.

Under the Dutch Presidency, the EU Ministerial Conference on trafficking in women for sexual exploitation was held in April 1997 and the *Hague Ministerial Declaration on European Guidelines for Effective Measures to Prevent and Combat Trafficking in Women for the Purpose of Sexual Exploitation*[18] was adopted. This Declaration set out a number of measures to be taken at national and regional levels. For instance, it called for co-operation among Member States in such areas as prevention, investigation and prosecution. It also stressed the need to facilitate communication between different actors. In addition, the provision of assistance to victims of trafficking of human beings was regarded as important and the Declaration proposed a list of measures for this purpose. The views of the European Parliament and the Commission in this regard were

---

OJ C 268/141 (16/9/93); and *European Parliament Resolution on the Communication from the Commission to the Council and the European Parliament "For Further Actions in the Fight against Trafficking in Women,"* A5-0127/2000 (19/5/00).

16 *Ibid.*

17 COM(96) 567 final (20/11/96). Under this Communication, trafficking was defined as "the transport of women from third countries into the European Union (including perhaps subsequent movements between Member States) for the purpose of sexual exploitation."

18 *The Hague Ministerial Declaration on European Guidelines for Effective Measures to Prevent and Combat Trafficking in Women for the Purpose of Sexual Exploitation* (26/4/97).

taken into consideration by Member States, as their policy documents were referred to in this Declaration.

In line with some of the policy objectives set out above, certain initiatives were taken. To begin with, the activities of the EDU and Europol should be analysed. The bulk of their work in the beginning was devoted to intelligence exchange and analysis. In 1996, out of 2,053 cases referred to the EDU for inquiry by Member States, 167 cases were linked to illegal immigration networks.[19] In the same year, the EDU initiated a Balkan Route project, in which it developed a strategic analysis of clandestine immigration networks involving Turkish nationals and organisations.[20] In 1997, inquiries relating to illegal immigration networks increased from 8 % (167 cases) to 19 %, and the EDU additionally dealt with 81 cases specifically related to trafficking of human beings.[21]

When the EDU was replaced by Europol, its scope of activities in relation to trafficking of human beings was expanded. In addition to ongoing intelligence analysis in such areas as the Balkan Region, West Africa, and Eastern Europe (Ukraine and Moldova),[22] Europol has hosted expert meetings and provided training for law enforcement officials to strengthen their capability to combat trafficking.[23] It also conducts joint investigations with law enforcement agencies of Member States, and co-ordinates common border control operations. In 2004, for instance, Europol supported an initiative to combat trafficking of Chinese migrants, which resulted in the arrest of 5 traffickers and the interception of 273 illegal migrants.[24] In addition, Europol promotes co-operation with non-EU Member States such as Canada, Iceland, Monaco and the United States by concluding operational agreements on co-operation.[25]

In addition to the EDU and Europol, several actions were adopted under the Justice and Home Affairs provisions. One example is the *Joint Action of 29 November 1996, establishing an incentive and exchange programme for persons responsible for combating trade in human beings and the sexual exploitation of children*, also known as the *STOP Programme*.[26] Established on the basis of

19 EDU, *Report on the Activities of the EUROPOL DRUG UNIT in 1996* (1997), p. 1.

20 *Ibid.*, p. 2.

21 EDU, *Annual Report for 1997* (1998), p. 5.

22 Europol, *Annual Report 2001* (2002), pp. 11 and 12.

23 European Commission, *Trafficking in Human Beings: The European Response* (Background Document to the European Conference on Trafficking in Human Beings (18-20 September 2002), p. 18 (hereinafter EU Background Document). Some of the training sessions are also co-financed under the STOP II Programme, details of which will be shown below.

24 Europol, *Annual Report 2004*, p. 11.

25 EU Background Document, *supra*, p. 23.

26 96/700/JHA, OJ L 322/7 (12/12/96).

Article K.3[27] of the Maastricht Treaty, the *STOP Programme* ran from 1996 to 2000. The main aim was to establish a framework whereby public and law enforcement officials, civil servants, and members of the judiciary could hold meetings, undergo training, exchange and disseminate information and conduct research on trafficking.

Another pertinent initiative was the *Joint Action of 24 February 1997, concerning action to combat trafficking in human beings and sexual exploitation of children.*[28] This required Member States to review their relevant national laws and make trafficking for sexual exploitation a criminal offence.[29] It also called for the enhancement of enforcement actions including investigation and technical assistance.[30] Police and judicial co-operation and co-ordination within and among Member States, and protection to victims of trafficking and sexual exploitation were also regarded as important.[31] Any action taken by Member States was to be assessed by the end of 1999.[32]

Further, The *Daphne Initiative* (1997-1999)[33] was established in 1997 by the European Parliament in response to growing instances of violence against children, young persons and women.[34] This Initiative was not adopted under the Justice and Home Affairs provisions, unlike the *STOP Programme* described above, and activities covered must relate to training and exchange, support for pilot projects and the European network, studies and research, dissemination of information, and co-operation between NGOs and the public authorities.[35] Out of 149 projects implemented between 1997 and 1999, 16 projects dealt with trafficking of human beings. [36] They included the establishment of a support

27 Now Article 31.

28 97/154/JHA, OJ L 63/2 (4/3/97). Trafficking of human being was defined as "any behaviour which facilitates the entry into, through, residence in or exit from the territory of Member States for the purpose set out in point B(b) and (d) (sexual exploitation)."

29 Title II, *ibid.*

30 Title III, *ibid.*

31 *Ibid.*

32 This Joint Action was repealed with the adoption of the Framework Decision on Trafficking in Human Beings in July 2002. See below for detail.

33 *The Daphne Initiative: Measures for Combating Violence against Children, Young Persons and Women, Call for Proposals,* OJ C 136/14 (1/5/97).

34 European Commission, *The Daphne Initiative 1997-1999: Overview and External Evaluator's Report of the 1998 Initiative* (2001), p. 6.

35 *Ibid.*

36 The project numbers were as follows: 97/43/W, 97/118/WC, 97/132/C, 97/408/W, 98/043/WC, 98/057/W, 98/070/W, 98/126/WC, 98/245/W, 98/273/WC, 99/093/W, 99/105/W, 99/146/C, 99/201/W, 99/210/W, 99/319/WC. For more information, see the Daphne Toolkit at http://www.daphne-toolkit.org/.

network for victims of trafficking, the facilitation of psychological assistance, information/awareness-raising campaign, and training and capacity building in the States of origin.

Other measures have complemented the EU's action against trafficking. In the area of immigration, measures such as visa requirements,[37] expulsion,[38] and an initiative known as *ODYSSEUS*[39] were pertinent to trafficking of human beings, as they were designed to prevent illegal migration facilitated by traffickers. In relation to organised crime, *FALCONE*[40] touched upon issues relating to the phenomenon.[41] In examining the development of policies and programmes under the Maastricht Treaty, it becomes clear that the main approach of the EU towards trafficking was to promote functional co-operation among law enforcement and judicial authorities in Member States.

---

37 See, among others, *Council Regulation (EC) No 1683/95 of 29 May 1995 laying down a uniform format for visas*, OJ L 164/1 (14/7/95); *Joint Action of 4 March 1996 adopted by the Council on the basis of Article K.3 of the Treaty on European Union on airport transit arrangements*, 96/197/JHA, OJ L 63/8 (13/3/96); and *Council Regulation (EC) No 574/1999 of 12 March 1999 determining the third countries whose nationals must be in possession of visas when crossing the external borders of the Member States* OJ L 72/2 (18/3/99).

38 *Council Recommendation of 22 December 1995 on concerted action and cooperation in carrying out expulsion measures,* OJ C 5/3 (10/1/96); and *Council Recommendation of 30 November 1994 concerning the adoption of a standard travel document for the expulsion of third-country nationals* OJ C 274/18 (19/9/96).

39 *Joint Action of 19 March 1998 adopted by the Council on the basis of Article K.3 of the Treaty on European Union, introducing a programme of training, exchanges and cooperation in the field of asylum, immigration and crossing of external borders (Odysseus- Programme)*, 98/244/JHA, OJ L 99/2 (31/3/98). Under *ODYSSEUS*, more than half of the programmes implemented in 1999 (75) related directly or indirectly to trafficking of human beings. *Third Report of the Commission to the European Parliament and the Council on the implementation of GROTIUS, STOP and OISIN Programmes, and Second Report of the Commission to the European Parliament and the Council on implementation of ODYSSEUS and FALCONE Programmes* (1999).

40 *Joint Action of 19 March 1998 adopted by the Council, on the basis of Article K.3 of the Treaty on European Union, establishing a programme of exchanges, training and cooperation for persons responsible for action to combat organised crime (Falcone programme)*, 98/245/JHA, OJ L 99/8 (31/3/98).

41 In 2000, for instance, case studies of criminal organisations engaging in trafficking in migrants (2000/FAL/107) and research on organised crime and illegal migrants (2000/FAL/165) were funded under the *FALCONE* Programme. European Commission, *Report on the Activities of the FALCONE Programme (Financial Year 2000)*(February 2001).

3.2.2 Policies and Programmes under Treaty of Amsterdam

The entry into force of the Treaty of Amsterdam marks a significant development in relation to trafficking of human beings, as the Treaty introduced a provision for the approximation of national laws among Member States.[42] This is to be achieved through the adoption, by the Council, of framework decisions in accordance with Article 34 of the Maastricht Treaty as revised by the Treaty of Amsterdam, and the *Council Framework Decision on combating trafficking in human beings*[43] was thus adopted in 2002. Three key elements are a common definition of the act; a uniform threshold for minimum penalties applicable to trafficking of human beings; and the provision of protection and assistance to victims.[44]

The adoption of this Framework Decision is significant for several reasons. First, the EU recognised that merely seeking functional co-operation was not sufficient to deal with trafficking of human beings, as asymmetries in legislative frameworks among Member States were counterproductive in dealing effectively with trafficking. [45] This underscores the limitations inherent in Title VI of the Maastricht Treaty, in that it was not designed to bridge variations in national laws and regulations on the practice. Second, Member States, at the time when the Maastricht Treaty entered into force, were quite reluctant to seek active co-operation in the area of Justice and Home Affairs, as this area entailed national security implications, and therefore was still considered to be a matter of domestic concern.[46] Nevertheless, while States may still be reluctant to cede control over Justice and Home Affairs, it may be argued that the transnational nature of trafficking has prompted them to reassess the level of co-operation required in this sphere.

---

42 Another significant contribution of the Treaty of Amsterdam is that some parts of the third pillar were incorporated into the first pillar, as evidenced in Articles 61-69 of the EC Treaty (Title IV on Visa, Asylum, Immigration, and Other Policies Related to Free Movement of People). One initiative in relation to trafficking was taken in April 2004 when the Council adopted the *Council Directive, 2004/81/EC of 29 April 2004, on the residence permit issued to victims of action to facilitate illegal immigration or trafficking in human beings who cooperate with the competent authority*, OJ L 261/19 (6/8/04) (hereinafter Directive on Residence Permit). See below for detail.

43 OJ L 203/1 (1/8/02).

44 Articles 1, 3 and 7, *ibid.*

45 *Proposal for a Council Framework Decision on combating trafficking in human beings*, COM(2000) 854 final/2 (hereinafter Proposal for the Framework Decision).

46 McGuinness, D, and E. Barrington, 'Immigration, Visa and Border Controls in the European Union,' in Barrett (ed.), *Justice Cooperation... supra*, p. 157. See also Turnbull, P, 'The Fusion of Immigration and Crime in the European Union: Problems of Cooperation and the Fight against the Trafficking in Women,' in Williams (ed.), *Illegal Immigration... supra*, p. 195.

In practical terms, the Framework Decision can be used to strengthen EU action by promoting a common approach. For instance, a common definition of trafficking will assist law enforcement agencies of Member States to identify it, making it easier for them to promote co-operation in investigation and prosecution of traffickers within or outside of their domestic jurisdictions. Approximating the levels of penalties among Member States will also reduce situations where certain traffickers receive lesser punishments than others simply because of the jurisdiction in which they are prosecuted. Moreover, from the point of view of victims, the Framework Decision will require Member States to offer protection.

Another initiative is the Directive on Residence Permit. The legal basis of this is Article 63(3)(b) of the EC Treaty, which allows the Council to adopt measures in relation to illegal immigration and residence.[47] Several provisions are worth mentioning. To begin with, the Directive obliges Member States to give victims a so-called "a reflection period" that would allow them to decide whether or not they wish to co-operate with the authorities.[48] The Directive also states that the authorities should give a short-term residence permit of at least six months to victims, which is subject to renewal if they are willing to co-operate.[49] Member States are also to ensure access to, among other things, accommodation, emergency medical and psychological treatment, and social welfare during the reflection period, and additional measures such as access to the labour market, education and rehabilitation for those who hold the short-term residence permits are stipulated.[50] Finally, the residence permits can be granted not only to those trafficked, but also those smuggled.[51] However, the Directive makes it clear from the outset that its main purpose is to enhance measures to combat illegal migration, and that it is not intended to arrange protection for victims.[52] Therefore, the protection of human rights is not a primary objective.

A similar measure to the Directive on Residence Permit is the regime of subsidiary protection.[53] A Proposal for a Council Directive on this was devel-

---

47 In accordance with Article 249 of the EC Treaty, a directive shall be binding as to the result to be achieved, upon each Member State to which it is addressed, but shall leave to the national authorities the choice, form and methods.

48 Article 6 of the Directive on Residence Permit, *supra*. The length of such period is to be determined in accordance with the national law of each Member State.

49 Article 8(3), *ibid.*

50 Articles 7, 11 and 12, *ibid.*

51 Article 1, *ibid.*

52 *Ibid.* See also *Proposal for a Council Directive on the short-term residence permit issued to victims of action to facilitate illegal immigration or trafficking in human beings who cooperate with the competent authority*, COM (2002) 71 final (11/2/02).

53 *Council Directive 2004/83/EC of 29 April 2004, on minimum standards for the qualification and status of third country nationals and stateless persons as refugees or as per-*

oped in 2001.[54] Subsidiary protection is to be granted to those who do not strictly fit into the definition of refugees under the *Convention Relating to the Status of Refugees* 1951 (Refugee Convention),[55] but instead have a fear of suffering serious and unjustified harm, including torture, indiscriminate violence and other violations of human rights.[56] If one qualifies for subsidiary protection, a Member State is obliged to issue a residence permit lasing at least one year.[57] The major difference between the Directive on Qualification and the Directive on Residence Permit is that the former does not require those in need of subsidiary protection to co-operate with law enforcement authorities. As a result, the categories of people to be protected are expanded.

In relation to other initiatives, those implemented under the Maastricht Treaty have been extended. For instance, the STOP Programme was replaced by STOP II by the *Council Decision of 28 June 2001 establishing a second phase of the programme of incentives, exchanges, training and cooperation for persons responsible for combating trade in human beings and the sexual exploitation of children*.[58] One important aspect of STOP II is that the phrase "assisting victims" was added for the implementation of the programme under Article 3, thereby recognising that trafficking is a human rights issue. At the end of 2002, STOP II was replaced by an initiative known as *AGIS* (framework programme on police and judicial co-operation in criminal matters) which will last until the end of 2007.[59] In 2004, out of 111 projects financed by the *AGIS*, 10 related to trafficking of human beings.[60] In addition, the EU also extended until 2008 the *Daphne Initiative* which had originally been established by the European Parlia-

---

sons who otherwise need international protection, OJ L 304/12 (30/9/04) (hereinafter Directive of Qualification).

54 *Proposal for a Council Directive on minimum standards for the qualification and status of third country nationals and stateless persons as refugees or as persons who otherwise need international protection*, COM(2001) 510 final.

55 189 UNTS 150, as amended by the Protocol Relating to the Status of Refugees 1967, 606 UNTS 267.

56 Article 15 of the Directive on Qualification, *supra*.

57 Article 24(2), *ibid*.

58 2001/514/JHA, OJ L 186/7 (7/7/01).

59 Council Decision 2002/630/JHA, OJ L 203/5 (1/8/02).

60 *List of Project Financed in 2004* .

ment in 1996.[61] Approximately 60 projects were funded in 2004, and 3 of them were directly concerned with trafficking of women and children.[62]

Finally, the Commission established a consultative group known as the *Expert Group on Trafficking in Human Beings*, in line with a recommendation proposed in the *Brussels Declaration on Preventing and Combating Trafficking in Human Beings*, which followed the European Conference on Preventing and Combating Trafficking in Human Beings held in September 2002.[63] In August 2003, the Commission appointed the Expert Group consisting of representatives of governments, international organisations, NGOs and scholars who have experience and expertise on trafficking.[64] The main function of this Expert Group is to advise the Commission on the development of EU action against trafficking.[65] In line with its mandate, the Expert Group has so far published a report[66] and issued opinions on various aspects of the EU action against trafficking.[67]

3.2.3 Analysis of EU Actions against Trafficking

Many commentators are in agreement that the inclusion of the Justice and Home Affairs provisions (Title VI) in the Maastricht Treaty was a significant step forward as they established a basic framework for co-operation in this area.[68] The adoption of these provisions was also important in relation to trafficking of

---

61 *Decision No. 293/2000/EC of the European Parliament and of the Council of January 24 2000 adopting a programme of Community action (the Daphne programme) (2000 to 2003) on preventive measures to fight violence against children, young persons and women*, OJ L34/1 (9/2/00); and *Decision No 803/2004/EC of the European Parliament and of the Council of 21 April 2004 adopting a programme of Community action (2004 to 2008) to prevent and combat violence against children, young people and women and to protect victims and groups at risk (the Daphne II programme)*, OJ L 143/1 (30/4/04).

62 *Selected Projects in 2004.*

63 *Commission Decision of 25 March 2003 on setting up a consultative group known as the 'Expert Group on Trafficking in Human Beings' (2003/209/EC)*, OJ L 79/25 (26/3/03).

64 Article 3, *ibid.*

65 Article 2, *ibid.*

66 *Report of the Expert Group on Trafficking in Human Beings* (December 2004).

67 See for instance, *Opinions on the Green Paper on an EU Approach to Managing Economic Migration Presented by the Commission* (May 2005); *Opinion on the Tampare II Agenda* (October 2004); and *Opinion on Reflection Period and Residence Permit* (May 2004).

68 See for example, O'Keeffe, D, 'Can the Leopard Change its Spots? Visas, Immigration and Asylum-- Following Amsterdam,' in O'Keeffe and Twomey (eds.), *Legal Issues of the Amsterdam Treaty* (Oxford: Hart Publishing)(1999); and Barrett, G,

human beings. Policies and programmes relating to the practice were virtually non-existent before the coming into force of the Maastricht Treaty. However, the Justice and Home Affairs provisions have paved the way for the adoption of policies and programmes and enhanced the capability of the EU to deal with trafficking.[69] The adoption of the Treaty of Amsterdam is also significant, as it has made it possible for the EU and Member States to seek a unified approach to the phenomenon. Nevertheless, the effectiveness of EU action against trafficking can be questioned.

3.2.3.1 Legal Nature of Measures Taken by the EU

Although the conventions were legally binding, the legal nature of other instruments adopted under the Maastricht Treaty was not clear. It was argued, for example, that joint positions did not have significant legal effects.[70] It was noted in this respect that a "joint position in the context of the third pillar has to be understood as a joint declaration or recommendation without a legally binding effect on Member States."[71] The legal effects of the joint actions were also vague as they were not defined under the Maastricht Treaty.[72]

'Cooperation in Justice and Home Affairs in the European Union - An Overview and Critique,' in Barrett (ed.), *Justice Cooperation…*, *supra*.

69 Turnbull asserts that trafficking is an area under Justice and Home Affairs which has produced some success, *supra*, p. 203.

70 Barrett, *supra*, p. 24, citing O'Keeffe.

71 Müller-Graff, P. C, 'The Legal Bases of the Third Pillar and Its Position in the Framework of the European Union,' 31 *Common Market Law Review* 493 (1994), p. 509. Meyring, however, argues that not having legal effect (Joint Positions) "does not exclude any legal obligation arising under general international law." Meyring, B, 'Intergovernmentalism and Supranationality: Two Stereotypes for a Complex Reality,' 22 *European Law Review* (1997) 221, p.232.

72 Some, however, argued in support of the legal effect of Joint Action. The Advocate General in *Commission v. Council* ((C-170/96) [1998] I-2765), stated that Joint Action was a binding instrument which has legal effects. Müller-Graff also did not deny a possibility of legally binding effect of the Joint Actions "in a sense of Union law," (which is comparable to the legal effect of public international law), as opposed to Community law under the first pillar. He seems to suggest the existence of two separate legal orders in distinguishing Union law from Community Law. Anderson, *et al.*, also argue in a similar vein that Joint Actions may be classified as "manifestations of a new category of European law called 'Union law,' or perhaps even 'Union quasi-legislation'." They caution, however, that its relationship with both Community law and national law remains to be determined. Anderson, M, *et al.*, *Policing the European Union* (Oxford: Clarendon Press)(1995), pp. 202 and 203. Meyring argues that the legal effect of Joint Actions (and Joint Positions) comes from procedural rules applying to their adoption. He points to the existence of dates for entry into force in relation to Joint Actions, and maintains that this creates an obligation on the part of Member States. Meyring, *ibid.*, p. 233.

All of this created a situation where Member States did not undertake the joint positions or actions. As shown above, the Joint Action of 1997, among others, required Member States to take measures to protect victims of trafficking and to report back to the Council at the end of 1999. Before the entry into force of this Joint Action, Belgium was the only Member State to have laws and polices on the protection of victims of trafficking.[73] Between the entry into force of the Joint Action and the reporting deadline at the end of 1999, only a few took initiatives in relation to the protection of victims of trafficking.[74] This illustrates that most Member States did not follow this Joint Action. The failure of this Joint Action was also explicitly recognised by the Commission.[75]

In a similar vein, the legal nature of framework decisions is not entirely clear. While Article 34 provides that framework decisions are binding, it also stipulates that they do not have direct effect, meaning that they are not enforceable before national courts of Member States.[76] This creates the possibility that Member States cannot be held accountable for non-compliance with, or non-implementation of, the Framework Decision. It has been argued that while framework decisions lack direct effect, Article 34 does not exclude the possibility of implementing measures under framework decisions having direct

73 *Ministerial Circular Concerning the Granting of Residence Permits and Work Permits (Work Cards) to Foreigners Who Are Victims of Trafficking in Human Beings* (of 7 July 1994) and *Instructions to the Foreigners Department (Office des Etrangers), the Prosecuting Authorities, the Police and the Social Law Inspection Service and Social Inspection Services Concerning Assistance to Victims of Human Trafficking* (of 13 January 1997). Council of Europe, *Trafficking in Human Beings: Compilation of the Main Legal Instruments and Analytical Reports Dealing with Trafficking in Human Beings at International, Regional and National Levels (Volume II: National Texts)*, EG (2000) 2 rev. 1, (Strasbourg: Council of Europe)(2001), pp. 24 - 28.

74 Austria established the Intervention Centre for Victims of Trafficking in Women in 1997. Italy adopted *Legislative Decree No. 286/98 on Immigration and Aliens -- Article 18 Referring to the Granting of Temporary Residence Permits* (25 July 1998) and *Presidential Decree No. 394/99 on Rules of Implementation of the Consolidation Act* (31 August 1999) (allocation of funds for assistance and social integration). Portugal enacted the *Act 244/98* stipulating the possibility of exempting those who cooperate with authorities from visa requirements for residence permits and *Act 93/99* (14 July 1999) which covers witness protection of victims of trafficking. Council of Europe, *ibid*. However, there are general criminal and other laws in Member States which, although not directly related to trafficking, can be used to provide assistance to victims of crimes in general.

75 Proposal for the Framework Decision, *supra*.

76 For the notion of direct effect, see, among others, Case 26/622, *NV Algemene Transporten Expeditie Onderneming van Gend en Loos v. Netherlandse Administratie der Belastingen* [1963] ECR 1.

effect.[77] Another commentator also notes that the principle of "indirect effect," a notion that national measures giving effect to international obligations must be interpreted in light of the parent obligations, may be applicable to framework decisions.[78] Nevertheless, a certain degree of uncertainty on the legal effect of framework decisions still remains due to a lack of jurisprudence on these framework decisions by the European Court of Justice.[79]

3.2.3.2 Restrictive Immigration Laws and Policies

It is fair to state that the EU policies and measures for immigration control briefly mentioned above do contribute to the suppression of trafficking to some extent, and are consistent with, or even complement, trafficking policies and programmes as shown above. After the terrorist attack on the United States on 11th September, 2001, the EU has been promoting an even tougher approach to immigration control in the name of the fight against terrorism.[80] Tightening immigration control on this ground may be a natural reaction, as there is a close link between terrorism and organised crime.[81]

However, immigration policies and programmes adopted at the EU level raise a series of concerns. As noted elsewhere, many people flee their States of origin due to persecution and therefore qualify as refugees under the Refugee Convention. The EU and Member States have developed various laws and policies in order to protect such people.[82] However, these measures have been simul-

77 Craig P, and G. de Burca, *EU Law: Text, Cases and Materials* (3rd ed)(Oxford: Oxford University Press)(2003), p. 179.

78 Peers, S, *EU Justice and Home Affairs Law* (Harlow: Longman)(2000), p. 49.

79 Under Article 35 of the Maastricht Treaty as revised by the Treaty of Amsterdam, the ECJ has jurisdiction to give preliminary rulings on the validity and interpretation of framework decisions.

80 *Written Statement Submitted by Centre Europe - Tiers Monde (CETIM)*, E/CN.4/2002/NGO/90, para. 6.

81 Bantekas, I, 'International Law of Terrorist Financing,' 97 *American Journal of International Law* 315 (2003), p. 318; and Mylonaki, E, 'The Manipulation of Organised Crime by Terrorists: Legal and Factual Perspectives,' 2 *International Criminal Law Review* 213 (2002). See, further, United Nations Security Council Resolution 1373 (International Co-operation to Combat Threats to International Peace and Security Caused by Terrorist Acts)(2001), S/RES/1373.

82 See, for example, *Convention determining the State responsible for examining applications for asylum lodged in one of the Member States of the European Communities* (Dublin Convention), OJ C 254/1 (19/8/97); *Council Decision of 4 March 1996 on an alert and emergency procedure for burden-sharing with regard to the admission and residence of displaced persons on a temporary basis (96/198/JHA)*, OJ L 63/10 (13/3/96); *Joint Action of 26 April 1999 adopted by the Council on the basis of Article K.3 of the Treaty on European Union, establishing projects and measures to provide practical support in relation to the reception and voluntary repatriation of refugees,*

taneously criticised because they are designed to stem the flow of asylum seekers and refugees into EU Member States in practice.[83] This poses a problem not only for those trafficked who qualify as refugees but also for those who are not refugees but suffer from human rights abuses.

An irony arising from these restrictive immigration policies and programmes is that they encourage the growth of the trafficking business. These policies limit the opportunity for legal migration to the territories of Member States, and therefore people will naturally resort to traffickers. Further, not all of those trafficked enter and stay illegally in the EU territory as illustrated elsewhere. This means that enforcement against illegal migration does not necessarily lead to the curtailment of trafficking of human beings. In sum, reconsideration and reformulation of the EU immigration laws and policies are necessary.

3.2.3.3 Failure to Protect Victims of Trafficking

An analysis of the EU action also reveals that the protection of victims of trafficking is not a priority for the EU and Member States. While the Commission and the European Parliament have consistently expressed the views that the protection of the human rights of those trafficked should be an integral part of the EU policy on trafficking, they are not followed in practice. The Framework Decision on trafficking is a case in point. It is important to note that the *Council Framework Decision on standing of victims in criminal proceedings*[84] is applicable to trafficking victims, as it is specifically referred to under the Framework Decision. It sets out a list of measures to be taken by Member States to protect those who participate in criminal proceedings against traffickers, such as legal aid, witness protection and compensation. The evidence obtained from those trafficked is necessary to prosecute and punish traffickers, and therefore providing protection to those who are willing to co-operate may be a reasonable and justified step from the point of view of Member States.

Nevertheless, the Framework Decision on the Victims' Standing only applies to victims who participate in criminal proceedings, and does not oblige Member States to provide wider support outside of these proceedings. A problem arises

displaced persons and asylum seekers, including emergency assistance to persons who have fled as a result of recent events in Kosovo (1999/290/JHA) OJ L 114/2 (1/5/99); *Council Decision of 28 September 2000 establishing a European Refugee Fund (2000/596/EC)*, OJ L 252/12 (6/10/00); and *Council Directive 2001/55/EC of 20 July 2001 on minimum standards for giving temporary protection in the event of a mass influx of displaced persons and on measures promoting a balance of efforts between Member States in receiving such persons and bearing the consequences thereof*, OJ L 212/12 (7/8/01).

83 Morrison and Crosland, *supra*, pp. 31-39; and Ward, I, 'Identifying the European Other,' 14 *International Journal of Refugee Law* 219 (2002), pp. 229-235.

84 OJ L82/1 (22/3/01).

when these criminal proceedings are terminated (e.g. due to a lack of sufficient evidence) or completed (i.e. traffickers are convicted or acquitted). Under these circumstances, Member States can withdraw all support once victims have no further value from the criminal justice viewpoint. Another problem is that those who do not co-operate with law enforcement authorities are most likely to face enforcement actions, resulting in deportation to their States of origin even when they are exploited and victimised to a great extent during the course of their journey. The same is true for the Directive on Residence Permits mentioned earlier as it is to be used to facilitate co-operation with law enforcement authorities. Viewed in these contexts, these instruments can be used in a discriminatory manner to distinguish those who deserve protection from those who do not, and there is a danger of victims being used merely as a tool to achieve the EU's main objective: enhancement of law enforcement against trafficking.

The regime of subsidiary protection is advantageous in this regard as it does not specifically require those trafficked to co-operate with law enforcement authorities. However, some argue that its scope has become narrower through amendments made by the Council. For instance, the extent of the "serious harm" to be suffered by the victims in the original proposal was wider as it did not limit itself to particular types of human rights violations.[85] However, the actual Directive is limited to the death penalty or execution.[86] In addition, protection afforded to victims of trafficking under the Directive is narrow in that it does not go beyond the granting of temporary residence permits, unlike the Directive on Residence Permits which also provides for such measures as vocational training and medical assistance.[87]

3.2.4 A Need for a Holistic Approach

The overall EU action against trafficking represents a criminal justice response, in that the main aim is the suppression of the practice through crime and immigration control. This is quite similar to the national responses to trafficked examined in Chapter 2. While this is an important part of an overall strategy, a criminal justice response alone is not sufficient. As stressed throughout this book, successful actions against trafficking necessitate the EU and Member States to go beyond criminalisation of the act, punishment of traffickers, and reduction of the flow of trafficked migrants, and address a range of wider issues related to trafficking.

To begin with, the endemic problem of corruption must be addressed. States in transition such as the Central and Eastern European States - some of which are new Members of the EU – are particularly vulnerable to such prac-

85 Proposal, *supra.*

86 Piotrowicz and Van Eck, *supra,* p. 113.

87 Directive on Qualification, *supra.*

tices as noted elsewhere. The European Commission and the Council of Europe have, since 1996, been assisting the Central and Eastern European States to deal with corruption through a programme known as *OCTOPUS*, by providing expertise and technical assistance.[88] This type of programme should be extended to Member States in Western Europe as corruption is a problem which exists regardless of the types of political, social, and economic system. Moreover, they must also incorporate instruments on corruption, such as the *Criminal and Civil Conventions for Corruption* 1999[89] in order to show commitment to deal with corruption.

Further, the causes and consequences of trafficking must be addressed. While States of origin may inevitably be responsible for the flow of migrants, States of destination, including Member States of the EU, are also responsible. The demand for trafficked people is a case in point. Traffickers would not keep trafficking people to the territories of the EU Member States, were it not for the strong demand for cheap and/or forced labour.[90] Some of the measures, such as implementing laws on slavery and forced labour and opening up legal channels to migrate for employment, may be promoted at the EU level to oblige Member States to take further action in this regard. This is a reasonable option, given that there is a growing demand for labour in the territories of the EU.[91]

In relation to the consequences of trafficking, in addition to forced labour and slavery, one of the endemic problems facing migrants in the territories of the EU Member States is racism and/or xenophobia. Instances of racial abuse, physical and verbal, promoted by citizens and public officials, often resulting in the restriction of migrants' rights and freedoms, have been reported in some Member States,[92] and these clearly constitute serious violations of human rights. Member States therefore must take steps to eliminate racism and xenophobia.

Finally, the transnational nature of trafficking requires the EU and Member States to establish a good working relationship with States of origin and transit to control the supply side of trafficking of human beings. Poverty, a lack of

88 Council of Europe, *The Prevention of Corruption in Central and Eastern Europe: Activity Report (Provisional)* (Strasbourg: Council of Europe)(2002).

89 ETS Nos. 173 and 174. As of August 2005, Austria, France, Germany, Greece, Italy, and Spain have not ratified the Criminal Convention, and Austria, Belgium, Denmark, France, Germany, Ireland, Italy, Luxembourg, the Netherlands, Portugal, Spain and the United Kingdom either have not signed or ratified the Civil Convention. While the European Community as a whole can become a signatory to these two Conventions, it has not done so.

90 IOM, *Trafficking in Unaccompanied Minors for Sexual Exploitation in the European Union* (Brussels: IOM)(2001), pp. 10-12.

91 Drew, *supra,* p. 490.

92 *Written Statement Submitted by Society for Threatened Peoples*, E/CN.4/2003/NGO/253.

employment, and humanitarian crises are among the major factors contributing to the movement of people as noted elsewhere. While the primary duty to address these issues rests upon States of origin, they often lack the means to do so. The EU, being a powerful economic and political organisation, is in a good position to assist them technically and financially. The EU and the Member States have a very good reason to do this, as the restoration of economic, social and political stability in States of origin can reduce the incentive for people to migrate.

It should be recognised in this respect that the EU has been at the forefront in providing economic, social and political assistance to developing States. This is reflected in, among other things, the *Tacis Programme* (Technical Assistance to Commonwealth of Independent States). It was originally established under the *Council Regulation No. 1279/96 of 25 June 1996*,[93] and renewed by the *Council Regulation No. 99/2000*[94] with an estimated budget of 3,138 million Euro for 6 years (2000-2006).[95] The *Tacis Programme* covers a wide range of issues such as economic development, environmental protection, rural economies, and nuclear safety, and therefore is not specifically directed towards trafficking of human beings. Nevertheless, the phenomenon has been identified as a priority area, and some anti-trafficking initiatives are being implemented in Belarus, Moldova and Russia under this Programme.[96]

It is submitted that one way to promote a holistic approach to trafficking in the context of the EU is to make use of the first and second pillars. The proposed EU Constitution is worth noting in this respect. If and when adopted, the EU will have exclusive or shared competence in a wide variety of relevant areas,[97] making it possible for the EU and the Member States to adopt an inte-

93 OJ L 165/1 (4/7/96).

94 OJ L 12/1 (18/1/00). This programme is managed by the Directorate-General of External Relations.

95 Written Correspondence from Mr. Alistair MacDonald, Head of Unit, Directorate of Eastern Europe, Caucasus, Central Asian Republics of the External Relations Directorate General (26/8/02); and *Report from the Commission: The Tacis Programme Annual Report 1999*, COM (2000) 835 final.

96 See website of the Directorate General External Relations of the European Commission for more detail at http://europa.eu.int/comm/external_relations/index.htm.

97 Articles I-11 to I -18 of *Treaty Establishing a Constitution for Europe*. Under Article I-13, the EU would have exclusive competence over monetary policy for the Member States which have adopted the euro, common commercial policy, customs union, the conservation of marine biological resources under the common fisheries policy, and establishment of the competition rules necessary for the functioning of the internal market. It has shared competence, among other things, over internal market, area of freedom, security, and justice, and economic, social and territorial cohesion in accordance with Article I-14.

grated approach. Further, the EU will be able to promote and enhance the Area of Freedom, Security and Justice by adopting legally binding instruments such as European laws (with direct effect) and European framework laws in relation to common immigration and asylum policies (including the fight against trafficking of human beings), and police and judicial co-operation.[98]

The Expert Group mentioned above has much potential in this respect. Since it represents a wide variety of interests coming from different actors, the Group can serve as a vehicle to promote an integrated approach to deal with trafficking. In so doing, the value of the human rights framework should be emphasised, as it has the potential for promoting a holistic approach to deal with the act. If the EU and Member States can achieve these together with their partners, they may be able to curtail this rapidly growing phenomenon sooner rather than later.

3.3 International IGOs: UNIAP, IOM and ILO

3.3.1 United Nations Inter-Agency Project on Trafficking (UNIAP)

Within the United Nations system, there are several key organisations which have been at the forefront in dealing with the trafficking of human beings. The United Nations Office of Drugs and Crime (UNODC) is one example. In conjunction with the United Nations Interregional Crime and Justice Research Institute (UNICRI), the UNODC launched the *Global Programme Against Trafficking in Human Beings* in 1999 to strengthen national and international efforts to combat the phenomenon.[99] Another key agency is the Office of the United Nations High Commissioner for Human Rights (OHCHR). The main function of the Office is to promote human rights norms and principles with regard to trafficking through the Commission on Human Rights, Sub-Commission on Promotion and Protection of Human Rights (Sub-Commission), and various other mechanisms created under international human rights law and the Commission on Human Rights.[100] The recent activities initiated by the OHCHR include the adoption of the Recommended Principles and Guidelines.[101] There are other organisations such as the United Nations Children's Fund (UNICEF)[102] and the

98 Article III-265- III-277, *ibid.*

99 The main objectives of the Programme are 1) Data Collection; 2) Promotion of Best Practices and 3) Promotion of International Strategy against Trafficking. *Global Programme against Trafficking in Human Beings: An Outline for Action* (February 1999). More information can also be obtained from their website at http://www.unodc.org/unodc/en/trafficking_human_beings.html.

100 Interview with Ms. Jyoti Sanghera, Advisor on Trafficking to the UN High Commissioner for Human Rights (20/10/03).

101 *supra.*

102 http://www.unicef.org.

United Nations Development Fund for Women (UNIFEM)[103] which have the mandate to deal with the subject matter.

The focus of this book, however, is on the UNIAP. It was established in 1999[104] by the Ted Turner Fund (UN Foundation) as a pilot project to promote an inter-agency co-operation[105] and managed by the Office of the Resident Co-ordinator in Thailand through a full time Project Manager and his/her assistant.[106] There are two Phases to the UNIAP. Phase I lasted from June 2000 until May 2003 and Phase II began in December 2003 and will continue until June 2006.[107] Phase I can be characterised as more activity-orientated, in that it was involved in co-ordinating a wide variety of projects in the field. The implementation of projects was carried out through three Committees. The first was the Project Steering Committee. It was an inter-country committee with representatives of the governments, UN agencies, NGOs, and community based organisations (CBOs) and provided inputs to the UNIAP projects.[108] The second was the Project Working Committee which consists of 12 IGOs and 8 NGOs.[109] This Committee supported the Project Office by monitoring the implementation of activities, fostering co-ordination, and providing technical and management support.[110] The final Committee was the National Project Committee. Its mem-

103 http://www.unifem.org.

104 *United Nations Development Programme: Project of the Mekong Sub-Region*, 98/Sep/NDP/194 (RAS/98/H01/A/IV/31) (hereinafter Project Document). Before the establishment of the UNIAP, trafficking of human beings in Mekong sub-region was dealt with by the UN Working Group on Trafficking of Women and Children which did not have a clear organisational structure. This consisted of : Children-Asianet, ECPAT International, United Nations Economic Commission for Asia and the Pacific (ESCAP), International Labour Organization (ILO). International Organization for Migration (IOM), Mekong Region Law Centre (MRLC), United Nations Joint Programme on HIV/AIDS (UNAIDS), United Nations Office of Drug Control and Crime Prevention (UNDCP), United Nations Development Programme (UNDP), United Nations Educational, Scientific, and Cultural Organization (UNESCO), United Nations Population Fund (UNFPA), OHCHR, UNICEF, and UNIFEM.

105 Interview with Mr. Phil Robertson, Project Manager of the UNIAP (5/7/05).

106 *Project of the Mekong Sub-region: Project Revision*, RAS/00/Ho1/C/JB/31, p. 7 (hereinafter Project Revision).

107 *UNIAP Project Document: Version VI* (November 2003) (hereinafter Project Document Version VI).

108 *Ibid.*

109 They included Child Workers in Asia, ECPAT International, ESCAP, FACE, GAATW, ILO, IOM, MRLC, OHCHR, Oxfam, Save the Children Alliance, UNAIDS, UNDCP, UNDP, UNESCO, UNFPA, UNHCR, UNICEF, UNIFEM, and World Vision International.

110 Project Revision, *supra*, p. 7

bership included representatives of the governments, UN agencies, and national/international NGOs and CBOs.[111] Similar to the Project Working Committee, the National Committee in each State of the Mekong Sub-region was charged with, among others, implementation of activities and fostering co-ordination with relevant agencies in the region.[112]

The main objective of the UNIAP, as set out in the original Project Document, has been to "reduce the incidence of trafficking of women and children in the Mekong sub-region by enhancing the capacities of organisations and persons (especially women) and improving sub-regional communication and cooperation."[113] It was, therefore, not intended to introduce a new framework to deal with trafficking of human beings. Rather, the UNIAP was envisaged to strengthen the existing network by promoting co-operation. Four priority areas were identified in assessing the need of the Mekong Sub-region: 1) data collection, information and research; 2) enhancement of community-based initiatives according to local needs; 3) legal remedies and human rights; and 4) strategic analysis and impact evaluation.[114]

Various activities have been initiated or co-ordinated by the UNIAP in order to achieve these objectives. In the area of data collection and research, for instance, the UNIAP co-ordinated the studies of migration patterns and trafficking in such States as Myanmar and Laos.[115] In relation to community based initiatives, the UNIAP, with assistance from the Save the Children UK, started various training programmes on life and vocational skills for approximately 97,000 children in Myanmar.[116] In the area of human rights, the UNIAP participated in the drafting of the *UN Recommended Principles and Guidelines on Human Rights and Human Trafficking*, and took part in a seminar on gender equality and trafficking in October 2002.[117] Finally, in relation to strategic analysis and impact evaluation, a research officer from the UNICEF has provided a detailed analysis on the work of the UNIAP, and produced reports. This research and analysis exercise resulted in the creation of a pilot project which documented the experience of children from their starting point of trafficking to

---

111 *Ibid.*

112 *Ibid.* The National Committees, however, were discontinued from Phase II. The UNIAP instead supports government-generated national co-ordinating structures. Project Document Version VI, *supra*.

113 Project Document, *supra*, p. 13.

114 *Ibid.*, p. 7.

115 UNIAP Management Office, *Semi-Annual Project Report for the United Nations Foundation and the United Nations Fund for International Partnerships* (August 2002), p. 2 (hereinafter Semi-Annual Report 2002).

116 Save the Children UK Southeast Asia & the Pacific Regional Office, *First Progress Report to UNIAP/UNOPS* (August 2002).

117 Semi-Annual Report 2002, *ibid.*, p. 10.

the end in order to understand the *modus operandi* and proposed anti-trafficking measures to protect potential victims.[118]

In comparison to the Phase I, the focus of the Phase II is slightly different, in that the responsibility of monitoring and implementing field activities has gradually been shifting from the UNIAP to the national governments in the Mekong Sub-Region.[119] An important step taken in this regard is the establishment of the COMMIT (Coordinated Mekong Ministerial Initiative against Trafficking) Process. This is an initiative taken by six governments of the Mekong Sub-region in 2003, and the UNIAP currently serves as its secretariat.[120] The main objective of the COMMIT Process is "to agree on common measures of achievement for the six participating countries with respect to the prevention of trafficking, prosecution of perpetrators and protection of the rights of victims."[121]

One major initiative taken within the framework of the COMMIT Process was the adoption of the *Memorandum of Understanding on Cooperation against Trafficking in Persons in the Greater Mekong Sub-region* and *Sub-regional Action Plan: Areas for Cooperation and Activities* in October 2004. In the Action Plan, six governments have agreed to promote cooperation and co-ordination in the areas of information exchange, investigation and prosecution of traffickers, and victim identification and their reintegration/repatriation. The COMMIT Process is in its infant stage, and therefore takes some time to judge its effectiveness and the effort put by the UNIAP. However, adoption of these documents at least shows their willingness to co-operate together not only to prohibit and prevent trafficking, but also to protect victims who have been caught up in the process.

3.3.2 *International Organisation for Migration (IOM)*

The IOM was established for the purpose of facilitating the organised transfer of migrants by providing assistance to those who would otherwise be unable to migrate.[122] It has been dealing with the trafficking of human beings since 1994. In

118 *Ibid.*, p. 10.

119 This is not to state, however, that the UNIAP no longer implements any project. It has identified 4 programme areas which the UNIAP can take an initiative: 1) Building the Knowledge Base; 2) Strategic Analysis and Priority Setting; 3) Targeted Intervention and Catalytic Research; and 4) Advocacy. See Project Revision Document Version VI, *supra*.

120 Interview with Mr. Robertson, *supra*.

121 *Ibid.*

122 Article 1 of the Constitution of the International Organisation for Migration 1987 (hereinafter IOM Constitution). Its predecessor was known as the Intergovernmental Committee for European Migration. The original Constitution was adopted in 1987 and the IOM came into being in 1989.

November of that year, the Council[123] approved a plan of action for trafficking of human beings in its Resolution No. 908 (LXIX). This resolution formulated an objective of the IOM in relation to trafficking, which is "to curtail migrant trafficking and protect the rights of migrants caught up in the practice."[124] The mandate to deal with trafficking of human beings was extended by Council Resolution No. 923 (LXXI) in 1995.[125] This resolution, among others, stipulated that the "IOM is committed to the principle that humane and orderly migration benefits migrants and society and acts to ... work towards effective respect of the human dignity and well-being of migrants."[126] Trafficking of human beings was therefore clearly regarded as a human rights issue.

This emphasis on human rights was maintained by the recent policy on trafficking in human beings, entitled *Trafficking in Migrants: IOM Policy and Responses.*[127] It starts by adopting a working definition of trafficking:

> For IOM, trafficking occurs when:
> - a migrant is illicitly engaged (recruited, kidnapped, sold, etc) and/or moved either within national or across international borders;
> - intermediaries (traffickers) during any part of this process obtain economic or other profit by means of deception, coercion and/or other forms of exploitation under conditions that violate the fundamental human rights of the migrants.[128]

In adopting this working definition, the IOM stresses that it focuses not only on the process of trafficking, but also on the human rights of those trafficked, as enshrined in the *Universal Declaration of Human Rights 1998* and other instruments.[129]

In accordance with the objective stipulated in the earlier Resolutions, the IOM implements various programmes in relation to trafficking. Its activities are divided into six categories: 1) seminar and fora; 2) information gathering and research; 3) technical co-operation; 4) information dissemination; 5) return

---

123 It is a policy making body which consists of representatives of Member States. Articles 6 to 11 of the IOM Constitution, *ibid.*

124 IOM Policy on Trafficking, *supra*, paras. 25 and 26.

125 *Ibid.*, para. 23.

126 *Ibid.*

127 *Ibid.*

128 With the adoption of the Trafficking Protocol, the IOM adopted its definition of trafficking. IOM, *IOM's Role in Preventing and Combating Trafficking in Human Beings* (A paper presented at the European Conference on Preventing and Combating Trafficking in Human Beings: Global Challenge for the 21st Century, 18-20 September 2002), p. 1 (hereinafter IOM Conference Paper 2002).

129 IOM Policy on Trafficking, *supra*.

and reintegration activities; and 6) counselling and medical support. The IOM organises seminars and fora for the purpose of sharing information among the different actors involved. In the past, the IOM has organised roundtable discussions on trafficking with government officials and other concerned parties in Armenia,[130] Azerbaijan[131] and Tajikistan,[132] and hosted a conference on human trafficking and smuggling in the Asia-Pacific region.[133] In relation to research, the IOM has conducted country based case studies in many parts of the world. States examined include Albania,[134] Cambodia,[135] Dominican Republic,[136] Georgia,[137] the Russian Federation,[138] Turkey,[139] Ukraine,[140] and the Former Yugoslavia.[141]

In addition, the IOM also conducts information campaigns to raise awareness. In Peru and Ecuador, for instance, the IOM regional office carried out a campaign through television, radio, newspaper, and other forms of advertisement.[142] The information campaign was designed to educate the general public

130 *IOM in Eastern Europe and Central Asia*, Issue 5 (October-December 2001), p. 3 (hereinafter Eastern Europe Issue 5).

131 *IOM in Eastern Europe and Central Asia*, Issue 6 (January-March 2002), p. 1 (hereinafter Eastern Europe Issue 6).

132 *IOM in Tajikistan Newsletter* No. 1 (September 2001), p, 4.

133 *Trafficking in Human Beings Quarterly Bulletin* No. 25, Spring 2002.

134 *Research Report on Third Country National Trafficking Victims in Albania: Inter-Agency Referral System (IARS) for Return and Reintegration Assistance to Victim of Trafficking* (Tirana, Albania: IOM)(2002).

135 *Path of Exploitation: Studies on the Trafficking of Women and Children between Cambodia, Thailand, and Vietnam* (Geneva: IOM)(1999).

136 *Trafficking in Women from the Dominican Republic for Sexual Exploitation* (Geneva: IOM)(1996).

137 *Hardship Abroad or Hunger at Home: A Study of Irregular Migration from Georgia* (Geneva: IOM)(2001).

138 Hughes, D, *Trafficking for Sexual Exploitation: The Case of the Russian Federation.* (Geneva: IOM)(2002).

139 *Transit Migration in Turkey* (Ankara: IOM)(1995).

140 *Information Campaign Against Trafficking in Women from Ukraine* (Geneva: IOM)(1998). For information on trafficking in CIS States in general, see *Migration Information from CIS States* (Geneva: IOM)(2000).

141 *Return and Reintegration - Counter-Trafficking- Situation Report in Kosovo* (Kosovo: IOM)(2001).

142 Electronic Correspondence from Mr. Manfred Ritter, Regional Officer for Programme in Andean Region (3/9/02).

about the danger of emigrating abroad illegally. Similar information campaigns have been implemented in such States as the Czech Republic.[143]

Technical co-operation programmes are designed to enhance the capability of governments to suppress trafficking more effectively. [144] In April 2002, the IOM organised immigration training for border guards from Kyrgyzstan, Tajikistan, Kazakhstan, and Uzbekistan.[145] Over a three-day period, 32 border guards received practical training on identifying false documents and exchanged information on trafficking of human beings. Similar training workshops were also held in February and March 2002 for government officials of Armenia, Azerbaijan, and Georgia.[146] In Belgium, IOM Brussels is currently developing a training manual for law enforcement agencies in South Eastern Europe as part of capacity building exercise.[147]

In addition, voluntary repatriation and reintegration activities are also important components of the IOM's work on trafficking.[148] In August 2001, for instance, the IOM in Sudan assisted the return of 73 Ugandans, who were abducted by a rebel group known as the Lord's Resistance Army. [149] These victims received medical/psychological assistance from NGOs and UNICEF in Sudan, and the IOM arranged return flights via Nairobi and also provided an escort service for them. In Mekong Sub-Region, a total of 548 women and children participated in repatriations promoted by the IOM between September 2001 and March 2003.[150]

---

143 Speech by the Deputy Director General of the IOM, entitled "Violence Towards Women: The Case of the Trade in Women for Prostitution and Response by the International Organzation for Migration" before Parliamentary Assembly of the Council of Europe, Sub-Commission on Violence towards Women (November 1999). The Deputy Director General also mentioned information campaigns in Bulgaria, Hungary and Ukraine.

144 *Technical Cooperation on Migration (TCM): IOM's Contribution towards Migration Policy-Making and Strengthened Migration Governance.* MC/INF/240 (October 1999). For a comprehensive study/research on IOM's TCM, see *Overview: IOM's Global TCM Expertise* (Geneva: IOM)(1999).

145 *IOM in Eastern Europe and Central Asia*, Issue 7 (April-June 2002), p. 6 (hereinafter Eastern Europe Issue 7).

146 Eastern Europe Issue 5, *supra*, p. 2.

147 This is known as EC CARDS (Community Assistance for Reconstruction, Development and Stabilisation) Regional Police Project (CARPO). It is expected to last until the summer 2006, and the author has been serving as an expert for this project.

148 *IOM Return Policy and Programmes*, MC/INF/236 (November 1997).

149 IOM Press Briefing Note (10/8/01).

150 *UN Inter-Agency Project Newsletter*, 'A Product of IOM Project: Return and Reintegration of Trafficked and Other Vulnerable Women and Children Between Selected Countries in Mekong Region,' Issue 11 (2003).

As for reintegration activities, the IOM in Thailand, in conjunction with the Thai Red Cross, has initiated a pre-return psycho-social assistance project. The manual for social workers and others was created, and the use of animation was relied upon to educate the general public, including those at risk of being trafficked.[151] In Romania, the IOM together with government and NGOs, opened a centre to provide temporary protection, including medical assistance and counselling for Romanian victims of trafficking.[152] By June 2002, 105 victims had benefited from services provided in that centre.[153] These activities have also been conducted in the Balkans region[154] and Ukraine.[155]

Finally, the IOM has also been active in providing health services which are needed for those affected by trafficking. In Ho Chi Minh City, Vietnam, the IOM in conjunction with local hospitals, the U.S. Centre for Disease Control (CDC) and the Australian government, conducted research on tuberculosis and its effects on migrants.[156] The IOM has also co-operated with the World Health Organisation (WHO) and the UNAIDS to provide health education all around the world.[157] In looking at the activities of the IOM, it can be stated that their strategy is more action orientated, in the sense that they actively engage themselves in field activities.

3.3.3 International Labour Organisation (ILO)

The ILO is an organisation mandated to deal with labour issues and regards trafficking as "a degrading misuse of human resources resulting in undignified and unproductive work."[158] The ILO is also a human rights organisation, in that it is charged with protection and promotion of human rights in relation to work

151 *Shattered Dreams: Activities Manual for Use with Life Skills Video* (2002).

152 IOM Bucharest, *IOM Counter-Trafficking Programmes in Romania* (June 2002).

153 *Ibid.* IOM Bucharest also established a network of 20 Romanian NGOs which provide a wide variety of services for victims of trafficking, such as transportation, counselling, job and life skills training, and legal assistance.

154 *IOM Participation in the Consolidated Appeals (CAP) for 2002*, p. 21. See further, *IOM Counter-Trafficking Strategy for the Balkans and the Neighbouring Countries* (Geneva: IOM)(2001).

155 IOM there opened a rehabilitation centre and a shelter for victims of trafficking with $170,000 provided by the Swedish International Development Cooperation Agency. *IOM in Eastern Europe and Central Asia*, Issue 2 (January-March 2001), p. 3.

156 *Migration Health Service 1999 Annual Report* (Geneva: IOM) (2000) (hereinafter IOM Health Report 1999), p. 17.

157 *Ibid.*

158 *Unbearable to Human Hearts: Child Trafficking and Action to Eliminate It* (Geneva: ILO)(2002), p. vii.

as stipulated in the *Declaration of Philadelphia* 1944.[159] In the context of trafficking, the ILO focuses on forced labour, the abuse of migrant workers, discrimination at work, and child labour,[160] and considers that all of these entail serious violations of human rights.

One of the important tasks which the ILO undertakes is to adopt Conventions. Some of these are applicable to certain aspects of trafficking. They include the *Forced Labour Convention (No. 29)* 1930, the *Migration for Employment Convention (Revised) (No. 97)* 1949, the *Abolition of Forced Labour Convention (No. 105)* 1957, the *Migrant Workers (Supplementary Provisions) Convention (No. 143)* 1973, and the *Worse Forms of Child Labour Convention (No, 182)* 1999.[161] The last Convention is of particular importance, as it stipulates that the worst forms of slavery include slavery and practices similar to slavery such as trafficking.[162]

The compliance of Member States with these Conventions is monitored by different bodies within the ILO. Parties to these Conventions are required to formulate a report for each Convention which they have signed or ratified, and transmit these reports to the Director-General of the ILO.[163] These reports are then examined by legal experts of the Committee of Experts on the Application of Conventions and Recommendations (CEACR).[164] The CEACR then submits an annual report to the International Labour Conference,[165] where it is examined by the Tripartite Committee on the Application of Standards of the International Labour Conference.[166] During the Conference, any employer and worker

159 It was adopted in May 1944. This Declaration sets out objectives and principles of the ILO, and was incorporated into the Constitution of the International Labour Organisation 1919 (hereinafter ILO Constitution) . The subsequent *Declaration on Fundamental Principles and Rights at Work* 1998 affirmed the ILO's commitment to the protection and promotion of human rights at work, and identified four fundamental principles: freedom of association, elimination of forced labour, abolition of child labour, and elimination of discrimination in the workplace, as enshrined in its international labour standards (as formulated in the forms of Conventions and Recommendations). *ILO at Work: Factpack (revised in 2000)*, Fact Sheet 2.1.

160 Boonpala, P, and J. Kane, *Trafficking of Children: The Problem and Responses Worldwide* (Geneva: ILO)(2001), p. 6.

161 All of these Conventions are available at http://ilolex.ilo.ch:1567/english/convdisp1.htm.

162 Article 3, *ibid.* See also ILO's Worse Form of Child Labour Recommendation No. 190 (1999). This Recommendation regards trafficking as a form of slavery, and calls for Member States to adopt legislation to criminalise the practice.

163 Article 22 of the ILO Constitution.

164 Explanatory Policy Paper, *supra*, p. 17.

165 It is held annually in June.

166 Explanatory Policy Paper, *supra*.

representatives of the Conference can lodge a complaint in cases where other Members are not "securing effective observance" of any Convention before the Commission of Inquiry appointed by the Governing Body.[167] The Commission of Inquiry, after examining the complaint, formulates a report containing its findings and recommendations.[168] The outcome is then distributed to the Governing Body and each of the States concerned in the complaint.[169] The States can either accept the recommendation, or refer the complaint to the International Court of Justice (ICJ).[170] In the event that any Member State fails to carry out recommendations proposed by the Commission of Inquiry or decisions of the ICJ, the Governing Body may recommend some forms of action to the Conference in order to secure compliance.[171]

In addition to monitoring implementation of Conventions, the ILO implements field programmes on trafficking. One such Programme is called the ILO International Programme on the Elimination of Child Labour (ILO-IPEC). Established in 1992 with 6 participating States, the ILO-IPEC now operates in more than 70 States.[172] Although the ILO-IPEC was not initially designed to deal with trafficking of human beings, its scope of activities has been expanded so that this is now included.[173] Activities on trafficking are generally categorised into five "intervention areas," namely direct action (prevention, education, skills training, etc.), capacity building (of governments and NGOs), awareness raising and advocacy, research, and policy/legislative support. Some of the examples on the ILO-IPEC Programmes are worth mentioning. In 1997, the ILO-IPEC launched a project entitled "Combating the Trafficking in Children and Their Exploitation in Prostitution and Other Intolerable Forms of Child Labour in South Asia and the Mekong Sub-Region."[174] This was essentially a research exercise conducted by the Institute of Population and Social Research at the

167 Article 26, of ILO Constitution, *supra.*

168 Article 28, *ibid.*

169 Article 29(1), *ibid.*

170 Article 29(2), *ibid.*

171 Article 33, *ibid.*

172 *IPEC Action Against Child Labour 2000-2001: Progress and Future Priorities* (2002), p. 11.

173 It began activities on trafficking in 1993 in such States as Thailand, Philippines, Cambodia and Nepal. IPEC Working Group on Trafficking, *Trafficking of Children for Labour and Sexual Exploitation: Overview of IPEC's Response to the Problem* (2001), p. 3. Between 2002 and 2003, approximately $ 20 million was allocated for combating trafficking of human beings. ILO, *ILO's Current Work on Combating Trafficking.*

174 *Combating Trafficking in Children for Labour Exploitation in the Mekong Sub-Region: A Proposed Framework for ILO-IPEC Action and Proceedings of a Mekong Sub-Regional Consultation.* (1998), p. 10 (hereinafter Framework for Action).

Mahidol University (Thailand), and contributed to better understanding of the extent of the problem in the region.[175]

This research exercise was followed by the Mekong Sub-Regional Consultation (July 1998) and the adoption of the Proposed Framework of Action (October 1998). [176] While the ILO recognised that the primary responsibility to combat trafficking rested on the national governments, it simultaneously stressed the need for partnerships with other concerned actors. The Proposed Framework for Action also envisaged the establishment of national focal points or taskforces which would be charged with management of programmes and co-ordination with partner organisations at the national level. In line with the transnational nature of trafficking, the ILO then proposed to implement programmes at national, bilateral and sub-regional levels. These include, but are not limited to, direct action programmes for prevention (e.g. awareness raising and provisions of alternatives such as education, jobs, etc.), reintegration (e.g. provisions of shelter and counselling), advocacy and campaign (ratification of international instruments), and capacity building (enhancement of national laws and enforcement, research activities, and in-country communication/networking).

An analysis of the ILO-IPEC programmes in the Mekong Sub-region reveals that they are generally implemented in line with this Framework for Action. Between October 1999 and January 2001, the ILO-IPEC, in close co-operation with the NGO DEPDC, implemented an Action Programme entitled "Preventing Young Girls in the North of Thailand from Being Lured into Child Labour: Intensifying DEPDC's Effort in Direct Service Provision for Girls at Risk and Mobilising Local and Provincial Resources and Action."[177] During this period, DEPDC and the ILO-IPEC organised study tours and camps, provided education on child labour, children's rights, health and other matters as well as vocational (job skill) training. Many children as well as parents, community leaders, teachers and others directly benefited from these programmes. The Action Programme was also said to establish a network of community leaders, law enforcement and other governmental agencies as well as NGOs in the Mae Sai region of Thailand.[178]

The ILO-IPEC also implements programmes related to trafficking in other regions of the world. In Latin America, the ILO-IPEC has implemented projects

175 The research exercises have also taken place in Nepal and West Africa. See *Nepal, Trafficking in Girls with Reference to Prostitution: A Rapid Assessment* (2001), and *Combating Trafficking in Children for Labour Exploitation in West and Central Africa* (2001).

176 Consisting of government representatives, NGOs and researchers. Framework for Action, *supra.*, p. 26.

177 DEPDC, *Progress Report B: Preparatory Outputs and Activities, Submitted to ILO-IPEC* (February 2001).

178 DEPDC, *Final Output Report* (May 2002).

which provide direct services to children who have already been exploited. In Cartagena and Barranquilla, Colombia, the ILO-IPEC funded a local NGO Fundación Renacer which administers day-time centres for child victims of exploitation.[179] These centres are used to provide psychological therapy, education, occupational and other training and serve as permanent homes for children. Similar services are also provided in Nicaragua and Costa Rica.[180]

In addition to ILO-IPEC, the ILO manages a specific programme on trafficking of human beings. A Programme entitled "Mekong Sub-regional Project to Combat Trafficking in Children and Women"(ILO-TICW Project) is a good example. This project started in February 2000.[181] The main focus of this programme is prevention through the creation of employment, education and vocational training, awareness-raising and advocacy, and capacity building at local and national levels. A number of activities have been implemented under the ILO-TICW Project. In Cambodia, the ILO and its implementing agency the *Cambodian Association for Assistance to Families and Widows* contributed to the enhancement of food security and income generation for approximately 150 families by organising agricultural skills training and demonstrations as well as social education between June 2001 and September 2002.[182] In Laos, a theatre group known as *Thiep Phong Phan Theatre Troop* was funded not only to help preserve their traditional form of entertainment, but also to initiate an awareness-raising campaign against trafficking through the use of traditional and modern media and entertainment.[183] The ILO in Laos has also been organising a series of meetings/training sessions for different actors involved. Similar programmes have also been implemented in other States such as Thailand, Vietnam and China.[184]

---

179 *Trafficking and Sexual Exploitation of Children: An Evaluation of ILO-IPEC Programmes in Thailand, Philippines, Colombia, Costa Rica and Nicaragua* (2001), p. 29 (herein after Trafficking and Sexual Exploitation).

180 *Ibid.*, pp. 21-46.

181 *Labour Migration and Trafficking within the Greater Mekong Sub-Region: Proceedings of Mekong Sub-Regional Expert Meeting and Explanatory Policy Paper* (Bangkok: ILO)(2001), pp. 8 and 9 (hereinafter Explanatory Policy Paper).

182 *Project Intervention: Cambodia* (June 2002).

183 *Project Interventions: Laos* (June 2002).

184 *Yunnan Province of China Situation of Trafficking in Children and Women: A Rapid Assessment* (2002); *Viet Nam Children in Prostitution in Hanoi, Hai Phong, Ho Chi Minh City and Can Tho:Rapid Assessment* (2002); and *Trafficking in Children into the Worst Forms of Child Labour in Thailand: Rapid Assessment Findings from Four Research Sites along the Thailand-Lao PDR and Thailand-Myanmar Border Areas* (2000). It should be noted, that the ILO currently does not implement programmes in Myanmar because it has sanctioned the government for not dealing

3.3.4 *Analysis of UNIAP, IOM and ILO*

There are several observations to be made in relation to the UNIAP, the IOM and the ILO. To begin with, it seems reasonable to maintain that the scope of activities of these organisations is wider than that of the EU. Given that Western Europe is a major destination for those trafficked, the main approach of the EU has been to prevent the flow of migrants into its territories. The activities of the UNIAP, the IOM and the ILO, however, range from preventive measures (e.g. awareness-raising and education) to return and reintegration (e.g. provision of escort services, shelter, counselling, etc.). In other words, they have been able to take a more holistic approach to trafficking than the EU. In addition, the focus on protection of the human rights of victims is more visible in relation to the activities of these three organisations. A further advantage of international IGOs such as the United Nations is that they are better suited to set the standards and norms in relation to trafficking to be accepted by the international community as a whole.[185]

It is also important to note that activities and programmes of the UNIAP, the IOM and the ILO are implemented mainly by governments, NGOs and other actors. This means that the major function of the international IGOs in relation to trafficking so far lies in the provision of funding and the co-ordination of activities for concerned actors involved. The UNIAP was established mainly for this purpose, while the IOM and the ILO rely heavily on their implementing partners, although these two IGOs do implement their own programmes. This underscores the point expressed elsewhere in this book that trafficking of human beings cannot effectively be addressed without co-operation from different actors at the national, regional and international levels.

The key point to be analysed, therefore, is whether or not these organisations have been able to promote effective co-ordination and co-operation. An examination reveals that there is no clear answer to this question, as there is a mixture of results. In Romania, for instance, activities conducted by national and foreign governmental agencies (e.g. USAID and FBI) and IGOs such as the UNAIDS, the UNDP, and the IOM are said to be well co-ordinated. The existence of the Romanian inter-ministerial committee on counter-trafficking as well as the IOM's Steering Committee have made it easy for concerned actors to communicate and co-ordinate their activities.[186] Similar co-ordination is said to take place in the Andean region of Latin America.[187]

---

with forced/child labour sufficiently. Interview with Ms. Eriko Kiuchi, Programme Officer of ILO Bangkok (27/6/05).

185 Through adoption of international treaties, for example. Interview with Mr. Robert England, former Resident Co-ordinator of the UN Office in Thailand (7/10/05).

186 Electronic Correspondence from by Mr. Dani Kozak, IOM Bucharest (14/10/02).

187 Electronic Correspondence from Mr. Ritter, *supra*.

Nevertheless, co-ordination can be difficult in other parts of the world. The Mekong sub-region is a good example. Given that this region has been affected by trafficking for a long time, the concentration of activities may be understandable. However, activities such as research, information campaign, training sessions, and provision of assistance, organised separately by the IOM, the ILO and other agencies, are similar in nature, and duplication of activities has been recognised.[188] One reason for this is that different IGOs are competing, instead of co-operating, with each other. It has been reported in this regard that the ILO in some States has implemented programmes with NGOs without co-ordination with other organisations such as the United Nations.[189] The Resident Co-ordinator, who manages the UNIAP, has expressed a similar view by stating that promotion of individual agencies takes precedence over team work and the promotion of the United Nations as a whole.[190]

What is needed therefore is an arrangement which would identify the strengths of each organisation, and design and implement programmes accordingly. The role of projects such as the UNIAP, therefore, is critical to reduce the instances of overlap and maximise scarce resources. In recognising the existence of similar activities conducted in the region, [191] the UNIAP has been instrumental in working for better communication and co-ordination. The GAATW, which has extensive experience of working with IGOs, is of the view that the level of communication and co-operation among IGOs have improved over the course of time.[192] It has also been reported that the UNIAP communicates with NGOs in the implementation of their programmes and provides assistance whenever possible.[193] In relation to the Phase II of the UNIAP, it has been noted the role is divided more in line with the expertise of each IGO. The ILO now works on preventive activities,[194] while the IOM emphases return and reintegration of victims of trafficking.[195] This ensures that IGOs do not interfere with each other's activities and maximises their resources and expertise. In view of these, it seems

188 *UN Inter-Agency Project Newsletter* 'Message from the Chair: Reflection on Phase I of UNIAP,' Issue 12 (2003).

189 Trafficking and Sexual Exploitation, *supra*. The research officer working for the UNIAP also notes that organisations working in the Mekong sub-region have a tendency to "define the issue according to their own mandate." Semi-Annual Report 2002, *supra*, p. 10.

190 UN Inter-Agency Newsletter, Issue 12, *supra*.

191 Electronic Correspondence from Mr. Phil Marshall, Project Manager, UNIAP (7/9/02).

192 Interview with Ms. Pattanaik, *supra*.

193 Electronic Correspondence from Ms, Nicholson, *supra.*

194 Interviews with Ms. Kiuchi and Ms. Engblom, *supra*.

195 Interview with Mr. Federico Soda, Programme Development Officer and Ms. Varaporn Chanapai, Assistant Project Co-ordinator of the IOM Bangkok (27/6/05).

reasonable to argue that the co-ordination and co-operation among different IGOs have seen some improvement over the course of time.

Aside from this issue of co-ordination, other factors must be taken into account in evaluating the roles played by these three organisations. Funding, for instance, is a relevant factor. As in any other field, securing adequate funding has been difficult. According to the report of the UNIAP, it required approximately $ 1.5 million in order for the UNIAP to carry out activities until the year 2005.[196] Although the UNIAP was able to secure enough funding to continue Phase II,[197] it has in the past been forced to withdraw resources from certain areas of work. This can be seen in the termination of the position of Regional Legal Policy Advisor, which was created in 2002.[198] Another related problem is that the competition among IGOs is fuelled by a lack of funding. IGOs often have to compete for funding to implement their own projects, and once they obtain enough funding to do their own business, they are said to lose interest in co-ordination and co-operation.[199]

A lack of funding has also affected the performance of implementing partners, especially NGOs in the field. AFESIP in Cambodia claims that the amount allocated by the UNIAP, $10,000, was not sufficient to implement a field program in relation to trafficking.[200] DEPDC, a Thai NGO which had worked with some IGOs in the past, also reports in a similar vein that it has been difficult to obtain sufficient funding to implement programmes effectively.[201] An added complication is the bureaucracy within IGOs which prevents them from providing funding in a timely manner. It takes between 6 to 8 months, sometimes longer, to obtain some financial assistance for NGOs to implement programmes.[202] This can affect small NGOs which rely heavily on external funding to continue their activities.

In addition, the safety and security of those working in the field are sometimes threatened. Save the Children UK expressed concerns over the safety of its staff members working in Myanmar on a UNIAP project. Some of the repatriation and reintegration activities have been difficult to implement, as they involved travelling to remote and insecure areas, which have been affected by conflicts

---

196 Semi-Annual Report 2002, *supra*, p. 2.

197 Interview with Mr. Phil Robertson, *supra*.

198 Electronic Correspondence from Mr. Brian Iselin, Regional Legal Policy Advisor of the UNODC (15/4/03).

199 Interview with Mr. England, *supra*.

200 Electronic Correspondence from Mr. Pierre Legros, Regional Advisor, AFESIP (28/8/02).

201 Electronic Correspondence from Ms. Nicholson (5/9/02), *supra*.

202 *Ibid.*, and Electronic Correspondence from Mr. Legros, *supra*.

between the government and ethnic groups.[203] Although instances of a similar nature have not publicly been reported elsewhere, the safety of staff members of NGOs and IGOs is a pressing issue in many parts of the world, particularly because of the involvement of criminals, organised or otherwise, in addition to external factors such as armed conflicts and other humanitarian crises.

Moreover, polices and programmes of these organisations are directed predominantly towards States of origin and transit, and are rarely applied to the States of destination. In other words, although much attention has been given to the supply side, controlling the demand for trafficked human beings has not been addressed adequately. The UNIAP explored in this Chapter has been created to deal with trafficking in the Mekong sub-region, the major region of origin for trafficked people. However, a similar initiative does not exist in States of destination, most of which are Western States. The IOM and the ILO also focus much on States of origin/transit, and not much has been done except for research purposes. In addition, there is no evidence to date to suggest that Member States of the EU, popular destinations for many, have done much to tackle and reduce the demand for trafficked human beings. Arguably, many of the donors to these IGOs are powerful and wealthy developed States, and therefore this might have influenced the way in which these IGOs implement activities. It has been noted in this regard that donor States decide on the priority areas, and the UN Resident Co-ordinator has a little say in allocation of funding.[204] Whatever the reasons, it seems reasonable to argue that the IGOs have not entirely been able to implement a holistic approach to trafficking of human beings, although they continue to play an important role in the prevention/suppression of the practice and the protection of victims.

3.4 Conclusion

This Chapter examined how regional and international IGOs have been dealing with trafficking of human beings. The phenomenon has become a priority among them. Those examined in this Chapter as well as other organisations deal with different aspects of trafficking one way or another in modern times. This, of course, is a welcome sign, as a multilateral or a global effort is required to suppress trafficking of human beings. It is also encouraging to see that these IGOs are working closely with governments and NGOs. Nevertheless, their responses are not entirely effective, due to such reasons as a lack of a holistic approach, difficulty in co-ordination and co-operation, and other issues including shortage in funding.

Further, IGOs have not been able to address the human rights issues pertinent to the phenomenon effectively. The EU promotes a criminal justice response at the expense of the protection and promotion of the human rights of those

203 Save the Children UK, *supra*, p. 6.

204 Interview with Mr. England, *supra*.

trafficked. Other examined IGOs are slightly different, as a human rights perspective is incorporated into various policies and initiatives. However, because these organisations are not taking a holistic approach, it becomes difficult to maintain that the human rights aspects of trafficking, particularly in States of transit and destination, are adequately addressed. What exactly are the human rights issues pertinent to trafficking, and how are human rights norms and principles enforced? This is the focus of the next two Chapters. They re-examine the process of trafficking from the beginning to the end, identify applicable human rights norms and principles that make up the human rights framework, and articulate human rights obligations imposed upon non-State and State actors.

Chapter 4

Trafficking of Human Beings as a Human Rights Abuse: Obligations and Accountability of Non-State Actors

4.1 Introduction

One of the main themes running through this book is that trafficking of human beings is a human rights issue. In Chapter 1, it was shown that an increasing number of actors view the practice from a human rights perspective. Chapters 2 and 3, among others, examined how this perception is reflected in laws, policies, enforcement, and various programmes related to trafficking at the national, regional and international levels. The main conclusion reached so far is that, although it is easy to regard trafficking as a human rights issue, it can be difficult in practice to address the human rights aspects of the phenomenon.

It is submitted that one reason why it is difficult to promote a human rights framework in relation to trafficking is that a comprehensive analysis of the practice utilising an application of the established human rights norms and principles has not been undertaken. As a result, many important questions remain unanswered, such as: What exactly are the human rights norms and principles applicable to trafficking? Does international human rights law establish and articulate obligations in relation to this practice? If so, what is their nature? What are the levels of obligations imposed upon State actors and non-State actors? Does the Trafficking Protocol have the potential to promote the human rights approach to the practice?

The next two Chapters seek to answer these questions in an attempt to establish a human rights framework, not only to understand, but also to address trafficking and the wider issues surrounding the practice. This Chapter focuses on the obligations and accountability of non-State actors. It begins by highlighting some human rights issues relevant to the causes, processes, and consequences of trafficking, such as poverty, discrimination, inhuman or degrading treatment, forced labour, and law enforcement practices. The Chapter then examines the obligations and accountability of non-State actors, such as organised criminal groups, under international human rights law. Although the duties of non-State actors are recognised in several international human rights instruments and widely supported by different actors, non-State actors do not have legal obligations under international human rights law. The importance of human rights norms and principles, however, is not to be underestimated as they may be enforceable indirectly. It will be shown that criminal and civil proceedings offer an alternative means by which the human rights norms and principles can be enforced at the national level, and therefore indirect application of human rights law is a viable option. At the international level, it is argued that trafficking can be regarded as a crime against humanity, and therefore the involvement of the International Criminal Court becomes a possibility. In conclusion, accountability of non-State actors who abuse human rights during the process of trafficking can still be addressed at different levels.

4.2 Human Rights Analysis of Trafficking

4.2.1 Causes of Trafficking

As highlighted elsewhere in this book, a common cause of trafficking is poverty.[1] Due to the poor economic conditions in their States of origin, many people migrate to developed States in order to seek better opportunities.[2] The fact that poverty has a negative impact on the enjoyment of human rights is explicit in the freedom from want in the Preambles of the *Universal Declaration of Human Rights* 1948 (UDHR), the ICCPR, the ICESCR, [3] and also recognised by UN human rights mechanisms such as the Commission on Human Rights,[4] the Committee on Economic, Social and Cultural Rights[5] and the Independent Expert on Human Rights and Extreme Poverty.[6] To be more specific, poverty affects economic, social and cultural rights, such as rights to work, food, hous-

---

1 For the link between poverty and trafficking and smuggling of human beings, see *Report of the Independent Expert on Human Rights and Extreme Poverty*, E/CN.4/2003/52, paras. 30-35.

2 *Report of the Special Rapporteur on Sales of Children, Child Prostitution and Child Pornography: Mission to Morocco*, E/CN.4/2001/78/Add.1, para. 21; and *Review of Reports, Studies and Other Documentation for the Preparatory Committee and the World Conference: Contribution Submitted by the Special Rapporteur on Violence against Women*, A/CONF.189/PC.3/5 (2001), para. 77.

3 *Statement Adopted by the Committee on Economic, Social and Cultural Rights*, E/C.12/2001/10 (Statement of CESCR).

4 Commission on Human Rights Resolution 2005/16 (Human Rights and Extreme Poverty), E/CN.4/RES/2005/16.

5 Statement of CESCR, *supra*. The Committee defines poverty as "a human condition characterized by sustained or chronic deprivation of the resources, capabilities, choices, security and power necessary for the enjoyment of an adequate standard of living and other civil, cultural, economic, political and social rights."

6 See recent reports of the Independent Expert on Human Rights and Extreme Poverty, E/CN.4/2004/43 and E/CN.4/2005/49.

ing, adequate standard of health, and education.[7] In addition, civil and political rights such as life, liberty and security are also affected by poverty.[8]

Another interlinked cause of trafficking is discrimination on account of race, gender and other grounds.[9] Racism sometimes leads to a lack of employment opportunities for people belonging to certain racial or ethnic groups, and forces them to seek employment elsewhere.[10] In a similar vein, gender discrimination is a reason why women turn to traffickers. They are marginalised economically, socially and politically in many parts of the world and therefore are unable to enjoy many basic rights enjoyed by men. This has led to the feminisation of poverty, and forced women to leave so that they can find economic opportunities abroad.[11] Violence against women, as well as traditional family structures, which subordinate women sexually or otherwise, also promote their movement.[12]

Moreover, humanitarian crises also trigger movements of people. Some people may be persecuted by States of origin on account of race, religion, nationality, membership to a particular social group or political opinion.[13] Others escape their States of origin due to international or internal armed conflicts.[14] A

7 Articles 6, 11 and 12 of ICESCR, *supra.*

8 Articles 6 and 9 of ICCPR, *supra*; and General Comment No. 6 (The Right to Life)(1982), in which the Human Rights Committee touches upon the obligation of States to take positive steps to reduces instances of infant mortality and malnutrition (para. 6), *Compilation of General Comments and General Recommendations adopted by the Human Rights Treaty Bodies*, HRI/GEN/1/Rev.5 (herein after Compilation of General Comments). See also Articles 2 and 7 of ECHR, *supra*; Articles 4 and 7 of ACHR, *supra*; and Articles 4 and 6 of African Charter, *supra.*

9 The principle of non-discrimination is enshrined in Article 2(2) of ICESCR, *supra*; Article 2(1) of ICCPR, *ibid*; CEDAW, *supra*; *International Convention on the Elimination of All Forms of Racial Discrimination* 1965 (CERD), 660 UNTS 195; and Article 2 of CRC, *supra.*

10 *Report of the Asia-Pacific Regional Seminar of Experts on Migrants and Trafficking in Persons with Particular Reference to Women and Children*, A/CONF.189/PC.2/3 (2001), paras. 9, 12, 18, 71, 83 and 85 (hereinafter Asia Report). See also *Response to the Report "Draft Guidelines: A Human Rights Approach to Poverty Reduction Strategies*," CERD/C/62/Misc.22 (2003).

11 *Special Rapporteur on Women* (2000), *supra.*

12 *Ibid.*, paras. 54 and 57.

13 *Written Statement Submitted by the Organization for Defending Victims of Violence (ODVV)*, E/CN.4/2002/NGO/97. The definition of a refugee is given in the Refugee Convention, *supra.*

14 *Report of the Special Rapporteur on the Situation of Human Rights in Myanmar*, E/CN.4/2004/33; *Report of the Special Rapporteur on the Human Rights in Afghanistan*, E/CN.4/2003/39; *Report of the Special Rapporteur on the Situation of Human Rights in Iraq*, E/CN.4/2004/36; and *Written Statement Submitted by the Colombian Commission of Jurists*, E/CN.4/2003//NGO/112.

wide variety of civil and political rights such as rights to life, liberty and security, and freedom from torture, can be violated in times of humanitarian crises.[15] It is also apparent that a set of economic, social and cultural rights, such as rights to work, health, food and housing,[16] can be deeply affected. Many people have no choice but to escape their States of origin under these circumstances, and one way to do so is to seek assistance from traffickers.[17]

4.2.2 Process of Trafficking

Several human rights issues arise during the process of trafficking. For instance, families and relatives in States of origin become indebted to traffickers because they share the cost of transportation.[18] A lack of official means to obtain loans is evident in many States of origin, and this is said to create informal networks of lenders who charge a high rate of interest.[19] Consequently, many lose their house, land and other property[20] and they become susceptible to slavery and bonded labour.

The process of recruitment and transportation also raises a set of human rights concerns. In some cases, people are forcibly recruited. Traffickers use violence and intimidation and other tactics to traffic people internally or internationally.[21] Abduction or kidnapping of children for adoption, organ extraction, or participation in armed conflicts are practices evidenced in some parts of the world.[22] Instances of torture, inhuman or degrading treatment[23] are also common during the process of trafficking. In addition, many of those trafficked are forced to travel in overcrowded trucks and shipping containers for long periods of time.[24] Because of these conditions, many people suffer from exhaustion,

15 Articles 6, 7, and 9 of ICCPR, *supra*; Articles 2, 3, and 5 of ECHR, *supra*; Articles 4, 5, and 7 of ACHR; and Articles 4-6 of African Charter, *supra*.

16 Articles 6, 11 and 12 of ICESCR, *supra*; and General Comment No.7 (The Right to Adequate Housing) (1997) of the Committee on Economic, Social and Cultural Rights, para. 6, Compilation of General Comments, *supra*.

17 Morrison and Crosland, *supra*.

18 *Special Rapporteur on Migrants* (2002), *supra*, para. 34.

19 *Ibid.*

20 *Ibid.*

21 *Report of Special Rapporteur on Violence against Women: Mission to Bangladesh, Nepal and India*, E/CN.4/2001/73/Add.2, para. 14.

22 Special Rapporteur on Sales of Children (1999), *supra*, paras, 57, 75, 76, 85, and 86; Shannon, *supra*, p. 121; and Human Rights Watch, *Stolen Children: Abduction and Recruitment in Northern Uganda* (2003).

23 Article 7 of ICCPR, *supra*; Article 3 of ECHR, *supra*; Article 5 of ACHR, *supra*; and Article 5 of African Charter, *supra*; and *Convention against Torture and Other Cruel, Inhuman or Degrading Treatment or Punishment* 1984, G.A. Res. 39/46.

24 Human Rights Advocate (2002), *supra,* paras. 12 and 13.

dehydration and malnutrition[25] and their health deteriorates as a result. Moreover, it has been reported that many traffickers, as well as smugglers, abandon people during the course of their journey and sometimes use physical and sexual violence as a means to demand more money for their services.[26] Finally, the right to life[27] is also relevant as there are cases where people lose their lives. In 2001, for instance, an overcrowded ship with migrants on board sank off the coast of Indonesia and 356 people died as a result.[28] Such cases of fatalities have also been reported in Ireland, Libya, Mexico, Niger, the United Kingdom and the United States of America.[29]

4.2.3 Consequences of Trafficking

In States of destination, many of those are exploited by transnational corporations, farmers, restaurant owners and others, and forced to work long hours with minimal pay in order to clear their debts imposed by traffickers,[30] raising the issues of slavery and forced labour.[31] A related issue is the conditions in which they are held. Those working in the agricultural sector, for instance, are exposed to dangerous chemicals, and their health is affected as a result.[32] The right to just and favourable conditions of work, therefore, is commonly denied.[33] Because of their illegal status, such people are unable or unwilling to seek medical assistance due to a fear of enforcement actions.[34] Moreover, instances of physical, mental or sexual abuse, especially against migrant women, have been

25 *Report of the Special Rapporteur on Migrants: Mission to the Border between Mexico and the United States of America*, E/CN/4/2003/85/Add.3, para. 4 (Special Rapporteur on Migrants in Mexico and US).

26 *Ibid.*, para. 19; and *Written Statement Submitted by Human Rights Advocates International*, E/CN.4/1999/NGO/96, para. 5. For a link between sexual violence, including rape and torture, inhuman or degrading treatment, see *Prosecutor v. Furundzia*, Case IT-95-17/1, Trial Judgment, 10 December 1998, para. 170.

27 Article 6 of ICCPR; Article 2 of ECHR; Article 4 of ACHR; and Article 4 of African Charter.

28 Special Rapporteur on Migrants (2002), *supra*, para. 32.

29 Human Rights Advocate (2002), *supra*, paras. 4-14.

30 Special Rapporteur on Women (2000), *supra*, para. 66; and *Report of the Special Rapporteur on Migrants Workers*, E/CN.4/2001/83, para. 54.

31 Article 8 of ICCPR, *supra*; Article 4 of ECHR, *supra*; Article 6 of ACHR, *supra*; and Article 5 of African Charter, *supra*.

32 Article 12 of ICESCR, *supra*; and Human Rights Advocates (2002), *supra*, para. 3.

33 Article 7 of ICESCR, *supra*; and General Comment No. 14 (The Right to the Highest Attainable Standard of Health)(2000), para. 15, Compilation of General Comments, *supra*. See also Articles 2 and 3 of the *European Social Charter (Revised)*, ETS No. 163 (1996).

34 Special Rapporteur on Migrants (2002), *supra*, paras. 36 and 50.

reported.[35] Furthermore, freedom of movement[36] is often restricted. Traffickers may take identity documents away from those trafficked as a way to gain control over them,[37] lock them in sweatshops, factories and brothels, and threaten them by hinting at the possibility of enforcement action and retaliation against their family members.[38]

Moreover, racism and xenophobia are serious human rights issues in States of destination.[39] It has been noted, for instance, that racism and xenophobia have made it easier for people to justify the exploitation of those trafficked in sex and other industries.[40] The term "illegal immigrants," which applies to many of those trafficked, has negative connotations in many societies and this sometimes leads to instances of violence and racism.[41] These illegal immigrants are also blamed for deficiencies in the health, education and social security systems in States of destination in many cases.[42] Once again, their illegal status makes it difficult for them to report instances of racism and violence, and therefore perpetrators are rarely punished.[43]

Finally, law enforcement practices in States of destination raise a set of human rights concerns.[44] For instance, cases of law enforcement authorities shooting directly at people at borders, resulting in injuries or deaths, have been reported.[45] In making arrests, some enforcement officers ask for money or sexual favours in return for release, and refusal to do so may result in prolonged detention.[46] A concern has also been raised in relation to the conditions of detention.

---

35 *Report of the Secretary-General on Violence against Women Migrant Workers,* E/CN.4/2000/76; and *Report of the Special Rapporteur on Migrants: Mission to Philippines*, E/CN.4/2003/85/Add.4, paras. 15 and 16.

36 Article 12 of ICCPR, *supra.*

37 *Report of the Special Rapporteur on Migrants*, E/CN.4/2000/82, para. 63; and King, T, 'The Modern Slave Trade,' 8 *U.C. Davis Journal of International Law and Policy* 293 (2002), p.309.

38 Special Rapporteur on Women (2000), *supra,* para. 39; and Ryf, *supra*, p. 51.

39 For a general discussion, see *Reports, Studies and Other Documentation for the Preparatory Committee and the World Conference: Contribution by the Special Rapporteur on the Human Rights of Migrants,* A/CONF.189/PC.1/19 (2001).

40 Anderson, B, and J. O'Connell Davidson, *Is Trafficking in Human Beings Demand Driven? A Multi-Country Pilot Study* (Geneva: IOM)(2003), p. 42.

41 Special Rapporteur on Migrant Workers (2001), *supra*, para. 67.

42 *Ibid.*, para. 69.

43 *Ibid.*, para. 68.

44 For discrimination against aliens in the criminal justice system, see *Discrimination in the Criminal Justice System: Final Working Paper*, E/CN.4/Sub.2/2002/5.

45 Special Rapporteur on Migrants in Mexico and US, *supra*, paras. 27- 29.

46 *Report of the Special Rapporteur on Migrants*, E/CN.4/2003/85, para. 22; and *Report of the Special Rapporteur on the Rights of Non-Citizens*, E/CN.4/Sub.2/2002/25/

Detention centres in which trafficked people are held are often unhygienic,[47] and instances of torture[48] have been reported. Furthermore, other rights, such as the right to be informed of charges being made against them, access to the judicial processes, interpreters, legal advice, and consular assistance are also restricted or non-existent.[49] From all of this, it is apparent that trafficking of human beings entails a wide variety of human rights concerns.

4.3 Obligations and Accountability of Non-State Actors

4.3.1 Development under International Human Rights Law

Having identified the key human rights norms and principles in relation to trafficking, it is now necessary to determine how and to what extent international human rights law may be used to address the practice. Although there are cases where States may be complicit in trafficking through corruption,[50] for example, the practice is mainly carried out by non-State actors such as organised criminal groups. This prompts the need for an examination of the extent to which international human rights law imposes obligations upon these non-State actors who commit human rights abuses. The general conclusion reached is that although there is a growing trend for recognising legal obligations of non-State actors and for holding them accountable under international human rights law, the current status remains that they do not bear legal obligations, and therefore cannot be held directly accountable. This is clear from the development of international human rights law.

Perhaps the best place to start this analysis is to look at the position of non-State actors under international law. The traditional view is that States are the bearers of obligations under international law. This is derived from the idea that they are the subject of international law and accordingly take on direct rights and responsibilities.[51] Consequently, States can be held legally account-

Add.3, para. 4.

47 Special Rapporteur on Migrants, *ibid.*, paras. 58 and 61; and *Written Statement Submitted by the Organization for Defending Victims of Violence (ODVV)*, E/CN.4/2002/NGO/104, para. 4.

48 Special Rapporteur on Migrant Workers (2001), *supra*, para. 82. For a general examination of torture in detention, see *Report of the Special Rapporteur on Torture*, E/CN.4/2001/66.

49 Special Rapporteur on Migrants (2003), *supra*, paras. 22, 27, 29, and 30.

50 See Chapter 2 on national case studies. See also *Report of the Special Rapporteur on Migrants: Mission to Mexico*, E/CN.4/2003/85/Add.2, para. 19; and Corene, R, 'The Victimization of Women through Human Trafficking - An Aftermath of War?' 10 *European Journal of Crime, Criminal Law and Criminal Justice* 152 (2002), p. 154.

51 McCorquodale, R, 'The Individual and the International Legal System,' in Evans (ed.), *International Law* (Oxford: Oxford University Press)(2003), p. 301.

able in cases when they breach obligations established by international instruments. In the area of international human rights law, it is generally recognised that individuals are the holders of rights, while States are the holders of duties to protect and promote those rights.[52] This suggests that non-State actors do not have obligations and therefore cannot be held accountable under international human rights law.

Nevertheless, it has increasingly been maintained that the traditional view is outdated and that accountability for non-State actors should be re-examined, in line with the global changes which have facilitated the growth of powers on the part of non-State actors and the consequent limits imposed upon the powers of States.[53] It has been argued in particular that non-State actors have obligations because they are also holders of duties to promote and protect human rights.[54] The idea that individuals are duty holders is also reflected in some of the existing human rights instruments. Such non-binding instruments as the

52 Jochnick, C, 'Confronting the Impunity of Non-State Actors: New Fields for the Promotion of Human Rights," 21 *Human Rights Quarterly* 56 (1999), p. 59.

53 *Ibid.* p. 63. See also Mertus, J, 'From Legal Transplants to Transformative Justice: Human Rights and the Promise of Transnational Civil Society,' 14 *American University International Law Review* 1335 (1999).

54 Clapham, A, *Human Rights in the Private Sphere* (Oxford: Clarendon Press)(1993) pp. 93 and 95; and Paust, J. J, 'The Other Side of Rights: Private Duties under Human Rights Law,' 5 *Harvard Human Right Journal* 51 (1992). See further Newman F.C, and K. Vasak, 'Civil and Political Rights," in Vasak (ed.), *The International Dimensions of Human Rights* (Westport: Greenwood Pres)(1982), pp. 125 and 152; Meron, T, *Human Rights in Internal Strife: Their International Protection* (Cambridge: Grotius)(1987), p. 34; Buergenthal, T, *International Human Rights in a Nutshell* (St. Paul: West Publishing Company)(1988), pp. 52, 128, and 177-179; Addo, M.K (ed.), *Human Rights Standards and the Responsibility of Transnational Corporations* (The Hague: Kluwer Law International)(1999); Anderson J.C, 'Respecting Human Rights: Multinational Corporations Strike Out," 2 *University of Pennsylvania Journal of Labour and Employment Law* 463 (2000), p. 467; McCorquodale, R, 'Human Rights and Global Business," in Bottmley and Kinley (eds.), *Commercial Law and Human Rights* (Aldershot: Ashgate)(2002); Ramasastry, A, 'Corporate Complicity: From Nuremberg to Rangoon, An Examination of Forced Labour Cases and Their Impact on the Liability of Multinational Corporations,' 20 *Berkeley Journal of International Law* 91 (2002), p. 96; Megret, F, and F. Hoffmann, 'The UN as a Human Rights Violator? Some Reflections on the United Nations Changing Human Rights Responsibilities,' 25(2) *Human Rights Quarterly* 281 (2003); *Human Rights Principles and Responsibilities for Transnational Corporations and Other Business Enterprise*, E/CN.4/Sub.2/2002/WG.2/WP.1; *Report of the Sessional Working Group on the Working Methods and Activities of Transnational Corporations on Its Fourth Session*, E/CN.4/Sub.2/2002/13; and *Reports of the Special Rapporteur on Human Rights and Human Responsibilities,* E/CN.4/2002/107 and E.CN.4/2003/105.

UDHR,[55] the *American Declaration on Rights and Duties of Man* 1948,[56] the *Declaration on the Right and Responsibility of Individuals, Groups and Organs of Society to Promote and Protect Universally Recognized Human Rights and Fundamental Freedoms* 1999[57] as well as legally binding instruments such as the ICCPR and the ICESCR,[58] the ECHR,[59] the ACHR,[60] and the African Charter[61] explicitly provide that individuals have duties to other individuals and/or to their community.

Some of the human rights mechanisms also talk about the duties of non-State actors in the promotion and protection of human rights. In relation to the right to health, for instance, the Committee on Economic, Social and Cultural Rights stated that international financial institutions "should pay greater attention to the protection of the right to health in their lending policies, credit agreements and structural adjustment programmes."[62] In relation to poverty, the United Nations High Commissioner for Human Rights stressed the responsibilities imposed upon non-State actors.[63] In addition, in elaborating the rights of the child under the ICCPR, the Human Rights Committee expressed its view that the responsibility to protect children rests not only upon States, but also upon families and society.[64] Moreover, the Special Rapporteur on Sales of Children, Child Prostitution and Child Pornography goes further to argue that "international human rights law has long imposed direct obligations on the private sector."[65] All of this marks a significant development in international human rights law, as it reflects the growing recognition that human rights abuses committed by non-State actors must be also addressed.

---

55 Article 29, *supra*.

56 Chapter II (Articles 29-38), OEA/Ser.L/V/II.71.

57 A/RES/53/44.

58 Preambles, *supra*.

59 Article 17, *supra*.

60 Articles 29 and especially 32, *supra*.

61 Articles 27-29, *supra*.

62 General Comments No. 14, *supra*; and No. 12(The Right to Adequate Food)(1999), in which the Committee (para. 20) stated that "all members of society - individuals, families, local communities, non-governmental organizations, civil society organizations, as well as the private business sector - have responsibilities in the realization of the right to adequate food," Compilation of General Comments, *supra*.

63 *Seminar on Human Rights and Extreme Poverty*, HR/GVA/POVERTY/SEM/2001/4 (February 2001).

64 General Comment No. 17 (Rights of the Child) (1989), para. 6, Compilation of General Comments, *supra*.

65 *Report of the Special Rapporteur on Sales of Children Child Prostitution and Child Pornography*, E/CN.4/2001/78, para. 52.

These views, however, must be treated with caution. In order to hold that international human rights law imposes direct obligations upon non-State actors and that they can be held directly accountable, it must be shown that international human rights law is directly enforceable against them. In other words, a horizontal application of international human rights law at the international level must be established. In examining the current status of international human rights law, it becomes apparent that a horizontal application is not possible. As a result, non-State actors do not bear legal obligations and therefore cannot be held directly accountable.[66] The Human Rights Committee makes this clear by stating that "obligations are directed to States and do not, as such, have direct horizontal effect as a matter of international law."[67] This position is also supported by jurisprudence in which claims against non-State actors have been deemed inadmissible.[68] In view of all of this, it is concluded that the obligations imposed upon non-State actors are moral, rather than legal, in character at the international level.

What is the value of moral obligations then? One could certainly argue that moral obligations have no value at all because it is doubtful that non-State actors such as organised criminal groups care much about the human rights of victims in conducting their business. Nevertheless, the moral obligations retain certain value for other non-State actors involved in the process. Take private companies, for example. As stressed throughout this book, they may become part of trafficking by employing child or cheap labour. While international human rights law does not impose obligations upon them, many companies have voluntarily

---

66 Rodley, N, 'Can Armed Opposition Groups Violate Human Rights,' in Mahoney and Mahoney (eds.), *Human Rights in the Twenty-First Century: A Global Challenge* (Dordrecht: Martinus Nijhoff Publishers)(1993), pp. 297-318; and Schabas, W. A, 'Punishment of Non-State Actors in Non-International Armed Conflict,' 26 *Fordham International Law Journal* 907 (2003), p. 908.

67 General Comment No. 31(Nature of the General Legal Obligation Imposed on States Parties to the Covenant)(2005), CCPR/C/21/Rev.1/Add.13, para. 8.

68 *F.G.G. v The Netherlands*, Communication No. 209/1986, CCPR/C29/D/209/1986, in which the Human Rights Committee held that communications directed against non-States actors to be inadmissible. In *G.R.B. v. Sweden*, Communication No. 83/1997, CAT/C/20/D/83/1997, the Committee against Torture stated that allegations of a risk of torture at the hands of Sendeero Luminoso, a non-State entity controlling significant portions of Peru, fell outside the scope of Article 3 of the Convention (para. 6.5). It is worth noting, however, that the Committee, in *Elmi v. Australia* (Communication No. 120/1998, CAT/C/22/D/120/1998), held that in the exceptional circumstance of State authority that was wholly lacking, acts by groups exercising quasi-governmental authority could fall within the definition of Article 1, and thus call for the application of Article 3 (para. 6.5). For an examination of this case, see, McCorquodale R, and R. La Forgia, 'Taking off the Blindfolds: Torture by Non-State Actors,' 1(2) *Human Rights Law Review* 189 (2002).

agreed to be bound by code of conduct and other non-legally binding rules.[69] Such a trend has undoubtedly been influenced by the human rights movement and law at the national, regional and international levels. It is submitted, therefore, that moral obligations can play an important part in encouraging non-State actors to promote and protect the human rights of others.

4.3.2 Indirect Enforcement of Human Rights Norms and Principles: Criminal and Civil Proceedings

All of this does not mean, however, that international human rights law is irrelevant in efforts to combat trafficking of human beings. The human rights norms and principles may be applied indirectly through national courts and tribunals, and the horizontal application of human rights law is possible at this level.[70] The benefit of horizontal application is that it empowers victims by providing them with a means to hold individual perpetrators legally accountable for human rights abuses.[71] This can be achieved in two ways. The first is to bring criminal proceedings against perpetrators.[72] In the context of trafficking, many States have already enacted specific laws and regulations to prohibit the act.[73] The victims can rely on these laws and regulations to see to it that traffickers are prosecuted and punished.

---

69 See Addo, *supra* and Anderson (2000), *supra.*

70 On this topic, see Klein, D. F, 'A Theory for the Application of Customary International Law of Human Rights by Domestic Courts,' 13 *Yale Journal of International Law* 332 (1988); Koh, H.H, 'Is International Law Really State Law?' 111 *Harvard Law Review* 1824 (1998); Dickson, B, 'The Horizontal Application of Human Rights Law,' in Hegarty and Leonard (eds.), *A Human Rights: An Agenda for the 21st Century* (London: Cavendish)(1999); Paust, J. J, 'Customary International Law and Human Rights Treaties Are Laws of the United States,' 20 *Michigan Journal of International Law* 301 (1999); Cooper, J, 'Horizontality: The Application of Human Rights Standards in Private Disputes,' in English and Havers (eds.), *An Introduction to Human Rights and the Common Law* (Oxford: Hart)(2000); Bixler, A, 'Private Enforcement of International Human Rights Law: Could a Small Church Group Successfully Combat Slavery in the Sudan?' 3 *Chicago Journal of International Law* 511 (2002); and Moon, G, 'Complying with Its International Human Rights Obligations: The United Kingdom and Article 26 of the International Covenant on Civil and Political Right,' 3 *European Human Rights Law Review* 283 (2003).

71 Slye, R.C, 'International Law, Human Rights Beneficiaries, and South Africa: Some Thoughts on the Utility of International Human Rights Law,' 2 *Chicago Journal of International Law* 59 (2001), pp. 73 and 74.

72 Pilkerton, C.M, 'Traffic Jam: Recommendations for Civil and Criminal Penalties to Curb the Recent Trafficking of Women from Post-Cold War Russia,' 6 *Michigan Journal of Gender and Law* 221 (1999).

73 Trafficking Report 2005, *supra.*

The second is to initiate civil actions against traffickers.[74] Such civil proceedings are more likely to be successful than criminal ones because "the burden of proof is by a preponderance of the evidence rather than beyond a reasonable doubt."[75] Civil actions also have the effect of empowering victims more, because they can be initiated by victims, giving them a degree of control, whereas the decision to bring criminal prosecutions lies mainly with States.[76] A classic example of a civil proceeding is *Filartiga v. Pena-Irala*[77] from the United States, in which the Court of Appeals applied the *Alien Tort Claims Act*[78] to adjudicate on the case of deliberate torture inflicted upon a plaintiff.[79] In the case of the United States, the *Torture Victim Protection Act*,[80] and more appropriately, the *Victims of Trafficking and Violence Protection Act*[81] can be invoked to initiate

74 See in general, Murphy, J.F, 'Civil Liability for the Commission of International Crime as an Alternative to Criminal Prosecution,' 12 *Harvard Human Rights Journal* 1 (1999); Van Schaack, B, 'In Defense of Civil Redress: The Domestic Enforcement of Human Rights Norms in the Context of the Proposed Hague Judgements Convention,' 42 *Harvard International Law Journal* 141 (2001); and Bradley, C. A, 'The Costs of International Human Rights Litigation,' 2 *Chicago Journal of International Law* 457 (2001). For a discussion on an obligation for non-State actors to provide compensation under international human rights law, see, *Right to a Remedy and Reparation for Victims of Violations of International Human Rights and Humanitarian Law: Note by the High Commissioner for Human Rights*, E/CN.4/2003/63, para. 18.

75 Hyland, *supra*, p. 51.

76 *Ibid.*

77 630 F.2d 876 (1980).

78 28 U.S.C. § 1350. For a discussion of the Alien Tort Statute, see, Lu, J, 'Jurisdiction over Non-State Activities under the Alien Tort Claims Act,' 35 *Columbia Journal of Transnational Law* 531 (1997).

79 See also *Tel-Oren v. Libyan Arab Republic*, 726 F. 2d 744 (1984); *Forti v. Suareaz-Mason*, 672 F. Supp. 1531 (1987); *Doe v. Karadzic*, 866 F. Supp. 734 (1994) ; *Kadic v. Karadzic*, 70 F.3d 232 (1995); *Abebe-Jira v. Negewo*, 72 F. 3d 844 (1996); and *Doe v. Islamic Salvation Front*, 993 F. Supp. 3 (1998). For a discussion of civil actions against torture, see Scott, C (ed.), *Torture as Tort: Comparative Perspectives on the Development of Transnational Human Rights Litigation* (Oxford: Hart Publishing)(2001).

80 Section 2, 106 Stat. 73 (1992), 28 USCA § 1350 (1991). On application of the Statute to private corporations, see Ramasastry, *supra*, pp. 121-130; and Ramsey, M. D, 'Multinational Corporate Liability under the Alien Tort Claims Act: Some Structural Concern,' 24 *Hastings International and Comparative Law Review* 361 (2001).

81 Section 111, *supra*. For discussions on this Act, see Ryf, *supra*; Tiefenbrun, *supra*; Hartsough, *supra*; Candes, M. R, 'The Victims of Trafficking and Violence Protection Act of 2000: Will It Become the Thirteenth Amendment of the Twenty-First Century?' 32 *University of Miami Inter-American Law Review* 571 (2001); Feve, S, and C. Finzel, 'Trafficking of People,' 38 *Harvard Journal on Legislation* 279 (2001);

civil actions. Such laws which allow actions in tort also exist in States such as Belgium,[82] the Netherlands,[83] and the United Kingdom.[84] To summarise, although international human rights law cannot be enforced directly against non-State actors, indirect enforcement is an option.

4.3.3 Individual Criminal Responsibility: Trafficking as a Crime against Humanity

4.3.3.1 Definition of Crime Against Humanity

At the international level, the principle of individual responsibility under international criminal law is applicable to trafficking of human beings as a way to enforce human rights norms and principles indirectly, similar to criminal proceedings at the national level. Violations of international criminal law and human rights law are inter-linked,[85] and the principle of individual criminal responsibility for committing crimes under international law has long been established.[86]

---

and Nelson, K.E, 'Sex Trafficking and Forced Prostitution: Comprehensive New Legal Approaches,' 24 *Houston Journal of International Law* 551 (2002).

82 Pearson, *supra*, pp. 100 and 101.

83 *Victim Act Tewrwee* 1995, *ibid.*, p. 81.

84 Sections 130 and 143 of the *Powers of Criminal Court Act (Sentencing)* 2000 (c. 6); and *Proceeds of Crime Act* 1995 (c.11).

85 Cassese, A, *International Criminal Law* (Oxford: Oxford University Press)(2003), p. 64. See also Meron, T, *Human Rights and Humanitarian Norms as Customary International Law* (Oxford: Clarendon Press)(1989); Sunga, L.S, *Individual Responsibility in International Law for Serious Human Rights Violations* (Dordrecht: Martinus Nijhoff Publisher)(1992); Bassiouni, M. C, *Crimes Against Humanity in International Criminal Law* (Dordrecht: Martinus Nijhoff Publishers(1992); Meron, T, 'International Criminalization of Internal Atrocities,' 89 *American Journal of International Law* 554 (1995); and Ratner, S. R, and J.A. Abrams, *Accountability for Human Rights Atrocities in International Law: Beyond the Nuremberg Legacy* (2nd ed)(Oxford: Oxford University Press)(2001).

86 See for instance, Articles 227-230 of the *Treaty of Versailles* 1919; Article 6 of the *Charter of International Military Tribunal* 1945; Article 6 of the *Charter of the International Military Tribunal for the Far East* 1946; *Control Council Law No. 10 (Punishment of Persons Guilty of War Crimes, Crimes against Peace and against Humanity)* 1945;Article 4 of the *Convention on the Prevention and Suppression of the Crime of Genocide* 1948; Article 3 of the *International Convention on the Suppression and Punishment of the Crime of Apartheid* 1973; Article 7 of the *Statute of the International Crime Tribunal for the Former Yugoslavia* 1993; and Article 6 of the *Statute of the International Crime Tribunal for Rwanda* 1994. Van den Wyngaert, C (ed.), *International Criminal Law: A Collection of International and European Instruments* (2nd ed) (The Hague: Kluwer Law International)(2000). For commentaries on these instruments, see Finch, G, 'The Nuremberg Trial and International Law,' 41 *American Journal of International Law* 20 (1947); Wright, Q, 'The Law of the Nuremberg Trial,' 41 *American Journal of International Law* 38 (1947); Hosoya,

This was reaffirmed in the *Rome Statute of the International Criminal Court 1998*.[87] Among different categories of crimes established, trafficking of human beings may be designated as a crime against humanity. It is worth noting in this regard that in the case of *Kunarac*, the Trial Chamber of the ICTY held that enslavement, as a crime against humanity, included trafficking of human beings.[88]

All of this warrants a careful analysis as it raises a possibility of trafficking being treated as an international crime. Under the Rome Statute, a crime against humanity is defined as:

> any of the following acts when committed as part of a widespread or systematic attack directed against any civilian population, with knowledge of the attack:
> (a) Murder;
> (b) Extermination;
> (c) Enslavement;
> (d) Deportation or forcible transfer of population;
> (e) Imprisonment or other severe deprivation of physical liberty in violation of fundamental rules of international law ;
> (f) Torture;
> (g) Rape, sexual slavery, enforced prostitution, forced pregnancy, enforced sterilization or any other form of sexual violence of comparable gravity;
> (h) Persecution against any identifiable group or collectivity on political, racial, national, ethnic, cultural, religious, gender as defined in paragraph 3, or other grounds that are universally recognised as impermissible under

---

C. *et al.* (eds.), *The Tokyo War Crime Trial: An International Symposium* (Tokyo: Kodansya)(1986); O'Brien, J. C, 'The International Tribunal for Violations of International Humanitarian Law in the Former Yugoslavia,' 87 *American Journal of International Law* 639 (1993); Meron, T, 'War Crimes in Yugoslavia and the Development of International Law,' 88 *American Journal of International Law* 78 (1994); Akhavan, P, 'The International Criminal Tribunal for Rwanda: The Politics and Pragmatics of Punishment,' 90 *American Journal of International Law* 501 (1996); Bekker, P.H.F, 'Application of the Convention on the Prevention and Punishment of the Crime of Genocide,' 92 *American Journal of International Law* 502 (1999); and Green, L. C, *The Contemporary Law of Armed Conflicts* (2nd ed) (Manchester: Manchester University Press)(2000).

87 Article 25, A/CONF.183/9. For commentaries on the Rome Statute in general, see, Cassese, A, P. Gaeta and J. Jones (eds.), *The Rome Statute of the International Criminal Court: A Commentary* (Oxford: Oxford University Press)(2002); and Lee, R. S, *The International Criminal Court: Elements of Crimes and Rules of Procedure and Evidence* (New York: Transnational Publisher)(2000).

88 *Kunarac* Trial Judgment, *supra,* para. 542.

international law, in connection with any act referred to in this paragraph or any crime within the jurisdiction of the Court;

(i) Enforced disappearance of persons;

(j) The crime of apartheid;

(k) Other inhumane acts of a similar character intentionally causing great suffering, or serious injury to body or to mental or physical health.[89]

Of particular importance is Article 7(2)(c) which states:

> "Enslavement" means the exercise of any or all of the powers attaching to the right of ownership over a person and includes the exercise of such power in the course of trafficking in persons, in particular women and children;[90]

The first point which needs to be addressed is the relationship between trafficking and enslavement. It was noted in Chapter 1 that trafficking and enslavement are not necessarily the same acts. This means that an additional ground or grounds may be necessary in order to establish trafficking as a crime against humanity in cases where the practice does not amount to slavery. In analysing Article 7 of the Rome Statute, it can be stated that trafficking can fall under some other acts. Forcible transfer of population under Article 7(1)(d) is one example. Together with deportation, the act is defined as "forced displacement of the persons concerned by expulsion or other coercive acts from the area in which they are lawfully present, without grounds permitted under international law."[91] According to the Preparatory Commission for the ICC, the term "forcible":

> is not restricted to physical force, but may include threat of force or coercion, such as that caused by fear of violence, duress, detention, psychological oppression or abuse of power against such person or persons or another person, or by taking advantage of a coercive environment.[92]

---

89 Article 7, *supra*. The Rome Statute entered into force on 1 July 2002. While this category of crime was considered as an extension of war crimes when it was defined for the first time under the Nuremberg Charter, it is generally accepted now that crimes against humanity can be committed during peace time as well. See Bassiouni, M.C, 'Crimes against Humanity" in Bassiouni (ed.), *International Criminal Law*(2nd ed.)(New York: Transnational Publishers)(1999), p. 523; Bassiouni, M.C, 'Crimes Against Humanity: The Need for a Specialized Convention," 31 *Columbia Journal of Transnational Law* 457 (1994); and Cassese (2003), *supra*, p. 64.

90 *Ibid.*

91 Article 7(2)(d), *ibid.*

92 *Report of the Preparatory Commission for the International Criminal Court, Finalised Draft Text of the Elements of the Crimes,* UN Doc. PCNICC/2000/INF/3/Add.2 (2000), p. 11.

The Rome Statute does not require proof of crossing an international border, but only that the civilian population was displaced.[93] In addition, unlike the enforced disappearance under Article (7)(1)(i), which must be committed with the authorization, support or acquiescence of, a State or a political organization,[94] there is no such requirement for forcible transfer of people. This means that it can be committed by non-State actors such as traffickers. Applying these interpretations to the definition of trafficking, it may reasonably be sustained that trafficking can be regarded as forcible transfer within the meaning of Article (7)(1)(d). However, those being deported or transferred must be lawfully present in a given State, and therefore trafficking of illegal migrants in foreign States does not constitute forcible transfer under the same Article.

In addition, torture under Article 7(1)(f) of the Rome Statute may be invoked as noted above. Torture and related practices can be committed by non-State actors without any involvement of public officials.[95] Moreover, trafficking may be regarded as "other inhuman acts" under Article 7 (1)(k). The conditions which must be satisfied are that such acts must be similar to other acts stipulated under a crime against humanity, and that they must entail the intentional causing of great suffering or serious injury to body or to mental or physical health. As stressed elsewhere, trafficking is coercive, and as such, may fall under this category. In sum, it is possible to apply other provisions when trafficking cannot be regarded as enslavement.

In addition to these specific acts stipulated in Article 7 of the Rome Statute, there are several other conditions which must be satisfied. A lack of jurisprudence under the ICC necessitates an analysis of the pre-existing jurisprudence established by the national and international tribunals to elaborate upon the meaning of a crime against humanity. In applying their interpretations to Article 7 of the Rome Statute, it becomes possible to hold that trafficking of human beings can be treated as a crime against humanity. To begin with, it stipulates that in order for conduct to constitute a crime against humanity, it must be "widespread or systematic."[96] The term "widespread" has been interpreted to mean the large-scale nature of the attack against civilians and the number of its

93 *Prosecutor v. Stakic*, IT-97-24, Trial Judgement, 31 July 2003, para. 680. However, the Trial Chamber in the past made a distinction between deportation and forcible transfer. Deportation presumed transfer beyond State borders, whereas forcible transfer related to displacements within a State. *Prosecutor v. Krstic*, IT-98-33, Trial Judgement, 2 August 2001, para. 521.

94 Article 7(2)(i) of Rome Statute, *supra*.

95 Cassese, A, 'Crimes against Humanity' in Cassese, Gaeta and Jones (eds.), *supra*, p. 374.

96 Article 7(1), *supra*.

victims[97] and therefore isolated acts committed by perpetrators cannot be considered as such.[98] Further, "systematic" conduct requires "the organised nature of the acts of violence." [99]

Another key phrase is "with the knowledge of the attack."[100] This suggests that criminal intent or *mens rea* is required. On this point, the ICTY held that

> the accused must have had the intent to commit the underlying offence or offences with which he is charged, and that he must have known "that there is an attack on the civilian population and that his acts comprise part of that attack, or at least that he took the risk that his acts were part of the attack.[101]

This does not mean, however, that the accused must know the details of the act itself.[102] Unlike genocide, which requires an intention to destroy a population on grounds of nationality, ethnicity, race or religion,[103] a discriminatory intent is not required under a crime against humanity.[104] It is worth noting further that while all perpetrators must have criminal intent, they may commit the act for a wide variety of reasons. On this point, it has been held that "the motives of the accused for taking part in the attack are irrelevant and a crime against humanity may be committed for purely personal reasons."[105]

In addition, in accordance with Article 7(2)(a) of the Rome Statue, a crime against humanity must be committed in pursuance or in furtherance of a State or organizational policy.[106] The formulation of this Article is wide enough to include acts committed by non-State actors, and such an interpretation has been

---

97 *Prosecutor v Tadic*, IT-94-1-T, Trial Judgement, 7 May 1997, para 648; *Prosecutor v Blaskic*, IT-95-14-T, Trial Judgement, 3 March 2000, para. 206; and *Prosecutor v Akayesu*, ICTR-96-4-T, Trial Judgement, 2 September 1998, para. 580.

98 Commentary on the Draft Code of Crimes against Peace and Security of Mankind, *Report of the International Law Commission on the Work of its Forty-Eighth Session* (1996) GAOR, 51st Sess, Supp No 10, UN Doc A/51/10.

99 *Tadic* Trial Judgement, *supra*, para. 648; *Blaskic* Trial Judgement, *supra*, para. 203; and *Akayesu* Trial Judgement, *supra*, para. 580.

100 Article 7(1) of Rome Statute, *supra*.

101 *Prosecutor v. Kunarac*, IT-96-23, Appeal Judgement, 12 June 2002, para. 102.

102 *Kunarac* Trial Judgement, *supra*, para. 434. See also Cassese (2003), *supra*, p.92.

103 Article 6 of Rome Statute, *supra*; and *Akayesu* Trial Judgment, *supra*, para. 498.

104 Except for persecution which requires a discriminatory intent. *Prosecutor v. Akayesu*, ICTR-96-4-T, Appeal Judgement, 1 June 2001, para. 467. In order for a conduct to constitute a crime against humanity under the ICTY Statute, however, the attack itself must be discriminatory, paras. 464 and 469. See also *Prosecutor v. Tadic*, IT-94-1-T, Appeal Judgment, 15 July 1999, para. 305.

105 *Kunarac* Trial Judgement, *supra*, para. 433.

106 Rome Statute, *supra.*

endorsed at national and international levels.[107] Although a policy to commit a crime against humanity requires that a State or an organisation actively promotes or encourages an attack against a civilian population,[108] it need not be expressly declared or clearly stated.[109] The existence of the widespread and systematic nature of a particular act itself may be enough to show that there was indeed a policy.[110]

In looking at these elements, it may be reasonably argued that trafficking of human beings can be designated as a crime against humanity. Given the number of people trafficked each year and States affected, it can be stated that trafficking is widespread. The act is also systematic as it requires organisation, as shown elsewhere. In addition, the definition of trafficking under the Trafficking Protocol suggests that traffickers must have knowledge of the attack on civilian populations. As noted above, a crime against humanity can be committed purely for personal reasons. This means that trafficking, which is carried out for personal financial or material gain, can also be regarded as such. Moreover, the term "organisational policy" under Article 7(2)(a) of the Rome Statute can be inter-

107 Opinion of the International Law Commission (ILC) on the work of its 43rd session, *1991 ILC Report*, p. 266 in which the ILC stated that individuals "with *de facto* power or organized in criminal gangs" are just as capable as State leaders of implementing a large-scale policy of terror and committing mass acts of violence"; Article 18 of the ILC Draft Code of Crime Against the Peace and Security of Mankind, which stipulates that a crime against humanity is committed "in a systematic manner or on a large scale and instigated or directed by a government or by any organization or group." *Yearbook of the International Law Commission, 1996*, vol. II(2). In the Commentary on this Article, the ILC states that "the instigation or direction of a Government or any organization or group, which may or may not be affiliated with a Government, gives the act its great dimension and makes it a crime against humanity imputable to private persons or agents of a State." Commentary on the Draft Code of Crimes against Peace and Security of Mankind, *supra*; *Tadic* Trial Judgement, *supra*, para. 655; *Akayesu* Trial Judgement, *supra*, para. 580; *Blaskic* Trial Judgment, *supra*, para. 205, in which the Trial Chamber asserted that the international community, in adopting the Rome Statute, confirmed that the crime against humanity could be committed by non-State actors; *Kadic v. Karadzic, supra*; the Opinion of the Advocate General in *Féderation National des Déportées et Internés Résistants et Patriots and Others v. Barbie*, Vol. 78, ILR 128 (1988), p. 147; Ratner, S.R, and J. S. Abrams, *Accountability for Human Rights Atrocities in International Law: Beyond the Nuremberg Legacy* (Oxford: Oxford University Press)(1997), p. 66; Robinson, D, 'The Elements of Crimes Against Humanity' in Lee (ed.), *International Criminal Court, supra,* p. 64; and Fry, J.D, 'Terrorism as a Crime Against Humanity and Genocide: The Backdoor to Universal Jurisdiction,' 7 *UCLA Journal of International Law and Foreign Affairs* 169 (2002), p. 187.

108 Cassese (2003), *supra*, p. 93.

109 *Blaskic* Trial Judgement, *supra*, para. 204.

110 *Kunarac* Appeal Judgment, *supra*, para. 98.

preted to include trafficking carried out by entities such as organised criminal groups, although this can in effect exclude trafficking perpetrated by those other than organised criminal groups. If similar interpretations are accepted by the ICC in the future, then trafficking of human beings can be elevated to the status of international crimes which are considered to be "most serious crimes of concern to the international community as a whole"[111] or *delicta juris gentium*, and traffickers may be treated as *hostes humani generic* (enemies of all mankind).

4.3.3.2 Some Implications for the International Legal System

There are several important implications for the international legal system if trafficking of human beings is accepted as a crime against humanity. First and foremost, cases involving trafficking of human beings can be tried by the ICC. In other words, direct control of the crime of trafficking may become possible at the international level.[112] There are mainly two advantages in doing so. First, States may be able to avoid retaliation or corruption in the forms of violence, intimidation and bribery on the part of traffickers. National governments and courts are more vulnerable to threats and corruption, as it may be easy for traffickers, such as organised criminal groups, to influence them in order to advance their trafficking business. However, being an independent international judicial organ with judges who have no personal interests or opportunities for gain, it is arguable that the ICC can be immune from the influence of traffickers and therefore that it is better suited to try cases of trafficking.

Second, victims of trafficking are able to participate in the proceedings against traffickers. At the investigation stage, the Prosecutor is able to receive information not only from States, but also from inter-governmental and non-governmental organisations as well as other reliable sources.[113] Victims can also make representations in order for the Pre-Trial Chamber of the ICC to determine whether or not to issue an authorization of investigation.[114] During the trial stage, the ICC can allow the interests and views of the victims to be presented, and protection measures for the victims involved, such as proceedings *in camera* can be provided.[115] Finally, the Rome Statute also provides for a trust

111 Article 5 of Rome Statute, *supra*.

112 Boister, N, 'Transnational Criminal Law?,' 14 *European Journal of International Law* 953 (2003), p. 962. He notes that transnational criminal law (which deals with transnational offences such as drug and human trafficking, as opposed to international criminal law which addresses crime of concern for the international community as a whole such as war crimes and crimes against humanity) does not create individual criminal responsibility under international law and therefore that States remain to be the locus of penal power, p. 972.

113 Article 15(2), *supra*.

114 Article15(3), *ibid.*

115 Article 68, *ibid.*

fund for victims, whereby the Court may award compensation.[116] In sum, the Rome Statute has the effect of empowering victims of trafficking by affording them access to international criminal justice.

Nevertheless, the role of the ICC is constrained by the limits imposed upon its exercise of jurisdiction. There are three ways in which the ICC can exercise jurisdiction. First, it can do so when a case is referred to the Prosecutor by States.[117] In this case, the consent of States where offences take place or States of the accused's nationality is required.[118] In addition, the Court would find a case inadmissible if it is being investigated and prosecuted at the national level.[119] Second, the ICC has jurisdiction over cases referred by the Security Council of the United Nations acting under Chapter VII of the United Nations Charter.[120] This is unlikely to happen in the context of trafficking as the act may not be easily treated as a threat to international peace and security to merit the invocation of Chapter VII. Third, the ICC can exercise jurisdiction upon an independent investigation initiated by the Prosecutor.[121] Similar to cases of referral by States, the consent of States is required.[122] It can certainly be argued from these that bringing a case of trafficking before the ICC is not practical, as the principle of national sovereignty and political interests of States may hinder it.

However, the possibility remains for the ICC to be involved. For instance, cases requiring the consent of States would be deemed admissible if it can be shown that they are either unwilling or unable to investigate, prosecute and punish perpetrators of the crime specified in the Rome Statute.[123] In the context of trafficking, such a situation can arise if States do not enact laws prohibiting trafficking, allow impunity of traffickers, or are not able to conduct independent and impartial proceedings due to corruption. In the case of referral by the Security Council, trafficking may reasonably be considered as a threat to international peace and security under certain circumstances which may include, but are not limited to, its link with terrorist activities[124] and instances of internal

116 Article 79, *ibid.*

117 Articles 13(a) and 14, *supra.*

118 Article 12 (2), *ibid.*

119 Article 17, *ibid.*

120 Article 13(b), *ibid.*

121 Article 13 (c), *ibid.*

122 Article 12 (2), *ibid.*

123 Article 17, *ibid.*

124 Security Council Resolution 1373 (2001), *supra*; and Security Council Resolution 1456 (2003)(High-Level Meeting of the Security Council: Combating Terrorism), S/RES/1456.

and international armed conflict.[125] Even when the exercise of jurisdiction by the ICC is hindered, trafficking as a crime against humanity can serve as a basis for the establishment of universal jurisdiction by States. The ICC is not able to exercise universal jurisdiction because the basis of its jurisdiction is territoriality and/or nationality.[126] Universal jurisdiction may be invoked when a crime constitutes a "joint concern of all States" and is "of such a gravity and magnitude" that it "warrants their universal prosecution and repression."[127] Simply put, "universal jurisdiction permits any State to apply its laws to punish an offence even when the State has no links of territory with the offence, or of nationality with the offender."[128] Universal jurisdiction over such offences as piracy, slave trade, genocide, war crimes and crimes against humanity has been established as a matter of customary law.[129] Although the Organised Crime Convention, the parent instrument to the Trafficking Protocol, does not touch upon universal jurisdiction, its exercise in relation to trafficking of human beings is increas-

125 Security Council Resolution 1296 (Protection of Civilians in Armed Conflict)(2000), S/RES/1296, provides, for instance (at para. 5) that "the deliberate targeting of civilian populations or other protected persons and the committing of systematic, flagrant and widespread violations of international humanitarian and human rights law in situations of armed conflict may constitute a threat to international peace and security." In Security Council Resolution 1460 (Children in Armed Conflict)(2003), S/RES/1460, the Council notes (para. 10) with concern the cases of sexual exploitation and abuse of women and children in humanitarian crisis.

126 Danilenko, G.M, 'The Statute of the International Criminal Court and Third States,' 21 *Michigan Journal of International Law* 445 (2000), pp. 455 and 456. An exception is when a case is referred by the Security Council under Chapter VII of the U.N. Charter, whose decision is mandatory in character whether or not a particular State is a party to the Rome Statute.

127 Cassese (2003), *supra*, pp 284 and 285. See also *Attorney General of Israel v. Eichmann*, 36 I.L.R. 277.

128 American Law Institute, *Restatement of the Law (Third): Foreign Relations Law of the United States*, 2 American Law Institute (1987), para. 404.

129 Orentlicher, D. F, 'Settling Accounts: The Duty to Prosecute Human Rights Violations of a Prior Regime,' 100 *Yale Law Journal* 2537 (1991), pp. 2555, 2593, and 2594; Lippman, M, 'Crime Against Humanity,' 17 *Boston College Third World Law Journal* 171 (1997); and Scharf, M. P, 'Application of Treaty-Based Universal Jurisdiction to Nationals of Non-Party States,' 35 *New England Law Review* 363 (2001), pp. 372 and 373. See also *R. v. Bow Street Metropolitan Stipendiary Magistrate ex parte Pinochet Ugarte (No. 1)*, 4 All E.R. 897 (H.L. 1998); and *Demjanjuk v. Petrovsky*, 612 F. Supp.544 (1985), in which the United States District Court held (at 556) that perpetrators of crimes against humanity and war crimes are subject to universal jurisdiction. The Court of Appeal in the same case also delivered the same opinion. 776 F. 2d, at 582.

ingly supported.[130] If it is accepted that trafficking constitutes a crime against humanity, this would not only send a message to traffickers that they would not be able to escape from the reach of the law, but also put more pressure on States to establish criminal jurisdiction, prosecute and punish traffickers.[131]

Further, trafficking as a crime against humanity has an important implication for immunities of those government officials and military personnel who become part of trafficking process. There are two types of immunity. The first type is known as personal immunity or immunity *ratione personae*, which is attached to a particular office and continues to be possessed by an official as long as he/she remains in the office.[132] This type of immunity exempts high ranking or senior officials such as heads of States and governments, and foreign ministers from civil or criminal jurisdiction in other States. It was noted by the ICJ in *Arrest Warrant Case* that these high ranking officials are exempt from arrest and prosecution in foreign courts even when they are suspected of committing international crimes.[133] Such a principle has also been accepted at the national level.[134] The ICJ, however, went further to state that senior officials may be subject to criminal proceedings before international criminal courts where they have jurisdiction.[135] All of this suggests that if high ranking officials are implicated for committing trafficking directly or indirectly, the ICC can step in and try them, provided that all the jurisdictional hurdles noted above are cleared, and that States of the nationals being prosecuted are parties to the Rome Statute.[136]

---

130 ECPAT Europe Law Enforcement Group, *Extraterritorial Legislation as a Tool to Combat Sexual Exploitation of Children* (Amsterdam: ECPAT)(1999); Seabrook, J, *No Hiding Place: Child Sex Tourism and the Role of Extraterritorial Legislation.* (London: Zee Books)(2000); and Trapalis, V, 'Extraterritorial Jurisdiction: A Step Toward Eradicating the Trafficking of Women into Greece for Forced Prostitution.' 32 *Golden Gate University Law Review* 207 (2002), p. 232. She asserts that trafficking of women should be regarded as *jus cogens*, p. 233.

131 It was noted in this connection that the establishment of the ICTY and the ICTR has encouraged the national courts in several European States to exercise jurisdiction to try international crimes. Orentlicher, D, 'Striking a Banalce: Mixed Law Tribunals and Conflicts of Jurisdiction,' in Lattimer and Sands (eds.), *supra*, pp. 225 and 227.

132 *Case Concerning the Arrest Warrant of 11 April 2000 (The Democratic Republic of Congo v Belgium), ICJ Report 2000*, paras. 51-55 (hereinafter Arrest Warrant Case); and Akande, D, 'International Law Immunities and the International Criminal Court," 98 *American Journal of International Law* 407 (2004), pp. 409 and 410.

133 *Ibid*, para. 58.

134 Akande, *supra*, p. 411.

135 Arrest Warrant Case, *supra*, para. 61.

136 Akande explains in this regard that a treaty establishing an international tribunal cannot remove immunities that international law grants to officials of States that are not parties to the treaty, *supra*, pp. 417 and 421.

The next type is functional immunity or immunity *ratione materiae*. This applies to acts performed in official capacity.[137] Immunity of this type can be applied to acts not only of serving State officials, but also of former officials while they were in the office.[138] Unlike the immunity *ratione personae*, State officials are not immune from criminal jurisdiction in foreign courts when they commit international crimes under immunity *ratione materiae*.[139] This type of immunity may be more relevant to trafficking of human beings, because lower ranking officials working in the field, such as the police, are more likely be implicated for the practice as noted elsewhere. Trafficking as a crime against humanity, then, can make a strong case for bringing the representatives of the governments, who attempt to hide behind the veil of immunity, to justice.

In relation to immunities for UN officials and experts on mission, including UN peacekeeping forces, a starting point is Article 105 of the United Nations Charter which provides:

> 1. The Organization shall enjoy in the territory of each of its Members such privileges and immunities as are necessary for the fulfilment of its purposes.
> 2. Representatives of the Members of the United Nations and officials of the Organization shall similarly enjoy such privileges and immunities as are necessary for the independent exercise of their functions in connexion with the Organization.[140]

In accordance with Article 105(3) of the Charter, the General Assembly adopted, in 1946, the *Convention on the Privileges and Immunities of the United Nations*.[141] The relevant provisions in this Convention are Articles V and VI. Article V relates to UN officials, while Article VI touches upon the immunity of 'experts on mission' who include Special Rapporteurs appointed by the Commission on Human Rights,[142] UN Civilian Police (UNCIVPOL) and military observers.[143] Further, there is general understanding that the Convention also applies to those

---

137 *Ibid.*, pp. 412 and 413.

138 *Ibid.*

139 Cassese, A, 'When May Senior State Officials Be Tried for International Crimes? Some Comments on the Congo v. Belgium Case,' 13 *European Journal of International Law* 853 (2002), pp. 865 and 871. See also Akande, *ibid,*. pp. 410 and 413.

140 United Nations Charter, *supra*.

141 1 UNTS 15.

142 *Advisory Opinion of 15 December 1989 on the Applicability of Article VI, Section 22, of the Convention on the Privileges and Immunities of the United Nations (1989), ICJ Report 1989.*

143 *Model Status-of-Force Agreement for Peace Keeping Operations: Report of the Secretary-General*, A/45/594 (1991).

involved in UN peacekeeping operations and transitional authorities.[144] The immunity accorded to these people is functional immunity discussed above,[145] and therefore can be waived if they commit international crime such as trafficking of human beings. In this regard, the Secretary-General of the United Nations has the right and duty to waive the immunity if it "impedes the course of justice."[146] In view of all of this, it seems reasonable to conclude that international human rights law, together with other legal principles, plays an important part in addressing the liability of non-State actors.

There are two more points to be made. First, trafficking as a crime against humanity opens the door for other criminal conducts to be categorised as international crimes in the future. Although States and the international community may still be reluctant to expand the scope of international crime(s), they must be able to recognise the changing nature of different criminalities at the national, regional and international levels in modern times, and should be willing to treat them as international crimes accordingly if they consider that they warrant universal repression and prevention. Second, the position of individuals under international criminal law is worth highlighting. In analysing the jurisprudence in relation to this branch of law, it can be stated that the vast majority of the defendants have been agents of States and/or part of armed forces. Trafficking as a crime against humanity reaffirms that non-State actors are capable of committing atrocities against innocent civilians, and that they cannot escape from the reach of international criminal law and justice.

4.4 Conclusion

This Chapter examined issues relating to accountability of non-State actors under international human rights law. The main conclusion reached was that although non-State actors cannot be held legally accountable under international human rights law, there are ways in which human rights abuses committed by them can be addressed. A remaining point to be examined, then, is the extent to which the States, the primary subjects under international human rights law, can be held accountable for trafficking of human beings committed by these non-State actors. This is the subject of the next and final Chapter of this book.

---

144 *Ibid,* para. 15. See further, Rawski, *supra*, pp. 109 and 110. He notes that absolute immunity may be granted to peacekeeping personnel at times. An example of this is Regulation 2000/47 passed by the UNMIK [United Nations Interim Administration Mission in Kosovo], which grants absolute immunity to personnel of KFOR (Kosovo Force), a NATO-led international force.

145 Sections 12 and 18, of the *Convention on Privileges and Immunities*, *supra.* See also Maginnis, V, 'Limiting Diplomatic Immunity: Lessons Learned from the 1946 Convention on the Privileges and Immunities of the United Nations,' 28 *Brooklyn Journal of International Law* 989 (2003), p. 1011-1013.

146 Sections 20 and 23, *ibid.*

It will be shown that certain obligations are imposed upon States under international human rights law in relation to trafficking of human beings.

Chapter 5

Trafficking of Human Beings as a Human Rights Violation: Obligations and Accountability of States

5.1 Introduction

Having illustrated that non-State actors are not held directly accountable under international human rights law, this Chapter proceeds to examine the extent of obligations imposed upon States. The development of international human rights law reveals that States have certain obligations with regard to trafficking committed by non-State actors, and consequently they can be held legally accountable. While there may be a number of obligations which are pertinent to trafficking, this Chapter explores four obligations applicable to all States regardless of their status as States of origin, transit or destination: obligations to 1) prohibit trafficking and related acts; 2) investigate, prosecute and punish traffickers; 3) protect victims of trafficking; and 4) address the causes and consequences of the practice. In addition, the ability of the Trafficking Protocol to promote a human rights framework will be assessed.

Further, the Chapter continues with an analysis of an interaction among different branches of international law in relation to trafficking. In particular, it examines how international human rights law, international criminal law and an emerging branch known as transnational criminal law, complement or contradict with each other in dealing with trafficking. Finally, the Chapter ends with a note on the importance of global governance in addressing transnational organised crime, including trafficking of human beings. The main conclusion reached is that certain human rights norms and principles derived from international human rights law are applicable to trafficking of human beings, and therefore States can be held directly accountable.

5.2 Obligations and Accountability of States[1]

5.2.1 *Obligation to Prohibit Trafficking of Human Beings and Related Acts*

Prohibition of trafficking of human beings through national legislation for the purpose of suppression and prevention is one obligation imposed upon States under international human rights law. While the exact wording varies, some of the existing human rights instruments explicitly require States to prohibit the practice. They include the 1949 Convention,[2] the CEDAW,[3] the CRC,[4] and its Optional Protocol on Sales of Children.[5] Regionally, the *Charter of Fundamental Rights of the European Union* 2000,[6] the Council of Europe *Convention on Action against Trafficking in Human Beings*,[7] the *Inter-American Convention on International Traffic in Minors* 1994[8] and the SAARC *Convention on Preventing and Combating Trafficking in Women and Children for Prostitution* 2002[9] are also pertinent.

This obligation to prohibit trafficking is strengthened when the right to life is involved. In *Osman v. United Kingdom*, the European Court of Human Rights held that States' primary duty to secure the right to life included "putting in place effective criminal law provisions to deter the commission of offences against the person."[10] It has been noted in this regard that prohibition extends not only to murder, but also other serious offences against the person.[11] This line of reasoning can be applied when trafficked victims are seriously injured or lose their lives during their journey or after they reach their destinations.

Other related acts are also prohibited under international human rights law. As shown elsewhere, those trafficked are coerced into the process by traffickers, and may experience acts amounting to torture, inhuman or degrading treat-

---

1 A shorter version of this section appears in Obokata, T, 'Human Trafficking, Human Rights, and the Nationality, Immigration and Asylum Act 2002,' 4 *European Human Rights Law Review* 410 (2003).

2 Articles 1-4, *supra.*

3 Articles 6 and 12, *supra.*

4 Article 35, *supra.*

5 Articles 1-3, *supra.*

6 Article 5(3), *supra.* This instrument does not have legal force.

7 *supra.*

8 Article 7, *supra.*

9 Article 3, *supra.*

10 (App. 23452/94), Judgment of 28/10/98, para. 115.

11 Mowbray, A, *The Development of Positive Obligations under the European Convention on Human Rights by the European Court of Human Rights* (Oxford: Hart Publishing)(2004), p. 16.

ment. States are placed under a clear obligation to prohibit these acts.[12] It is now settled that the prohibition of torture is part of customary international law[13] and *jus cogens*.[14] The prohibition of torture, inhuman or degrading treatments extends to acts committed by non-State actors. In this regard, the European Court of Human Rights held that:

> The obligation on the High Contracting Parties under Article 1 of the Convention to secure to everyone within their jurisdiction the rights and freedoms defined in the Convention, taken together with Article 3, requires States to take measures designed to ensure that individuals within their jurisdiction are not subjected to torture or inhuman or degrading treatment or punishment, including such ill-treatment administered by private individuals.[15]

Moreover, the prohibition of slavery and forced labour is a clear obligation established under human rights instruments such as the *Slavery Convention* 1926,[16] the

12 Convention against Torture, *supra*. Other instruments include, Article 5 of the UDHR *supra*; Article 7 of ICCPR, *supra*; Article 3 the ECHR, *supra*; Article 5 (2) of ACHR, *supra*; Article 5 of the African Charter, *supra*; *Inter-American Convention to Prevent and Punish Torture* 1985, OASTS No. 67; and *European Convention for the Prevention of Torture and Inhuman, Degrading Treatment or Punishment* 1987, ETS No. 126.

13 See, for example, *Filartiga v. Pena-Irala*, *supra*; *Prosecutor v. Delalic*, IT-96-21-T, Trial Judgement, 11 November 1998, para. 459; and General Comment No. 24 (Issues Relating to Reservations Made upon Ratification or Accession to the Covenant or Optional Protocols)(1994) of the Human Rights Committee, para. 8, Compilation of General Comments, *supra*.

14 *Prosecutor v. Furundzija*, IT-95-17/1, Trial Judgment, 10 December 1998, para. 153; and General Comment No. 24 , *ibid*., para. 10 ("the prohibition of torture has the status of a peremptory norm"). That the international proscription of torture has turned into *jus cogens* has been upheld by U.S. courts in *Siderman de Blake v. Republic of Argentina*, 965 F. 2d 699 (9th Cir. 1992) Cert. Denied; *Republic of Argentina v. De Blake*, 507 U.S. 1017,123L. Ed. 2d 444, 113 S. Ct. 1812 (1993); *Committee of U.S. Citizens Living in Nicaragua v. Reagan*, 859 F. 2d 929, 949 (D.C. Cir. 1988); and *Xuncax et al. v. Gramajo*, 886 F. Supp. 162 (D. Mass. 1995). Article 53 of the *Vienna Convention on the Law of Treaties* 1969, 1155 UNTS 33, provides that *jus cogens* is "a peremptory norm of general international law" which is "accepted and recognized by the international community of States as a whole as a norm from which no derogation is permitted and which can be modified only by a subsequent norm of general international law having the same character."

15 *A. v. United Kingdom* (App. 25599/94), Judgment of 23/9/98, para. 22.

16 *supra*.

Forced Labour Convention 1930,[17] the ICCPR,[18] the ICESCR,[19] and the Migrant Workers' Convention.[20] Similar to torture, the prohibition of slavery is also part of customary international law and constitutes *jus cogens*.[21] Thus, States' obligation to prohibit trafficking and related acts is clearly established under international human rights law.

5.2.2 Obligation to Investigate, Prosecute and Punish Traffickers

The obligation to investigate, prosecute and punish non-State actors, including traffickers, with "due diligence," is established by jurisprudence of international human rights law. One important case which touches upon this obligation is that of *Velasquez Rodriguez v. Honduras*.[22] In this case, it was held by the Inter-American Court of Human Rights that:

> The State is obliged to investigate every situation involving a violation of rights under the Convention. If the State apparatus acts in such a way that the violation goes unpunished and the victim's full enjoyment of such rights is not restored as soon as possible, the State has failed to comply with its duty to ensure the free and full exercise of those rights to persons within its jurisdiction. *The same is true when the State allows private persons or groups to act freely and with impunity to the detriment of the rights recognised in the Convention.*[23]

In a similar vein, the European Court of Human Rights, in elaborating on a duty to investigate in *Ergi v. Turkey*, held that:

> This obligation is not confined to cases where it has been established that killing was caused by an agent of the State. Nor is it decisive whether members of the deceased's family or others have lodged a formal complaint about the killing with the relevant investigatory authority. In the case under consideration, the mere knowledge of the killing on the part of the authorities gave rise *ipso*

---

17 *supra.*

18 Article 8, *supra.*

19 Article 10 (3), *supra.*

20 Article 11, *supra.*

21 For prohibition of slavery as *jus cogens*, see, among other things; American Law Institute, *Restatement*, *supra*, p. 167; Bassiouni, M.C, 'Enslavement as International Crime,' 23 *New York University Journal of International Law and Politics* 445 (1991); General Comment No. 24, *supra*, para. 8; and Rassam, *supra*, p. 303.

22 Ser. C, No. 1 (1988).

23 *Ibid.*, para. 176 (Emphasis added). The test of "due diligence" was expanded in para. 167. See also, Shelton, D, 'Private Violations, Public Wrongs, and the Responsibility of States,' 13 *Fordham International Law Journal* 23 (1989).

> *facto* to an obligation under Article 2 of the Convention to carry out an effective investigation into the circumstances surrounding the death.[24]

This obligation has also been endorsed by other human rights mechanisms including the Human Rights Committee,[25] and the Special Rapporteur on Violence against Women.[26] Some commentators go further to argue that this obligation to investigate constitutes customary international law.[27] The first step which must be taken to fulfil this obligation is to establish criminal jurisdiction, which in itself is an established general principle of international law.[28]

It is important to note here that a criminal justice response to trafficking, which dominates at the national level as noted earlier in this book, is a necessary component of a human rights framework. This is so because prohibition of the practice coupled with severe punishment can deter traffickers from abusing human rights. However, a criminal justice response must be facilitated in accordance with international human rights law. It was demonstrated earlier that some law enforcement practices violate the human rights of victims of trafficking. There are various obligations imposed upon States under such circumstances. States at the very minimum have an obligation to investigate cases of such violations and to punish those responsible.[29] In *Assenouv and Others v Bulgaria*, for instance, it was held by the European Court of Human Rights that States have a

24 *Ergi v. Turkey*, (App. 23818/94), Judgment of 28/7/98, para. 82. See also *Osman v. United Kingdom*, *supra*, paras. 115 and 116; *Z and Others v. United Kingdom* (App. 29392/95), Judgment of 10/5/01, para. 109. On the duty to investigate in the European context, see, Mowbray, A, 'Duties of Investigation under European Convention on Human Rights,' 51 *International and Comparative Law Quarterly* 437 (2002).

25 General Comment No. 7 (Torture, Inhuman or Degrading Treatment and Punishment)(1982), paras. 1 and 2, Compilation of General Comments, *supra*; and *Herrera Rubio v. Colombia*, Communication No. 161/1983, CCPR/C/31/D/161/1983, para. 11.

26 Special Rapporteur on Women (2000) *supra*, paras. 51-53. For the notion of "due diligence" in the context of violence against women perpetrated by non-State actors, see E/CN.4/1996/53, paras. 32-39 and E/CN/4/1999/68, paras. 23-25. See further, General Recommendation No. 19 (Violence against Women)(1992) of the Committee on the Elimination of Discrimination against Women, para. 9, Compilation of General Comments, *supra*; and Cook, R, 'State Responsibility for Violation of Women's Human Rights,' 7 *Harvard Human Rights Journal* 125 (1994).

27 Orentlicher (1991), *supra*; and Roht-Arriaza, N, 'State Responsibility to Investigate and Prosecute Grave Human Rights Violations in International Law,' 78 *California Law Review* 449 (1990).

28 *S.S. Lotus (France v. Turkey)*, 1927 P.C.I.J. (Ser.A) No.10, para. 70.

29 General Comments Nos. 7, *supra*, para. 1, and 20 (Replaces General Comment Concerning Prohibition of Torture and Cruel Treatment or Punishment)(1992) of

positive duty to investigate cases involving a breach of Article 3 (prohibition on torture), in line with a general duty to "secure" rights and freedoms to all persons under their jurisdictions under Article 1 of the European Convention.[30]

Another obligation relates to poor conditions of detention. In addition to the access to health care,[31] States must also improve poor conditions of detention. In *Dougoz v Greece*, the applicant, a Syrian national who was detained in Greece for drug related offences, successfully argued that the poor conditions of detention amounted to degrading treatment under Article 3 of the European Convention.[32] The Human Rights Committee further noted in this regard that treating all persons deprived of their liberty with humanity and with respect for their dignity is a fundamental and universally applicable rule, and the application of this rule cannot be dependent on the material resources available in the State party.[33] This means that States cannot present a lack of resources as an excuse for not being able to improve the conditions of detention.

These and other pertinent obligations extend to those against whom criminal charges are brought.[34] This means that States must also respect and protect the human rights of traffickers simultaneously. The rights which are particularly important in this regard are the rights to liberty and security, and to a fair trial. In relation to the right to liberty and security, States have a duty to inform arrested or detained persons of the reasons for their arrest and/or detention in a timely manner,[35] and any person arrested or detained must be brought "promptly" before a judge or other officer authorized by law to exercise judicial power.[36]

---

the Human Rights Committee, paras. 13 and 14, Compilation of General Comments, *supra*; and *Velasquez Rodriguez* Case, *supra,* para. 176

30 (App. 24760/94), Judgment of 28/10/98, para. 102.

31 *Ilhan v Turkey* (App. 22277/93), Judgment of 27/6/00, para. 87.

32 (App. 40907/98), Judgment of 6/3/01, paras. 46-49.

33 General Comment No. 21 (Replaces General Comment 9 Concerning Humane Treatment of Persons Deprived of Liberty (Art. 10)), Compilation of General Comments, *supra*, para. 4.

34 General Comment No. 7, *supra*. See also General Comments No. 8 (Right to Liberty and Security of Persons)(1982), and 9 (Humane Treatment of Persons Deprived of Liberty)(1982) of the Human Rights Committee, Compilation of General Comments, *ibid.*

35 Article 9(2) of ICCPR; and Article 5(2) of ECHR. The European Court of Human Rights defined the requirements of Article 5(2) in the case *Fox, Campbell and Hartley v United Kingdom* (App. 12244/86), Judgment of 27/3/91.

36 Article 9(3) of ICCPR, *supra*, and General Comment No. 8, *supra,* para. 2. The Human Rights Committee expressed an opinion that the delay must not exceed more than a few days in General Comment No. 8, while the European Court of Human Rights thought that detention lasting a little over 4 days was in breach of

As to the right to a fair trial, there are minimum procedural guarantees which must be afforded to the defendants. For instance, States have duties to inform charged persons, *in a language they understand*, of the detailed nature and cause of the accusations against them,[37] to afford adequate time and facilities for the preparation of defence,[38] and to provide free legal assistance to defendants,[39] even when they are foreign nationals.[40] All of this illustrates the contributions which international human rights law can bring in order to ensure that a criminal justice response meets the human rights standard. Therefore, it is possible for the human rights framework and the criminal justice response to co-exist.

5.2.3 Obligation to Protect Victims of Trafficking

Victims of trafficking are often seen as a threat to internal security because of their connection with criminal activities and organisations, and therefore such measures as detention and deportation are frequently taken, as has been stressed elsewhere in this book. A point which needs to be examined is the extent to which States are obliged to protect such victims. The development of international human rights law reveals that certain obligations exist. The human rights instruments specifically related to trafficking, such as the 1949 Convention,[41] the Optional Protocol to the CRC,[42] the Inter-American Convention on Trafficking in Minors,[43] and the Council of Europe Convention on Trafficking[44] contain provisions on protection of victims. Such an obligation can also be implied from Article 16(2) of the Migrant Workers' Convention which provides:

> Migrant workers and members of their families shall be entitled to effective protection by the State against violence, physical injury, threats and intimida-

---

Article 5(3) of the ECHR. *Brogan and Others v United Kingdom* (App. 11209/84), Judgment of 30/5/89, para. 62.

37 Article 14(3)(a) of ICCPR and Article 6(3) of ECHR (Emphasis added). See also *Brozicek v Italy* (App. 10964/84), Judgment of 19/12/89.

38 Article 14(3)(b) of ICCPR and Article 6(3)(b) of ECHR.

39 Article 14(3)(d) of ICCPR and Article 6(3)(c) of ECHR.

40 General Comment No. 15 (The Position of Aliens under the Covenant)(1986) of the Human Rights Committee. The Human Rights Committee was, however, cautious in stating that the right to fair trial should be guaranteed to those who enter into a State legally (paras. 6 and 7). Compilation of General Comments, *supra*. This suggests that if traffickers themselves are illegal migrants, then the refusal to grant the right may not be regarded as a violation of their human rights. See also, *Pakelli v Germany* (App. 3898/78), Judgment of 25/4/83.

41 Articles 16, 17 and 19, *supra*.

42 Articles 8, 9, and 10, *supra*.

43 Articles 6 and 16, *supra*.

44 Articles 10-17, *supra*.

> tion, whether by public officials or by private individuals, groups or institutions.[45]

A migrant worker is defined as "a person who is to be engaged, is engaged or has been engaged in a remunerated activity in a State of which he or she is not a national."[46] An interesting aspect of this Convention is that it applies to both documented (legal) and undocumented (illegal) migrants.[47] This means that the scope of its application can be extended to include trafficked as well as smuggled migrants.

In relation to other human rights instruments, the obligation to protect can be inferred from a general duty to secure, ensure, or restore rights, and to provide remedies.[48] The Inter-American Court of Human Rights has noted in this regard that "the obligation to respect and ensure the exercise of rights has an *erga omnes* character. The obligation is imposed upon States to benefit persons under their respective jurisdiction, irrespective of migratory status of the protected persons."[49] Article 2(3)(a) of the ICCPR also provides that States are under an obligation to ensure that "any person whose rights and freedoms as herein recognised are violated shall have an effective remedy, notwithstanding that the violation has been committed by persons acting in an official capacity."[50] Even though the wording may be different, a similar obligation is also

---

45 *supra.*

46 Article 2, *ibid.*

47 Article 5, *ibid.* For discussions on the Migrant Workers' Convention, see Bosniak, L.S, 'Human Rights, State Sovereignty and the Protection of Undocumented Migrants under the International Migrant Workers Convention,' 25 *International Migration Review* 737 (1991); Pena, L.R, 'Some Salient Human Rights in the UN Convention on Migrant Workers,' 2(2) *Asian and Pacific Migration Journal* 179 (1993); and Cholewinski, R, *Migrant Workers in International Human Rights Law: Their Protection in Countries of Employment* (Oxford: Clarendon Press)(1997).

48 Moore, J, 'From Nation State to Failed State: International Protection from Human Rights Abuses by Non-State Agents,' 31 *Columbia Human Rights Law Review* 81 (1999), pp. 92, 93 and 96. See also, Shelton, D, *Remedies in International Human Rights Law* (Oxford: Oxford University Press)(1999); and 'Private Violence, Public Wrongs, and the Responsibility of States, 13 *Fordham International Law Journal* 1 (1989/1990) by the same author.

49 *Judicial Condition and Rights of the Undocumented Migrants*, Advisory Opinion OC-18/03, Ser. A, No. 18 (2003), para. 109.

50 *supra.* The Human Rights Committee, in relation to prohibitions against torture, stated that "it is the duty of the State party to afford everyone protection through legislative and other measures as may be necessary against acts prohibited by article 7, whether inflicted by people acting in their official capacity, outside their official capacity or in a private capacity," General Comment No. 20, *supra*, para. 2.

established by such instruments as the CRC[51] and ECHR.[52] The obligation to protect also arises when States fail to take positive steps to prevent non-State actors from committing illegal acts. One of the cases which touched upon this is the *Case Concerning United States Diplomatic and Consular Staff in Tehran (Iran v. United States)*, in which the ICJ held that even when attacks of militants were not imputable to Iran, it was not "free of responsibility in regards to the attacks," as Iran was placed under an obligation to "take appropriate steps to ensure the protection of the United States Embassy and Consulates." [53] In the context of human rights, this duty to prevent violations committed by non-State actors was illustrated by the Inter-American Court in *Velasquez Rodriguez* Case.[54]

What types of protection are States obliged to provide to victims of trafficking? There is no precise answer to this question, as protection and remedial measures can take different forms. However, the term "protection" should not be narrowly construed. One example is the observance of the principle of *non-refoulement* or non-return.[55] This principle applies in particular to refugees.[56] It has been accepted that an obligation of States to respect this principle extends to cases where persecution is attributed to non-State actors when States are unwilling or unable to punish them. In a case involving a Ukrainian woman who was trafficked into the United Kingdom for prostitution, it was held that the inability of the government of the Ukraine to protect her made it more likely for her to be persecuted by traffickers if she was returned to Ukraine.[57] She was consequently granted asylum in the United Kingdom.[58] The principle of *non-refoulement* also

51 Articles 2 and 3 , *supra.*

52 Articles 1 and 13, *supra.*

53 *ICJ Report 1980*, paras. 58, 59, and 61. See also, *Commentaries to the Draft Article on Responsibility of States for Internationally Wrongful Acts, Report of the International Law Commission on the Work of Its Fifty-Third Session, Official Record of the General Assembly*, A/56/10, chp IV.E.2, p. 70.

54 *supra*, para. 172.

55 Article 33 of the Refugee Convention, *supra.*

56 Under Article 1 of the Refugee Convention, a refugee is defined as someone who has well-founded fear of being persecuted on grounds of his/her race, religion, nationality, or membership of a particular social group or political opinion, *ibid.*

57 *Secretary of State for the Home Department v. Lyudmyla Dzhygun* (Immigration Appeals Tribunal), Appeal no. CC-50627-99 (00TH00728), 13 April 2000. The Immigration Appeals Tribunal recognised that the respondent belonged to a particular social group under the definition of a refugee. For a discussion on the definition of a refugee and its application to trafficked people, see Raghu, *supra.*

58 See also recent cases before the Immigration Appeals Tribunals: *Secretary of State for the Home Department v. Josephine Ogbeide* (May 2002); *Secretary of State for the Home Department v. A.B.* (February 2003); *Secretary of State for the Home*

applies to cases where people are likely to face torture, inhuman or degrading treatment perpetrated by non-State actors.[59] Moreover, it has also been held in the past that expulsion of a person to a State where he/she would be subjected to slavery or forced labour might raise issues under the obligation to prohibit torture.[60]

One measure which should be taken to secure the principle of *non-refoulement* is to issue temporary or permanent residence permits so that those trafficked can legally reside in a given State. This measure has already been implemented in such States as Belgium, Italy, the Netherlands,[61] and the United States.[62] In the United Kingdom, although specific laws or regulations do not exist, temporary residence permits are provided on the basis that victims co-operate with law enforcement authorities to investigate, prosecute and punish traffickers as noted in Chapter 2. At the regional level, the Directive on Residence Permits was recently adopted by the EU.[63]

It should be stressed, however, that an approach which provides residence permits on the basis that victims co-operate with law enforcement authorities should be re-considered. Many victims are not willing to come forward to the authorities due to a fear of reprisal by traffickers or of enforcement actions. A desirable approach is to provide a certain period of time to all victims so that they can decide whether or not they wish to co-operate. This is constructive in building a sense of trust between victims and the authorities, and may well facilitate co-operation in the long run. This approach is taken by some States such as Belgium and the Netherlands.[64] At the EU level, the regime of subsidiary protection as noted in Chapter 3 is worth noting in this regard.

The point on the fact of being trafficked and recognition of refugee status is worth expanding. The United Nations High Commissioner for Refugees (UNHCR), a principal UN organisation charged with protection of refugees, has recognised the fact of being trafficked as possibly constituting gender-based persecution and therefore one of the Convention grounds for refugee recogni-

---

Department v. A (February 2003); *Secretary of State for the Home Department v. K* (August 2003); and *Secretary of State for the Home Department v. Tam Thi Dao* (September 2003). Anti-Slavery International (2003), *supra*, pp. 19 and 20.

59 *Bensaid v. United Kingdom* (App. 44599/98), Judgment of 6/2/01, para. 34.

60 Case of *Barar v. Sweden* (App. 42367/98) (unreported). Case Comment, 3 *European Human Rights Law Review* 330 (1999).

61 Pearson, *supra*.

62 Section 107 of the *Victims of Trafficking and Violence Protection Act* of 2000, *supra*.

63 See Chapter 3.

64 Pearson, *supra*.

tion, provided that States are unable or unwilling to protect them [65] If such a position is widely accepted, as has been the case with the United Kingdom, then more victims can be protected in the future. Nevertheless, this does not solve the problem for men and boys who are trafficked. The UNHCR is still in the process of formulating a policy on trafficking.[66] It is hoped that the organisation will take the plight and suffering experienced by other categories of people into consideration.

If victims wish to return, then voluntary repatriation must be facilitated. Instances of forced repatriation by States of destination[67] as well as a refusal to accept victims in States of origin[68] have been reported, and these practices can constitute violations of human rights. Voluntary repatriation is closely linked to one's right to freely return to his/her State of origin[69] and is enshrined in international human rights instruments such as the ICCPR,[70] the ACHR,[71] the CERD,[72] and the Migrant Workers' Convention.[73] These instruments serve as a legal basis to facilitate voluntary return. When States of destination decide to expel people in accordance with domestic law, international human rights law also stipulates that they must provide an opportunity to appeal against the decision to expel,[74] and that collective expulsion is prohibited.[75] Once returned

65 UNHCR, *Guideline on International Protection: Gender-Related Persecution in the Context of Article 1A(2) of the 1951 Convention and/or Its 1967 Protocol Relating to the Status of Refugees*, HCR/GIP/02/01 (7/5/02), para. 18.

66 As of January 2006.

67 *Written Statements Submitted by Federation of Associations for Defense and Promotion of Human Rights*, E/CN.4/2003/NGO/43.

68 *Written Statement Submitted by the Association of Refugees and Displaced Persons of the Republic of Bosnia-Herzegovina*, E/CN.4/1999/NGO/53; *Report of the Special Representative on Internally Displaced Person: East Timor*, E/CN.4/2000/83/Add.3, para. 48; and *Situation of Human Rights in Cambodia: Note by the Secretary General*, A/57/230 (2003), paras. 49-54.

69 *The Return of Refugees' or Displaced Persons' Property: Working Paper*, E/CN.4/Sub.2/2002/17, paras. 22-28.

70 Article 12 (4), *supra,* and General Comment No. 27 (Freedom of Movement)(1999), Compilation of General Comments, *supra*.

71 Article 22(5), *supra*.

72 Article 5(d)(ii), *supra*, and General Recommendation No. 22 (Refugees and Displaced Persons)(1996), Compilation of General Comments, *supra*.

73 Article 8, *supra*.

74 Article 13 of ICCPR, *supra*, and General Comment No. 15, *supra*.

75 Article 22(9) of ACHR, *supra*; Article 22 of the Migrant Workers' Convention, *supra*; Article 12 of African Charter, *supra*; and General Recommendation No. 30 (Discrimination against Non-Citizens) of the Committee on the Elimination of Racial Discrimination, CERD/C/64/Misc.11/rev.3 (2004), para. 26.

voluntarily and safely, States of origin should ensure that victims are re-integrated into society, by providing continuing physical and psychological support, education and training, and protection from retaliation by traffickers.[76]

In addition, effective investigations into cases of trafficking, leading to the prosecution and punishment of traffickers, is to be regarded as a form of redress available to victims.[77] This corresponds to the duty of States to investigate and punish as illustrated earlier. An integral part of this redress is the right of victims to participate in the investigation and judicial processes against traffickers. The participation of victims is beneficial from a criminal justice perspective, in that testimony and evidence provided by them should expedite investigation, prosecution and punishment. However, it is more important from a human rights perspective. Participation by victims allows them to have their voice heard, which has a therapeutic value.[78] It also assists them in handling their anger and trauma in a constructive way, which can lead to the restoration of their sense of control, dignity, and self-worth.[79]

There are several steps which must be taken in order to secure this right of victims to participate. Many of them are afraid to come forward to co-operate with law enforcement agencies due to a fear of reprisals by traffickers, as stated above. An important measure to be taken, then, is to ensure that they can remain in a State at least while criminal investigations or proceedings are under way. States should also secure effective witness protection to protect the identities of victims, coupled with such measures as free access to interpreters and legal advice.

States also have an obligation to protect the health of those trafficked, regardless of their legal status, by securing equal access to health facilities. This obligation was highlighted by the Committee on the Economic, Social and Cultural Rights, which stated that the "obligation to *respect* the right to health" included "refraining from denying or limiting equal access for all persons, including prisoners or detainees, minorities, asylum seekers and illegal immigrants."[80]

---

76 Hyland, *supra*, pp. 59-61. See also *The Right to Restitution, Compensation and Rehabilitation for Victims of Gross Violations of Human Rights and Fundamental Freedoms: Final Report of the Special Rapporteur*, E/CN.4/2000/62.

77 Such an interpretation of remedies has been accepted by the Inter-American Commission on Human Rights and the European Court of Human Rights. Roht-Arriaza (1995), *supra*, p. 34.

78 *Ibid.* p. 21.

79 *Ibid.* p. 19.

80 General Comment No. 14 *supra*, para. 34. See also Article 39 of the CRC which provides: "State Parties shall take all appropriate measures to promote physical and psychological recovery and social reintegration of a child victim of: any form of neglect, exploitation, or abuse; torture or any other form of cruel, inhuman or degrading treatment or punishment; or armed conflicts. Such recovery and reinte-

The European Court of Human Rights in the past also held that an issue may arise under Article 2 of the ECHR where it is shown that authorities put an individual's life at risk through the denial of health care which they have undertaken to make available to the population generally.[81] In this connection, the Court held that a failure of authorities to provide adequate medical treatment for seriously injured detainees could result in a breach of Article 2 of the Convention.[82] Further, the European Committee of Social Rights, which monitors the implementation of the *European Social Charter (Revised)* 1996,[83] recently held that "legislation or practice that denies entitlement to medical assistance to foreign nationals within the territory of a State Party, even if they are there illegally, is contrary to the Charter."[84]

In addition, as aliens, there is nothing more important for trafficked people than an opportunity to seek assistance from their own governments.[85] Therefore, access to consular assistance must be secured. States of destination have the duty to provide such access to consular assistance, while States of origin have the right to communicate with their own nationals to provide assistance in accordance with the *Vienna Convention on Consular Relations* 1963.[86] This Convention concerns both rights of States and individuals.[87] Moreover, a right

---

gration shall take place in an environment which fosters the health, self-respect and dignity of the child"; and General Comment No. 4 (Adolescent Health and Development in the Context of the Convention on the Rights of the Child)(2003), of the Committee on the Rights of the Child, CRC/GC/2003/4, para. 37.

81 *Cyprus v Turkey* (App. 25781/94), Judgment of 10/5/01, para. 219. It has been noted, however, that States have discretion to define their own level of health care provision. Only if a State fails to meet its own declared standard, could Article 2 be invoked. Mowbray, *supra*, p. 26.

82 *Velikova v Bulgaria* (App. 41488/98), Judgment of 18/5/00, paras. 74-76. See also *Anguelova v Bulgaria* (App. 38361/97), Judgment of 13/6/02.

83 *supra*.

84 *International Federation of Human Rights League v France*, Complaints No. 14/2003 (3/11/04), para. 32.

85 Except for those who fear persecution by States of origin.

86 Article 36, 596 UNTS 261.

87 Although the Vienna Convention is not a human rights instrument per se, the ICJ,in the *LaGrand Case (Germany v. United States)* stated that Article 36 of the Vienna Convention creates individual rights, *ICJ Report* 2002, para. 77. The Inter-American Court of Human Rights went further to state that consular assistance, as part of minimum due process guarantees, is recognised under Article 14 of ICCPR. *The Right to Information on Consular Assistance in the Framework of the Guarantees of the Due Process of Law*, Advisory Opinion OC-16/99, Ser. A, No. 16 (1999), paras. 80, 83, 84, 87, and 122-124. See also *Rules Governing the Detention of Persons Awaiting Trial or Appeal before the Tribunal or Otherwise Detained on the Authority of the Tribunal of the International Criminal Tribunal for the Former Yugoslavia,* IT/38/

of all people to equal treatment before national tribunals is established under international human rights law,[88] and States must take positive steps to secure "an effective right of access to the courts."[89]

Finally, compensation is an important form of remedy. It is important because an award of compensation serves to "affirm public respect for the victim and give public recognition of the wrongdoer's fault in failing to respect basic rights."[90] States of origin bear the primary responsibility in this regard, as the fact of people being trafficked illustrates their failure to prevent traffickers from abusing the human rights of those trafficked. However this obligation can also be imposed upon States of transit and destination, when they fail to fulfil pertinent human rights obligations illustrated above. The Committee on the Elimination of Racial Discrimination elaborates upon the general duty to provide compensation in the following terms:

> [T]he right to seek just and adequate reparation or satisfaction for any damage suffered ... is not necessarily secured solely by the punishment of the perpetrator of the discrimination; at the same time, the courts and other competent authorities should consider awarding financial compensation for damage, material or moral, suffered by a victim, whenever appropriate.[91]

The Inter-American Court of Human Rights adopted the same line of reasoning in the *Velasquez Rodriguez* Case by stating that the obligation to ensure the free and full exercise of those rights recognised by the Convention (ACHR) includes provision of compensation.[92] In a similar vein, when the right to life or prohibition against torture is involved, the European Court of Human Rights has held that the payment of compensation might be required.[93] These are pertinent to

---

REV.8 (1999), Rule 65; and Articles 16 and 23 of Migrant Workers' Convention, *supra*.

88 Advisory Opinion on Rights of Undocumented Migrants, *supra*, para. 109; General Comment No. 13 (Equality before Courts)(1984) of the Human Rights Committee, Compilation of General Comments, *supra*; Article 5(a) of CERD, *supra*; General Recommendation No. 20 (Non-Discriminatory Implementation of Rights and Freedom)(1996) in which the Committee on the Elimination of Racial Discrimination notes that the right to equal treatment applies to "all persons living in a given State"; and Article 18 of the Migrant Workers' Convention, *supra*.

89 *Airey v. Ireland* (App. 6289/73), Judgment of 9/9/79, para. 25.

90 Shelton, *supra*, p. 215.

91 General Recommendation No. 26 (Article 6 of the Convention)(2000), Compilation of General Comments, *supra*.

92 *Velasquez Rodriguez, supra*, paras. 166, 174 and 175.

93 *Z. v. United Kingdom, supra*, paras. 108 and 109. See also Article 14 (1) of the Convention Against Torture, *supra*, which provides that "Each State Party shall ensure

trafficking of human beings as noted earlier. States, however, must handle compensation with care. The victim's dignity can be affected by prolonged and excessive application procedures to obtain compensation, and compensation itself may be seen as "buying silence" or "blood money."[94] Therefore, States should take the best interests of victims into account in awarding compensation.

5.2.4 Obligation to Address the Causes and Consequences of Trafficking

As maintained consistently throughout this book, the effective prevention and suppression of trafficking requires a holistic approach which also addresses the causes and consequences of trafficking. International human rights law imposes certain obligations in this regard. One example of this is the obligation in relation to the reduction of poverty. This may be termed as an obligation of result, as opposed to an obligation of conduct. This distinction was developed by the United Nations International Law Commission in the 1970s when it was considering issues of State responsibility.[95] Simply put, States are required "to take or refrain from taking some specific action" under the obligations of conduct, while they are required "to ensure a particular situation or result," and can choose whatever the means necessary to fulfil this aim under the obligations of result.[96] It was noted in the context of human rights that the obligations of conduct are of immediate effect, whereas the obligations of result refer to progressive realisation of human rights.[97] In general, the former relates to civil and political rights, and the latter applies to economic, social and cultural rights.[98] However, it was simultaneously noted that there are two obligations of conduct which are pertinent to economic, social and cultural rights: obligations to guarantee rights without discrimination and to take steps towards the full realization

---

in its legal system that the victim of an act of torture obtains redress and has an enforceable right to fair and adequate compensation, including the means for as full rehabilitation as possible. In the event of the death of the victim as a result of an act of torture, his dependants shall be entitled to compensation."

94 Roht-Arriaza (1995), *supra*, p. 21; and McKay, F, 'Civil Reparation in National Courts for Victims of Human Rights Abuse', in Lattimer and Sands (eds.), *Justice for Crimes against Humanity*, *supra*, p. 287.

95 *State Responsibility in Report of the Commission to the General Assembly on the Work of its Twenty-Ninth Session*. Yearbook of International Law Commission Vol II (1-2) (1977), pp. 4-21 (1), and 11-30 (2).

96 *Ibid.* See also Rubenstein, P, 'State Responsibility for Failure to Control the Export of Weapons of Mass Destruction,' 23 *California Western International Law Journal* 319 (1993), p. 351

97 General Comment No. 3 (Nature of States Parties Obligations)(1990) of the Committee on Economic, Social and Cultural Rights, para. 1, Compilation of General Comments, *supra.*

98 *Ibid.*, paras. 1 and 9.

of the relevant rights within a reasonable time.[99] Several obligations of States in relation to poverty reduction can be identified by reference to obligations to *respect*, *protect* and *fulfil*. An obligation to *respect* requires States to refrain from interfering with the enjoyment of economic, social and cultural rights.[100] In the context of poverty reduction, States must respect "the resources owned by the individuals or groups seeking to make optimal use of their own knowledge and the freedom of individuals and groups to satisfy their own needs."[101] An obligation to *protect* means preventing abuses of rights by third parties.[102] States, therefore, must take necessary steps to ensure that entities such as international financial institutions do not infringe the rights of their citizens. Finally, an obligation to *fulfil* requires States to take appropriate administrative and other measures towards the full realization of economic, social and cultural rights.[103] In this connection, a failure to provide essential foodstuffs, primary healthcare, and basic housing,[104] and to take steps to devise/implement poverty reduction strategies[105] can incur accountability as violations.

Although States of origin may be ultimately responsible for eliminating poverty, the obligations in relation to poverty reduction extend to other States simultaneously. This is evident in Article 2(1) of the ICESCR which provides for international co-operation,[106] and the Committee on Economic, Social and Cultural Rights recognises in this respect that international co-operation for realisation of economic, social and cultural rights is an obligation of all States, in accordance with the Charter of the United Nations and other recognised principles of international law.[107] It was also noted that the phrase "to the maximum of its available resources" in Article 2(1) of the ICESCR was "intended by the drafters of the Covenant to refer to both the resources existing within a State and those available from the international community through international cooperation and assistance."[108] All of this suggests that all States, includ-

99 *Ibid.*, para. 1and 2.

100 *Maastricht Guidelines on Violations of Economic, Social and Cultural Rights* (1997), para. 6, reprinted in 20 *Human Rights Quarterly* 691 (1998).

101 *Report of the Independent Expert on Human Rights and Extreme Poverty*, E/CN.4/1999/48, para. 26.

102 Maastricht Guidelines, *supra*, para. 6.

103 *Ibid.*

104 General Comment No. 3, *supra*, para. 10.

105 On this, see OHCHR, *Draft Guidelines: A Human Rights Approach to Poverty Reduction Strategies* (September 2001).

106 *supra.*

107 General Comment No. 3, *supra*, para. 14.

108 *Ibid.* para. 13.

ing those of transit as well as destination, have a duty to assist States of origin to eliminate poverty.

Another inter-linked obligation is the prohibition of discrimination, which is a central cause, and often also a consequence of trafficking of human beings. At the very minimum, all States are obliged to enact legislation to eradicate discrimination on account of race, gender and other distinctions.[109] At a practical level, States are obliged to ensure the right of equal access to, among others things, health facilities,[110] food,[111] adequate housing,[112] and education.[113] In addition, when those trafficked are arrested and detained, they must be treated in a humane and non-discriminatory manner.[114] Moreover, when the principle of non-discrimination is violated, victims have the right to seek judicial remedies.[115]

Finally, all States have a duty to provide education to their citizens. In States of origin, a lack of education is one of the factors contributing to poverty. Therefore, States have an obligation to provide education[116] particularly to those at risk of being trafficked, so that they can engage in productive economic activities in the future. In all States, education should also be directed at promoting understanding, tolerance and friendship among all nations and all racial, ethnic or religious groups.[117] This can facilitate the elimination of the causes and consequences of trafficking such as discrimination on account of race and

---

109 Article 2 of ICESCR, *supra*, and General Comment No. 3, *ibid.*, para. 3; Article 2 of ICCPR, *supra*; Articles 2(d) and 4(a) of CERD, *supra* and General Recommendation No. 7 (Legislation to Eradicate Racial Discrimination)(1985) of the Committee on the Elimination of Racial Discrimination, Compilation of General Comments, *supra*; and Article 2 (b) of CEDAW, *supra*.

110 General Comment No. 14, *supra*, para. 43.

111 General Comment No. 12, *supra*, para. 18.

112 General Comment No. 7, *supra,* para. 10.

113 Article 10 of CEDAW, *supra*; Article 28 of CRC, *supra*, and General Comment No. 1 (Aims of Education)(2001) of the Committee on the Rights of the Child, para. 10, Compilation of General Comments, *supra*; Article 5(e) of CERD, *supra*; Article 13 of ICESCR, *supra*; and General Comment No. 13 (The Right to Education)(1999) of the Committee on Economic, Social and Cultural Rights, Compilation of General Comments, *ibid.*

114 Article 10 of ICCPR, *supra*; and General Comment No. 21, *supra*, para. 4; *Standard Minimum Rules for the Treatment of Prisoners* (1977), ECOSOC Resolution 2076 (LXII), para. 6.1; and *Body of Principles for the Protection of All Persons under Any Form of Detention or Imprisonment* (1988), A/RES/43/173, Principle 5.

115 Article 5 of CERD, *supra*; and General Comment No. 3, *supra*, para, 5.

116 General Comment No. 13, *supra*, para. 10; and General Comment No. 1 of the Committee on the Rights of the Child, *supra*, para. 10.

117 Article 13(1) of ICESCR, *supra*; and Article 29(1) of CRC, *supra*.

gender, including racial and gender related violence, in the long run. Moreover, it should also be a duty of all States, regardless of their status as one of origin, transit, or destination, to educate people on the dangers inherent in trafficking of human beings. When the potential victims are empowered through education, it becomes less likely for them to fall into the hands of traffickers.

5.3 Human Rights Framework and Trafficking Protocol

The Trafficking Protocol provides a comprehensive legal framework to facilitate global action against the phenomenon in modern times. Its main tactic, as noted elsewhere, is suppression and prevention, and therefore is in line with the human rights obligation to prohibit trafficking. In relation to the obligation to investigate, prosecute and punish traffickers, the Trafficking Protocol stipulates that States are under an obligation to co-ordinate information, provide sufficient training for law enforcement agencies, and co-operate in border control for the purpose of prevention.[118]

In addition, the Trafficking Protocol also provides that one of the aims of the instrument is to protect victims under Article 2(b). To this end, it contains a specific section on the protection of victims. Under Section II, States are obliged to provide such measures as psychological assistance, accommodation, educational and vocational training, and temporary or permanent residence permits.[119] Moreover, the facilitation of voluntary repatriation is provided for.[120] Finally, the Trafficking Protocol obliges States to address some causes and consequences of trafficking of human beings, such as poverty, underdevelopment, and the demand for trafficked people.[121] These provisions of the Trafficking Protocol clearly highlight its potential to facilitate the application of a human rights framework to the practice.

This is of course not to state that the Trafficking Protocol entirely meets the human rights standards set by international human rights law. There are other important issues discussed throughout this book, such as violence and/or discrimination against women and ethnic minorities and law enforcement practices, which are not covered in the Trafficking Protocol.

In addition, it may be argued that some human rights obligations stipulated in the Protocol are weak. Article 6 for instance, provides that States "shall consider" implementing measures for physical, psychological and social recovery for victims of trafficking. In a similar vein, Article 7 obliges States to consider, but not to adopt, legal measures to allow victims to remain in their territories at least on a temporary basis.

118 Articles 9-11, *supra.*

119 Articles 6 and 7, *ibid.*

120 Article 8, *ibid.*

121 Article 9, *ibid.*

All of this, however, should not be taken as a disadvantage because areas not covered in the Trafficking Protocol can be supplemented by international human rights law, and the applicable human rights norms and principles can be enforced through the established mechanisms at the international level. The Trafficking Protocol for its part can serve as a vehicle to promote international co-operation among different actors. Therefore, it should be an instrument recognised as a key for promoting and implementing a human rights framework, augmenting global action against the act.

5.4 Interaction among Different Branches of International Law

An examination of trafficking of human beings illustrates that the subject matter falls under different branches of international law simultaneously. In Chapter 4, it was illustrated that international criminal law may be utilised against traffickers. This Chapter has shown that international human rights law is pertinent to trafficking of human beings. In addition, the practice falls under an emerging branch of international law known as transnational criminal law. The characteristics of transnational criminal law may be better understood by comparing them with those of international criminal law. To begin with, transnational criminal law promotes "the indirect suppression by international law, through domestic penal law, of criminal activities that have actual or potential trans-boundary effects."[122] International criminal law, on the contrary, gives rise to "individual criminal responsibility for violation of international law before international tribunals."[123] In other words, direct control of criminal activities is possible at the international level.

Another difference between international criminal law and transnational criminal law is the exercise of jurisdiction by States.[124] As noted earlier, international crimes give rise to universal jurisdiction. This, however, is not necessarily the case for some transnational crimes, including money laundering and trafficking of human beings. This is illustrated by Article 15 of the Organised Crime Convention which provides for the territoriality or nationality principles as the basis for establishing jurisdiction.[125] Seen in this light, it becomes apparent that the Organised Crime Convention and the Trafficking and Smuggling Protocols belong to transnational criminal law as they are essentially the instruments which are designed to promote indirect suppression at the national level. Therefore, trafficking of human beings can be found at the intersection of three

122 Boister, *supra*, p. 955.

123 *Ibid.*

124 *Ibid.*, pp. 963-965.

125 *supra*. However, some argued that the principle of *aut dedere aut punire* (extradite or prosecute) reflected in transnational criminal law, including Organised Crime Convention, constitutes a subsidiary form of universal jurisdiction. Boister, *ibid.*, p. 964.

branches of international law: international human rights law, international criminal law and transnational criminal law.

All of this can be illustrated in the following diagram:

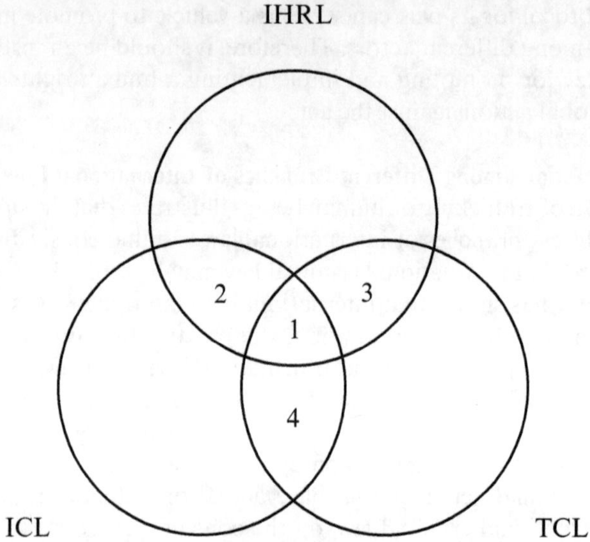

How are all of these translated into obligations imposed upon States in relation to trafficking of human beings? The common obligations imposed by all of three branches of international law (Area 1) are prohibition of the offence, punishment of traffickers, and protection of victims. The obligations jointly imposed by international human rights law and international criminal law (Area 2) include, but are not limited to, protection of the rights of the defendants, while the obligation to address the causes and the consequences of trafficking is imposed by transnational criminal law and international human rights law (Area 3). Finally, an example of obligations common to international criminal law and transnational criminal law (Area 4) is mutual legal assistance or international co-operation.

The existence of overlapping obligations among these branches of international law does not necessarily mean that international human rights law, transnational criminal law and international criminal law are in conflict with one another. It is submitted that they are mutually reinforcing instead. As noted earlier, the main purpose of international human rights law is protection of the basic rights of individual human beings. Therefore, the obligations are imposed not in relation to other States, but towards all individuals within their jurisdiction.[126] This means, among others, that international human rights law is not necessarily suited to promote international co-operation and mutual assistance because these are examples of obligations towards other States rather than individual human beings. This, however, can be compensated by transnational criminal law and international criminal law whose main aim is to facilitate and/or secure co-operation with other Parties.[127] Another benefit of utilising international criminal law is that it promotes direct control of international crimes through international tribunals as noted earlier, and therefore clearly spells out the contribution to be made not only by States, but also by the international community as a whole.

Another example in support of the above submission can be seen in some weaknesses inherent in transnational criminal law. While the Trafficking Protocol may be used to seek uniformity in the meaning of the offence itself and criminal liability among Member States, it is difficult to achieve harmonisation in reality. This was illustrated in Chapter 2 where the definitions of the offence of trafficking and the extent of punishment were shown to be different among Thailand, Poland and the United Kingdom. As noted by one scholar, all of this can affect the principle of legality, which demands States to use the same general principles, procedures and penalties in dealing with a particular offence. [128]

It has also been argued that transnational criminal law is not necessarily well equipped to promote and protect the human rights of defendants, as its main aim is to promote effective prohibition, prosecution and punishment.[129] Indeed, the Organised Crime Convention and the Trafficking Protocol say very little about the rights of defendants. The only provisions in the Organised Crime Convention are Articles 11(3) (Prosecution) and 16(13) (Extradition), which make a brief reference to rights of defence without elaboration,[130] and the Trafficking Protocol does not contain a single provision on the matter.

Aside from obligations imposed upon States, another important point to be noted is the principle of State sovereignty. One limitation imposed upon transnational criminal law is that the implementation of obligations is left to States. In other words, the principle of State sovereignty dominates.[131] To illustrate this further, the Organised Crime Convention has a specific provision protecting sovereignty of Member States. Article 4 provides:

---

126 Inter-American Court of Human Rights, *The Effect of Reservations on the Entry into Force of the ACHR (Articles 74 and 75)* (1982), Advisory Opinion OC 2-82, Ser. A, No.2, para. 29.

127 Cassese (2003), p. 15 and 16.

128 Boister, *supra*, p. 958.

129 *Ibid.*, p. 959.

130 *supra*.

131 Boister, *supra*, p. 956.

1. State party shall carry out their obligations under this Convention in a manner consistent with the principles of sovereign equality and territorial integrity of States and that of non-intervention in the domestic affairs of other States.

2. Nothing in this Convention entitles a State Party to undertake in the territory of another State the exercise of jurisdiction and performance of functions that are reserved exclusively for the authorities of that other State by its domestic law.[132]

This certainly can make it more difficult to seek effective co-operation and coordination among States.

These weaknesses inherent in transnational criminal law, however, may be compensated by international criminal law and international human rights law. The principle of legality has long been recognised as fundamental to the development of international criminal law.[133] Therefore, international criminal law could promote this principle so as to make sure that offences are clearly provided in written law (*nullum crimen sine lege scripta*), that criminal legislation abide by the rule of specificity (*nullum crimen sine lege stricta*), and that criminal rules are not retroactive (*nullum crimen sine proevia lege*).[134] Although the principle of legality in effect is designed to protect the rights of defendants, their protection can be strengthened with international human rights law, which provides detailed obligations including the right to liberty and security[135] and procedural guarantees such as adequate time for preparation, trial without delay, and right to legal representation.[136]

In relation to the principle of State sovereignty, the recognition of trafficking as an international crime makes it clear that the practice is not merely a domestic crime, and therefore that effective international co-operation is necessary to suppress and prevent the practice. In addition, it has long been sustained that State sovereignty is no longer an absolute concept in relation to the promotion and protection of human rights. Javier Perez de Cueller, the former UN Secretary-General, made this point clear:

---

132 *supra*.

133 Cassese (2003), *supra*, p. 31.

134 *Ibid.*, pp. 141 and 142.

135 Article 9 of ICCPR, *supra*.

136 Article 14 of ICCPR, *ibid.* The Rome Statute also contains several provisions in relation to protection of the rights of defendants. See for instance Articles 55 (Rights of Persons during Investigation), 66 (Presumption of Innocence), and 67 (Rights of the Accused), *supra*.

> It is now increasingly felt that the principle of non-interference within the essential domestic jurisdiction of States cannot be regarded as a protective barrier behind which human rights could be massively or systematically violated with impunity.[137]

Seen in this regard, international criminal law and international human rights law may be used to strengthen the argument that States can no longer hide behind the rubric of State sovereignty in relation to trafficking of human beings.

Finally, international criminal law represents a criminal justice response, in that the main emphasis is placed upon prohibition, prosecution and punishment. One drawback, as illustrated through this book, is that it is not designed to address the wider issues such as the causes and consequences of trafficking in depth. However, international human rights law and transnational criminal law, as represented in the Trafficking Protocol, can address this problem. What becomes apparent from all of these is that three branches of international law can assist each other to alleviate some of these problems. Therefore, it seems reasonable to argue that they are mutually reinforcing, and not necessarily conflicting, with each other.

5.5 Towards Global Governance?

In examining the responses to trafficking at the national, regional and international levels, it becomes apparent that global governance may be necessary. Williams and Baudin-O'Hayon note in this regard that the rise of transnational organised crime is a response to the failures of domestic governance.[138] They further argue that transnational organised crime is both a reflection of and a contributor to a new form of geopolitics, whose main characteristics no longer rest solely upon power, boundaries and territory, but on transnational flows of money, commodities and people.[139] All of this makes us realise that global governance over transnational organised crime, including trafficking of human beings, has a role to play.

137 *Report of the Secretary-General on the Work of Organization*, A/46/1 (13/9/91), p. 5. See further, Schreuer, C, 'The Waning of Sovereign State: Towards a New Paradigm for International Law?' 4 *European Journal of International Law* 447 (1993), pp. 468 and 469; Henkin, L, 'That "S" Word: Sovereignty, and Globalization, and Human Rights, Et Cetera' 68 *Fordham Law Review* 1 (1999), pp. 4 and 5; Shen, J 'National Sovereignty and Human Rights in a Positive Law Context,' 26 *Brooklyn Journal of International Law* 417 (2000); Aceves, W. J, 'Relative Normativity: Challenging the Sovereignty Norm Through Human Rights Litigation' 25 *Hastings International and Comparative Law Review* 261 (2002); and Ayoob, M, 'Humanitarian Intervention and State Sovereignty' 6 *International Journal of Human Rights* 81 (2002).

138 Williams and Baudin-O'Hayon, *supra*, p. 130.

139 *Ibid.*

What is global governance? Although this question has been a subject of intense debates and different people have different ideas,[140] the main characteristics can be identified. Under global governance, States are no longer regarded as the sole holders of power, and the role played by other actors such as NGOs, multi-lateral corporations and IGOs are seen as equally important.[141] It has been argued in this connection that the central characteristic of global governance lies in the reconfiguration or relocation of authority between different layers or infrastructures of governance: the suprastate (UN), the regional (EU, ASEAN, etc.), the transnational (civil society and business network), and the substate (community associations and local governments).[142] Global governance is not to be confused with the idea of global government, because the focus of its attention is placed upon interaction among these different actors, rather than advocating a creation of "global central public body" which legislates for the international community as a whole.[143]

In looking at various responses to trafficking illustrated in this book, several models for global governance can be identified. The first model, as represented by transnational criminal law and the Trafficking Protocol, places an emphasis on international co-operation and mutual legal assistance among States without much involvement of other actors. Therefore, States retain more power in this model. The main problem with this model is that some States are unable to contribute because they are politically or economically weak or corrupt and therefore conducive to the growth of organised crime.[144] Additionally, the principle of State sovereignty can make it more difficult to seek effective co-ordination as noted earlier.

The second model is based on international criminal law, under which direct control of the crime of trafficking is the key characteristic. An important aspect of this model is that IGOs, such as the ICC, are able to exercise more power in dealing with trafficking of human beings. One benefit of this model is that problems associated with weak or corrupt States may be alleviated, as international institutions are, as noted earlier, more immune from the influence of organised criminal groups. One possible problem, however, is that institutions such as the ICC may sometimes wield too much power in interpreting and even creating the law, which could interfere with or disrupt a structure of global governance based on participation by different actors.

Somewhat in between these two models lies a hybrid one which contains elements of both models. This is the model represented by international human

140 On this see Chapters 1-4 of *Governing Globalization* by Held and McGrew.

141 Held, D, and A. McGrew, 'Introduction', *ibid.*, p. 9.

142 *Ibid.*, pp. 9 and 10.

143 *Ibid.*

144 Williams and Baudin-O'Hayon, *supra*, pp. 139 and 140.

rights law. States remain the key actors in implementing human rights obligations applicable to trafficking of human beings. Nevertheless, implementation and observance of these obligations are constantly monitored by various human rights bodies at national, regional and international levels, compared to the other two branches of international law. This model, then, may be said to be a representative of global governance because it acknowledges the contributions made by all of those concerned more than any other models. In terms of what issues should be addressed under the rubric of global governance, this model also helps all of those concerned to acknowledge the importance of adopting a holistic approach, as stressed throughout this book.

It is difficult at this point to state precisely which model will work best to promote and maintain global governance over trafficking of human beings. All three branches of international law are necessary to compensate some weaknesses. Therefore, it may be that we need all three models for effective suppression and prevention. Given that trafficking of human beings has attracted attention only recently, the effectiveness of these models and the impact of the interaction of three branches of international law remain to be seen.

5.6 Conclusion

The purpose of this Chapter was to analyse the extent of human rights obligations in relation to trafficking of human beings imposed upon States. It identified four obligations to 1) prohibit trafficking, 2) investigate, prosecute, punish traffickers, 3) protect victims, and 4) address the causes and consequences of the practice. It has been shown that these obligations are firmly established under international human rights law. The main conclusion reached is that a human rights framework, through the promotion and implementation of human rights norms and principles, can usefully supplement global action against trafficking.

This main conclusion leads to several other observations. For one, a human rights analysis of trafficking reaffirms one of the fundamental principles that all human rights are indivisible and interdependent. Traditionally, human rights have been categorised into three generations of rights: first generation of civil and political rights; second generation of economic, social and cultural rights; and third generation of collective or group rights, self-determination and development.[145] A human rights analysis of trafficking underlines the fact that this practice affects economic, social, cultural as well as civil and political rights, and

145 For a critical analysis on this categorisation, see Wellman, C, 'Solidarity, the Individual and Human Rights' 22 *Human Rights Quarterly* 639 (2000); and Alston, P, 'A Third Generation of Solidarity Rights: Progressive Development or Obfuscation of International Human Rights Law?' 29 *Netherlands International Law Review* 207 (1982).

therefore that all human rights are interdependent and indivisible. This calls for a comprehensive analysis of trafficking which embraces all human rights.

At a practical level, a human rights analysis of trafficking also highlights the limitations of a criminal justice response to the practice, characterised by border control and punishment of traffickers and trafficked people. The effective action against the practice requires a holistic approach which addresses multi-faceted aspects of trafficking. A human rights approach is beneficial in this respect, as it provides a framework for understanding the nature of the problems intrinsic to the practice and for seeking not only legal, but also political, social and economic solutions.

However, a human rights analysis of trafficking also illustrates the current weaknesses in the enforcement of human rights norms and principles. Despite the fact that many aspects of trafficking are already covered by international human rights law, it is difficult to say that the human rights community, consisting of concerned actors at the national, regional and international levels, has been able to facilitate a human rights framework to address the phenomenon. Although it may be easy to blame States, the primary holders of duties under international human rights law, for not fulfilling human rights obligations, weaknesses in enforcement can also be attributed to the fact that the human rights aspects of trafficking have not been widely scrutinised. Therefore, the human rights obligations in relation to the practice have not been clearly spelled out. A task of the human rights community, then, is to move beyond reporting the cases of human rights violations pertinent to trafficking and to articulate human rights obligations. Unless the human rights community becomes more proactive, the value of a human rights framework to trafficking will not be fully realised.

Conclusion

The last decade has seen a significant development of responses to trafficking of human beings at the national, regional and international levels. The transnational nature of the act requires global action with the involvement of different actors. One of the major steps forward to address this was taken when the United Nations adopted the Trafficking Protocol. This instrument is crucial as it provides a definition of trafficking which can be utilised by different actors to formulate legislation and policies at national, regional and international levels. It also seeks to promote co-operation so as to consolidate the contributions made by different actors.

Trafficking of human beings undoubtedly is a criminal justice issue. It affects the territorial integrity of States as the practice in many cases involves the facilitation of illegal crossing of borders in violation of national immigration laws and policies. It also threatens the rule of law and the political foundation of States, because traffickers, particularly organised criminal groups, resort to violence and corruption as means to advance their business. The most common response, as shown throughout this book, has been crime and immigration control which aims to prosecute and punish traffickers and reduce the flow of trafficked people. The Trafficking Protocol augments this criminal justice response as it is essentially an instrument which seeks to promote the effective suppression and prevention of this practice.

Nevertheless, human rights dimensions of trafficking have increasingly been recognised in recent times. This suggests that a human rights framework to trafficking is also necessary in order to deal with the multi-faceted issues inherent in the phenomenon. The main purpose of this book was to elaborate on this and to establish a human rights framework to understand and address the phenomenon. In Chapter 1, although it was shown that different actors have adopted a wide variety of views in relation to trafficking, they are in agreement that the phenomenon entails human rights dimensions. It also highlighted some advantages of a human rights framework, such as its ability to promote a holistic approach to trafficking which addresses not only the process, but also wider issues, and the importance placed upon the protection of victims.

Chapters 2 and 3, among others, demonstrated that although it is easy to treat trafficking as a human rights issue, it can be difficult to promote a human rights framework to the practice in reality. At a national level, the main response of the governments has been a criminal justice one, in that the primary emphasis is placed on suppression of trafficking through the prosecution of traffickers and reduction of the flow of trafficked people. Although NGOs are proactive in taking a human rights approach, their work is affected by a series of problems such as a lack of funding and co-operation from governments and other sectors. At the regional and international level, a human rights approach, although considered as important, is not being promoted effectively due to such reasons as a lack of a holistic approach to address trafficking.

In Chapters 4 and 5, trafficking, including the causes and consequences of the practice, was analysed from a human rights perspective in order to identify applicable norms and principles. It then illustrated the key human rights obligations. It was shown that although international human rights law is not directly enforceable against non-State actors, this can be done indirectly by bringing civil and criminal proceedings against traffickers at the national level. It was also demonstrated that trafficking can be regarded as a crime against humanity and therefore there is the prospect of traffickers being tried before the ICC. As for States, there are certain obligations imposed upon them, and this book examined four obligations applicable to all States, regardless of their status as those of origin, transit or destination. The main conclusion reached is that a human rights framework can provide a valuable contribution to global action against trafficking.

Recommendations

There are several steps which should be taken at the national, regional and international levels so as to facilitate a human rights framework to address trafficking of human beings. At the national level, States bear the primary responsibility to promote a human rights framework. Relevant human rights issues raised throughout this book must be carefully considered and addressed through national legislation. This is essential because legislation makes obligations imposed upon those concerned, including the law enforcement authorities, clearer, and serves as a basis for holding them legally accountable for non-compliance.

The enforcement of human rights norms and principles at the national level can also be strengthened through the establishment of independent national human rights commissions. They have the potential not only to monitor the implementation of relevant human rights obligations relating to trafficking, but also to address complaints arising from non-compliance. The appointment of a National Rapporteur on Trafficking within these commissions and/or other government bodies may be beneficial in this respect. This has already been done in Nepal,[1] Belgium, Sweden, and the Netherlands.[2] Other governments should follow such examples. They can not only co-ordinate activities with other governmental bodies, but also act as a national focal point and facilitate co-operation with other actors regionally and internationally.

The role of actors other than governments should not be underestimated. In addition to reporting the cases of trafficking and putting more pressure on governments to act, the involvement of NGOs is essential in educating the general public about trafficking. Promotion of a human rights framework will be more meaningful when the citizens of the world, including the potential victims, are empowered through education and participation in global action against trafficking. This will be more effective, however, if NGOs can establish a good working relationship with local media and journalists who are better suited to disseminate information to the general public. In addition, legal practitioners have an important role to play. They can contribute by taking cases of trafficking before national courts and tribunals which in turn can promote the indirect enforcement of human rights norms and principles, so that traffickers are punished appropriately and victims are protected.

At the regional and international levels, mechanisms charged with the promotion and the protection of human rights must move beyond merely reporting the cases of trafficking, and roles and activities of different actors. They should be more proactive in addressing the phenomenon with the application of human rights norms and principles so as to promote a human rights framework. The development of jurisprudence on trafficking may be a useful starting point. Such principles as prohibition against torture and slavery/forced labour may reasonably be brought before regional bodies such as the European and Inter-American Courts of Human Rights and treaty monitoring mechanisms such as the Human Rights Committee and the Committee Against Torture. The potential of other bodies such as the ICC, the ICJ and the ILO should not be underestimated as they can contribute to the development and elaboration of human rights norms and principles as well. Once clear obligations are established, this can put more pressure on States to adopt a human rights framework to address trafficking.

The development of jurisprudence on economic, social and cultural rights has not been as progressive as civil and political rights, particularly because individual communications cannot be received by the Committee on Economic, Social and Cultural Rights. This is an area of concern, as some of the key human rights related to trafficking lie within this domain. Nevertheless, the Committee

1 National Human Rights Commission of Nepal at http://www.nhrc-nepal.org/?ID=203&AFD=0.

2 Smit, M (Bureau of the Dutch National Rapporteur on Trafficking), *Trafficking in Women: A Dutch Country Report* (April 2003).

has played, and continues to play a critical role in interpreting the ICESCR and articulating obligations through General Comments, and in monitoring implementation of obligations. Therefore, its role in relation to trafficking of human beings should not be underestimated.

Moreover, a channel of communication within the human rights community should also be strengthened. The subject matter falls under different mandates established by human rights instruments and by the Commission or Sub-Commission on Human Rights, and it has been noted that the co-ordination among these bodies must be improved.[3] It is worth noting in this respect that the Commission appointed a Special Rapporteur on Trafficking in Persons in April 2004 for a period of three years.[4] In addition to submitting an annual report on trafficking of human beings, the Special Rapporteur is required to co-operate with other concerned actors and co-ordinate activities.[5]

In promoting a human rights framework, the inclusion of potential or actual victims of trafficking is essential. The root causes of the act cannot be adequately addressed without understanding the conditions in which those at risk of being trafficked live. The preferred forms of protection may also vary among victims. In addition, the development of jurisprudence at the national, regional and international levels requires participation of victims in civil, criminal and human rights litigations. In sum, different actors must incorporate the wishes and the voices of these people in order to seek more effective promotion and implementation of a human rights framework in relation to trafficking of human beings.

Will a human rights framework contribute to global action against trafficking of human beings? This question is rather difficult to answer, given that it has not been widely promoted or implemented at the national, regional and international levels at this current moment. Therefore, it will take some time to judge its potential. The inherent weaknesses in enforcement of human rights norms and principles must also be addressed in order to fully appreciate its value. Nevertheless, the benefits of a human rights framework have clearly been illustrated throughout this book, and it is hoped that different actors will start using it to address trafficking.

Wider Issues and Future Research

There are various issues which this book has raised and yet has not elaborated upon. In relation to migration and human rights, the fact of being trafficked as a basis for granting refugee status is a topic which requires further exploration. It was shown that the United Kingdom has granted refugee status to some victims

---

3 Interview wish Ms. Sanghera, *supra*.

4 Commission Decision 2004/110, E/CN.4/2004/L.11/Add.6.

5 *Ibid.*

of trafficking and that the Office of the United Nations High Commissioner for Refugees has also been examining this aspect. If such a move is widely accepted, more victims can be protected. The potential of the Migrant Workers' Convention as a tool to protect victims of both trafficking and smuggling is also worth examining. It was noted earlier that they can be regarded as migrant workers under the Convention. However, the majority of those who have ratified the Convention so far are States of origin, illustrating the unwillingness of major States of destination, most of which are wealthy developed States, to guarantee equal rights to all migrant workers. Therefore, there is a need to promote the human rights principles and norms relevant to protection of migrant workers, and scholars can contribute in this regard.

The position of non-State actors under international human rights law is another topic which requires further examination. Human rights scholars and other actors have increasingly been recognising a need to address the human rights abuses committed by non-State actors. As research on this subject progresses and jurisprudence develops, there may be a time in the future when the direct accountability of non-State actors can be established through international human rights law. Another related topic is the position of the employees of IGOs such as the United Nations. It was shown in this book that instances have arisen where these individuals have taken part in trafficking. Future research should also elaborate on the position of IGO representatives under international law in general, and international human rights law in particular.

Finally, transnational criminal law, an emerging concept under international law, should be of interest to scholars of international law. It has been noted that study in this area of international law has been neglected,[6] and therefore some research on this topic would make a valuable contribution to the scholarship of international law. Further, theoretical and practical implications arising from the interaction of different branches of international law such as international human rights law, international criminal law and transnational criminal law, as has been shown in the study of trafficking, are worth further exploration.

All of this illustrates that trafficking of human beings is a complex topic for research. New issues will emerge as the phenomenon evolves over time. Although this book touched upon just one aspect of trafficking of human beings, it is hoped that it has contributed to the scrutiny of relatively new aspects of human rights and trafficking of human beings, and that research on different aspects of the phenomenon follows in order to promote better understanding and more effective response to this evil of the contemporary world.

6 Boister, *supra*, p. 956.

Annex 1

Protocol to Prevent, Suppress and Punish Trafficking in Persons, Especially Women and Children, supplementing the United Nations Convention against Transnational Organized Crime[1]

Preamble

The States Parties to this Protocol,

Declaring that effective action to prevent and combat trafficking in persons, especially women and children, requires a comprehensive international approach in the countries of origin, transit and destination that includes measures to prevent such trafficking, to punish the traffickers and to protect the victims of such trafficking, including by protecting their internationally recognized human rights,

Taking into account the fact that, despite the existence of a variety of international instruments containing rules and practical measures to combat the exploitation of persons, especially women and children, there is no universal instrument that addresses all aspects of trafficking in persons,

Concerned that, in the absence of such an instrument, persons who are vulnerable to trafficking will not be sufficiently protected,

Recalling General Assembly resolution 53/111 of 9 December 1998, in which the Assembly decided to establish an open-ended intergovernmental ad hoc committee for the purpose of elaborating a comprehensive international convention against transnational organized crime and of discussing the elaboration of, inter alia, an international instrument addressing trafficking in women and children,

Convinced that supplementing the United Nations Convention against Transnational Organized Crime with an international instrument for the preven-

1 A/RES/55/25 (Annex II), 8 January 2001

tion, suppression and punishment of trafficking in persons, especially women and children, will be useful in preventing and combating that crime,

Have agreed as follows:

I. General provisions

Article 1
Relation with the United Nations Convention against Transnational Organized Crime

1. This Protocol supplements the United Nations Convention against Transnational Organized Crime. It shall be interpreted together with the Convention.

2. The provisions of the Convention shall apply, mutatis mutandis, to this Protocol unless otherwise provided herein.

3. The offences established in accordance with article 5 of this Protocol shall be regarded as offences established in accordance with the Convention.

Article 2
Statement of purpose

The purposes of this Protocol are:

(*a*) To prevent and combat trafficking in persons, paying particular attention to women and children;

(*b*) To protect and assist the victims of such trafficking, with full respect for their human rights; and

(*c*) To promote cooperation among States Parties in order to meet those objectives.

Article 3
Use of terms

For the purposes of this Protocol:

(*a*) "Trafficking in persons" shall mean the recruitment, transportation, transfer, harbouring or receipt of persons, by means of the threat or use of force or other forms of coercion, of abduction, of fraud, of deception, of the abuse of power or of a position of vulnerability or of the giving or receiving of payments or benefits to achieve the consent of a person having control over another person, for the purpose of exploitation. Exploitation shall include, at a minimum, the exploitation of the prostitution of others or other forms of sexual exploitation, forced labour or services, slavery or practices similar to slavery, servitude or the removal of organs;

(*b*) The consent of a victim of trafficking in persons to the intended exploitation set forth in subparagraph (*a*) of this article shall be irrelevant where any of the means set forth in subparagraph (*a*) have been used;

(*c*) The recruitment, transportation, transfer, harbouring or receipt of a child for the purpose of exploitation shall be considered "trafficking in persons" even if this does not involve any of the means set forth in subparagraph (*a*) of this article;

(*d*) "Child" shall mean any person under eighteen years of age.

Article 4
Scope of application

This Protocol shall apply, except as otherwise stated herein, to the prevention, investigation and prosecution of the offences established in accordance with article 5 of this Protocol, where those offences are transnational in nature and involve an organized criminal group, as well as to the protection of victims of such offences.

Article 5
Criminalization

1. Each State Party shall adopt such legislative and other measures as may be necessary to establish as criminal offences the conduct set forth in article 3 of this Protocol, when committed intentionally.

2. Each State Party shall also adopt such legislative and other measures as may be necessary to establish as criminal offences:

(*a*) Subject to the basic concepts of its legal system, attempting to commit an offence established in accordance with paragraph 1 of this article;

(*b*) Participating as an accomplice in an offence established in accordance with paragraph 1 of this article; and (*c*) Organizing or directing other persons to commit an offence established in accordance with paragraph 1 of this article.

II. Protection of victims of trafficking in persons

Article 6
Assistance to and protection of victims of trafficking in persons

1. In appropriate cases and to the extent possible under its domestic law, each State Party shall protect the privacy and identity of victims of trafficking in persons, including, inter alia, by making legal proceedings relating to such trafficking confidential.

2. Each State Party shall ensure that its domestic legal or administrative system contains measures that provide to victims of trafficking in persons, in appropriate cases:

(*a*) Information on relevant court and administrative proceedings;

(*b*) Assistance to enable their views and concerns to be presented and considered at appropriate stages of criminal proceedings against offenders, in a manner not prejudicial to the rights of the defence.

3. Each State Party shall consider implementing measures to provide for the physical, psychological and social recovery of victims of trafficking in persons, including, in appropriate cases, in cooperation with non-governmental organizations, other relevant organizations and other elements of civil society, and, in particular, the provision of:

(*a*) Appropriate housing;

(*b*) Counselling and information, in particular as regards their legal rights, in a language that the victims of trafficking in persons can understand;

(*c*) Medical, psychological and material assistance; and

(*d*) Employment, educational and training opportunities.

4. Each State Party shall take into account, in applying the provisions of this article, the age, gender and special needs of victims of trafficking in persons, in particular the special needs of children, including appropriate housing, education and care.

5. Each State Party shall endeavour to provide for the physical safety of victims of trafficking in persons while they are within its territory.

6. Each State Party shall ensure that its domestic legal system contains measures that offer victims of trafficking in persons the possibility of obtaining compensation for damage suffered.

Article 7
Status of victims of trafficking in persons in receiving States

1. In addition to taking measures pursuant to article 6 of this Protocol, each State Party shall consider adopting legislative or other appropriate measures that permit victims of trafficking in persons to remain in its territory, temporarily or permanently, in appropriate cases.

2. In implementing the provision contained in paragraph 1 of this article, each State Party shall give appropriate consideration to humanitarian and compassionate factors.

Article 8
Repatriation of victims of trafficking in persons

1. The State Party of which a victim of trafficking in persons is a national or in which the person had the right of permanent residence at the time of entry into the territory of the receiving State Party shall facilitate and accept, with due regard for the safety of that person, the return of that person without undue or unreasonable delay.

2. When a State Party returns a victim of trafficking in persons to a State Party of which that person is a national or in which he or she had, at the time of entry into the territory of the receiving State Party, the right of permanent residence, such return shall be with due regard for the safety of that person and for the status of any legal proceedings related to the fact that the person is a victim of trafficking and shall preferably be voluntary.

3. At the request of a receiving State Party, a requested State Party shall, without undue or unreasonable delay, verify whether a person who is a victim of trafficking in persons is its national or had the right of permanent residence in its territory at the time of entry into the territory of the receiving State Party.

4. In order to facilitate the return of a victim of trafficking in persons who is without proper documentation, the State Party of which that person is a national or in which he or she had the right of permanent residence at the time of entry

into the territory of the receiving State Party shall agree to issue, at the request of the receiving State Party, such travel documents or other authorization as may be necessary to enable the person to travel to and re-enter its territory.

5. This article shall be without prejudice to any right afforded to victims of trafficking in persons by any domestic law of the receiving State Party.

6. This article shall be without prejudice to any applicable bilateral or multilateral agreement or arrangement that governs, in whole or in part, the return of victims of trafficking in persons.

III. Prevention, cooperation and other measures

Article 9
Prevention of trafficking in persons

1. States Parties shall establish comprehensive policies, programmes and other measures:

(*a*) To prevent and combat trafficking in persons; and

(*b*) To protect victims of trafficking in persons, especially women and children, from revictimization.

2. States Parties shall endeavour to undertake measures such as research, information and mass media campaigns and social and economic initiatives to prevent and combat trafficking in persons.

3. Policies, programmes and other measures established in accordance with this article shall, as appropriate, include cooperation with non-governmental organizations, other relevant organizations and other elements of civil society.

4. States Parties shall take or strengthen measures, including through bilateral or multilateral cooperation, to alleviate the factors that make persons, especially women and children, vulnerable to trafficking, such as poverty, underdevelopment and lack of equal opportunity.

5. States Parties shall adopt or strengthen legislative or other measures, such as educational, social or cultural measures, including through bilateral and multilateral cooperation, to discourage the demand that fosters all forms of exploitation of persons, especially women and children, that leads to trafficking.

Article 10
Information exchange and training

1. Law enforcement, immigration or other relevant authorities of States Parties shall, as appropriate, cooperate with one another by exchanging information, in accordance with their domestic law, to enable them to determine:

(*a*) Whether individuals crossing or attempting to cross an international border with travel documents belonging to other persons or without travel documents are perpetrators or victims of trafficking in persons;

(*b*) The types of travel document that individuals have used or attempted to use to cross an international border for the purpose of trafficking in persons; and

(*c*) The means and methods used by organized criminal groups for the purpose of trafficking in persons, including the recruitment and transportation of victims, routes and links between and among individuals and groups engaged in such trafficking, and possible measures for detecting them.

2. States Parties shall provide or strengthen training for law enforcement, immigration and other relevant officials in the prevention of trafficking in persons. The training should focus on methods used in preventing such trafficking, prosecuting the traffickers and protecting the rights of the victims, including protecting the victims from the traffickers. The training should also take into account the need to consider human rights and child- and gender-sensitive issues and it should encourage cooperation with non-governmental organizations, other relevant organizations and other elements of civil society.

3. A State Party that receives information shall comply with any request by the State Party that transmitted the information that places restrictions on its use.

Article 11
Border measures

1. Without prejudice to international commitments in relation to the free movement of people, States Parties shall strengthen, to the extent possible, such border controls as may be necessary to prevent and detect trafficking in persons.

2. Each State Party shall adopt legislative or other appropriate measures to prevent, to the extent possible, means of transport operated by commercial car-

riers from being used in the commission of offences established in accordance with article 5 of this Protocol.

3. Where appropriate, and without prejudice to applicable international conventions, such measures shall include establishing the obligation of commercial carriers, including any transportation company or the owner or operator of any means of transport, to ascertain that all passengers are in possession of the travel documents required for entry into the receiving State.

4. Each State Party shall take the necessary measures, in accordance with its domestic law, to provide for sanctions in cases of violation of the obligation set forth in paragraph 3 of this article.

5. Each State Party shall consider taking measures that permit, in accordance with its domestic law, the denial of entry or revocation of visas of persons implicated in the commission of offences established in accordance with this Protocol.

6. Without prejudice to article 27 of the Convention, States Parties shall consider strengthening cooperation among border control agencies by, inter alia, establishing and maintaining direct channels of communication.

Article 12
Security and control of documents

Each State Party shall take such measures as may be necessary, within available means:

(*a*) To ensure that travel or identity documents issued by it are of such quality that they cannot easily be misused and cannot readily be falsified or unlawfully altered, replicated or issued; and

(*b*) To ensure the integrity and security of travel or identity documents issued by or on behalf of the State Party and to prevent their unlawful creation, issuance and use.

Article 13
Legitimacy and validity of documents

At the request of another State Party, a State Party shall, in accordance with its domestic law, verify within a reasonable time the legitimacy and validity of travel or identity documents issued or purported to have been issued in its name and suspected of being used for trafficking in persons.

IV. Final provisions

Article 14
Saving clause

1. Nothing in this Protocol shall affect the rights, obligations and responsibilities of States and individuals under international law, including international humanitarian law and international human rights law and, in particular, where applicable, the 1951 Convention and the 1967 Protocol relating to the Status of Refugees and the principle of non-refoulement as contained therein.

2. The measures set forth in this Protocol shall be interpreted and applied in a way that is not discriminatory to persons on the ground that they are victims of trafficking in persons. The interpretation and application of those measures shall be consistent with internationally recognized principles of non-discrimination.

Article 15
Settlement of disputes

1. States Parties shall endeavour to settle disputes concerning the interpretation or application of this Protocol through negotiation.

2. Any dispute between two or more States Parties concerning the interpretation or application of this Protocol that cannot be settled through negotiation within a reasonable time shall, at the request of one of those States Parties, be submitted to arbitration. If, six months after the date of the request for arbitration, those States Parties are unable to agree on the organization of the arbitration, any one of those States Parties may refer the dispute to the International Court of Justice by request in accordance with the Statute of the Court.

3. Each State Party may, at the time of signature, ratification, acceptance or approval of or accession to this Protocol, declare that it does not consider itself bound by paragraph 2 of this article. The other States Parties shall not be bound by paragraph 2 of this article with respect to any State Party that has made such a reservation.

4. Any State Party that has made a reservation in accordance with paragraph 3 of this article may at any time withdraw that reservation by notification to the Secretary-General of the United Nations.

Article 16
Signature, ratification, acceptance, approval and accession

1. This Protocol shall be open to all States for signature from 12 to 15 December 2000 in Palermo, Italy, and thereafter at United Nations Headquarters in New York until 12 December 2002.

2. This Protocol shall also be open for signature by regional economic integration organizations provided that at least one member State of such organization has signed this Protocol in accordance with paragraph 1 of this article.

3. This Protocol is subject to ratification, acceptance or approval. Instruments of ratification, acceptance or approval shall be deposited with the Secretary-General of the United Nations. A regional economic integration organization may deposit its instrument of ratification, acceptance or approval if at least one of its member States has done likewise. In that instrument of ratification, acceptance or approval, such organization shall declare the extent of its competence with respect to the matters governed by this Protocol. Such organization shall also inform the depositary of any relevant modification in the extent of its competence.

4. This Protocol is open for accession by any State or any regional economic integration organization of which at least one member State is a Party to this Protocol. Instruments of accession shall be deposited with the Secretary-General of the United Nations. At the time of its accession, a regional economic integration organization shall declare the extent of its competence with respect to matters governed by this Protocol. Such organization shall also inform the depositary of any relevant modification in the extent of its competence.

Article 17
Entry into force

1. This Protocol shall enter into force on the ninetieth day after the date of deposit of the fortieth instrument of ratification, acceptance, approval or accession, except that it shall not enter into force before the entry into force of the Convention. For the purpose of this paragraph, any instrument deposited by a regional economic integration organization shall not be counted as additional to those deposited by member States of such organization.

2. For each State or regional economic integration organization ratifying, accepting, approving or acceding to this Protocol after the deposit of the fortieth instrument of such action, this Protocol shall enter into force on the thirtieth day after the date of deposit by such State or organization of the relevant instru-

ment or on the date this Protocol enters into force pursuant to paragraph 1 of this article, whichever is the later.

Article 18
Amendment

1. After the expiry of five years from the entry into force of this Protocol, a State Party to the Protocol may propose an amendment and file it with the Secretary-General of the United Nations, who shall thereupon communicate the proposed amendment to the States Parties and to the Conference of the Parties to the Convention for the purpose of considering and deciding on the proposal. The States Parties to this Protocol meeting at the Conference of the Parties shall make every effort to achieve consensus on each amendment. If all efforts at consensus have been exhausted and no agreement has been reached, the amendment shall, as a last resort, require for its adoption a two-thirds majority vote of the States Parties to this Protocol present and voting at the meeting of the Conference of the Parties.

2. Regional economic integration organizations, in matters within their competence, shall exercise their right to vote under this article with a number of votes equal to the number of their member States that are Parties to this Protocol. Such organizations shall not exercise their right to vote if their member States exercise theirs and vice versa.

3. An amendment adopted in accordance with paragraph 1 of this article is subject to ratification, acceptance or approval by States Parties.

4. An amendment adopted in accordance with paragraph 1 of this article shall enter into force in respect of a State Party ninety days after the date of the deposit with the Secretary-General of the United Nations of an instrument of ratification, acceptance or approval of such amendment.

5. When an amendment enters into force, it shall be binding on those States Parties which have expressed their consent to be bound by it. Other States Parties shall still be bound by the provisions of this Protocol and any earlier amendments that they have ratified, accepted or approved.

Article 19
Denunciation

1. A State Party may denounce this Protocol by written notification to the Secretary-General of the United Nations. Such denunciation shall become effec-

tive one year after the date of receipt of the notification by the Secretary-General.

2. A regional economic integration organization shall cease to be a Party to this Protocol when all of its member States have denounced it.

Article 20
Depositary and languages

1. The Secretary-General of the United Nations is designated depositary of this Protocol.

2. The original of this Protocol, of which the Arabic, Chinese, English, French, Russian and Spanish texts are equally authentic, shall be deposited with the Secretary-General of the United Nations.

IN WITNESS WHEREOF, the undersigned plenipotentiaries, being duly authorized thereto by their respective Governments, have signed this Protocol.

Annex 2

Protocol against the Smuggling of Migrants by Land, Sea and Air, supplementing the United Nations Convention against Transnational Organized Crime[1]

Preamble

The States Parties to this Protocol,

Declaring that effective action to prevent and combat the smuggling of migrants by land, sea and air requires a comprehensive international approach, including cooperation, the exchange of information and other appropriate measures, including socio-economic measures, at the national, regional and international levels,

Recalling General Assembly resolution 54/212 of 22 December 1999, in which the Assembly urged Member States and the United Nations system to strengthen international cooperation in the area of international migration and development in order to address the root causes of migration, especially those related to poverty, and to maximize the benefits of international migration to those concerned, and encouraged, where relevant, interregional, regional and subregional mechanisms to continue to address the question of migration and development,

Convinced of the need to provide migrants with humane treatment and full protection of their rights,

Taking into account the fact that, despite work undertaken in other international forums, there is no universal instrument that addresses all aspects of smuggling of migrants and other related issues,

---

1 A/RES/55/25 (Annex III), 8 January 2001.

Concerned at the significant increase in the activities of organized criminal groups in smuggling of migrants and other related criminal activities set forth in this Protocol, which bring great harm to the States concerned,

Also concerned that the smuggling of migrants can endanger the lives or security of the migrants involved,

Recalling General Assembly resolution 53/111 of 9 December 1998, in which the Assembly decided to establish an open-ended intergovernmental ad hoc committee for the purpose of elaborating a comprehensive international convention against transnational organized crime and of discussing the elaboration of, inter alia, an international instrument addressing illegal trafficking in and transporting of migrants, including by sea,

Convinced that supplementing the United Nations Convention against Transnational Organized Crime with an international instrument against the smuggling of migrants by land, sea and air will be useful in preventing and combating that crime,

Have agreed as follows:

I. General provisions

Article 1
Relation with the United Nations Convention against Transnational Organized Crime

1. This Protocol supplements the United Nations Convention against Transnational Organized Crime. It shall be interpreted together with the Convention.

2. The provisions of the Convention shall apply, mutatis mutandis, to this Protocol unless otherwise provided herein.

3. The offences established in accordance with article 6 of this Protocol shall be regarded as offences established in accordance with the Convention.

Article 2
Statement of purpose

The purpose of this Protocol is to prevent and combat the smuggling of migrants, as well as to promote cooperation among States Parties to that end, while protecting the rights of smuggled migrants.

Article 3
Use of terms

For the purposes of this Protocol:

(*a*) "Smuggling of migrants" shall mean the procurement, in order to obtain, directly or indirectly, a financial or other material benefit, of the illegal entry of a person into a State Party of which the person is not a national or a permanent resident;

(*b*) "Illegal entry" shall mean crossing borders without complying with the necessary requirements for legal entry into the receiving State;

(*c*) "Fraudulent travel or identity document" shall mean any travel or identity document:

(i) That has been falsely made or altered in some material way by anyone other than a person or agency lawfully authorized to make or issue the travel or identity document on behalf of a State; or

(ii) That has been improperly issued or obtained through misrepresentation, corruption or duress or in any other unlawful manner; or

(iii) That is being used by a person other than the rightful holder;

(*d*) "Vessel" shall mean any type of water craft, including non-displacement craft and seaplanes, used or capable of being used as a means of transportation on water, except a warship, naval auxiliary or other vessel owned or operated by a Government and used, for the time being, only on government non-commercial service.

Article 4
Scope of application

This Protocol shall apply, except as otherwise stated herein, to the prevention, investigation and prosecution of the offences established in accordance with article 6 of this Protocol, where the offences are transnational in nature and involve an organized criminal group, as well as to the protection of the rights of persons who have been the object of such offences.

Article 5
Criminal liability of migrants

Migrants shall not become liable to criminal prosecution under this Protocol for the fact of having been the object of conduct set forth in article 6 of this Protocol.

Article 6
Criminalization

1. Each State Party shall adopt such legislative and other measures as may be necessary to establish as criminal offences, when committed intentionally and in order to obtain, directly or indirectly, a financial or other material benefit:

(*a*) The smuggling of migrants;

(*b*) When committed for the purpose of enabling the smuggling of migrants:

(i) Producing a fraudulent travel or identity document;

(ii) Procuring, providing or possessing such a document;

(*c*) Enabling a person who is not a national or a permanent resident to remain in the State concerned without complying with the necessary requirements for legally remaining in the State by the means mentioned in subparagraph (*b*) of this paragraph or any other illegal means.

2. Each State Party shall also adopt such legislative and other measures as may be necessary to establish as criminal offences:

(*a*) Subject to the basic concepts of its legal system, attempting to commit an offence established in accordance with paragraph 1 of this article;

(*b*) Participating as an accomplice in an offence established in accordance with paragraph 1 (*a*), (*b*) (i) or (*c*) of this article and, subject to the basic concepts of its legal system, participating as an accomplice in an offence established in accordance with paragraph 1 (*b*) (ii) of this article;

(*c*) Organizing or directing other persons to commit an offence established in accordance with paragraph 1 of this article.

3. Each State Party shall adopt such legislative and other measures as may be necessary to establish as aggravating circumstances to the offences established in accordance with paragraph 1 (*a*), (*b*) (i) and (*c*) of this article and, subject to the basic concepts of its legal system, to the offences established in accordance with paragraph 2 (*b*) and (*c*) of this article, circumstances:

(*a*) That endanger, or are likely to endanger, the lives or safety of the migrants concerned; or

(*b*) That entail inhuman or degrading treatment, including for exploitation, of such migrants.

4. Nothing in this Protocol shall prevent a State Party from taking measures against a person whose conduct constitutes an offence under its domestic law.

II. Smuggling of migrants by sea

Article 7
Cooperation

States Parties shall cooperate to the fullest extent possible to prevent and suppress the smuggling of migrants by sea, in accordance with the international law of the sea.

Article 8
Measures against the smuggling of migrants by sea

1. A State Party that has reasonable grounds to suspect that a vessel that is flying its flag or claiming its registry, that is without nationality or that, though flying a foreign flag or refusing to show a flag, is in reality of the nationality of the State Party concerned is engaged in the smuggling of migrants by sea may request the assistance of other States Parties in suppressing the use of the vessel for that purpose. The States Parties so requested shall render such assistance to the extent possible within their means.

2. A State Party that has reasonable grounds to suspect that a vessel exercising freedom of navigation in accordance with international law and flying the flag or displaying the marks of registry of another State Party is engaged in the smuggling of migrants by sea may so notify the flag State, request confirmation of registry and, if confirmed, request authorization from the flag State to take appropriate measures with regard to that vessel. The flag State may authorize the requesting State, inter alia:

(*a*) To board the vessel;

(*b*) To search the vessel; and

(*c*) If evidence is found that the vessel is engaged in the smuggling of migrants by sea, to take appropriate measures with respect to the vessel and persons and cargo on board, as authorized by the flag State.

3. A State Party that has taken any measure in accordance with paragraph 2 of this article shall promptly inform the flag State concerned of the results of that measure.

4. A State Party shall respond expeditiously to a request from another State Party to determine whether a vessel that is claiming its registry or flying its flag is entitled to do so and to a request for authorization made in accordance with paragraph 2 of this article.

5. A flag State may, consistent with article 7 of this Protocol, subject its authorization to conditions to be agreed by it and the requesting State, including conditions relating to responsibility and the extent of effective measures to be taken. A State Party shall take no additional measures without the express authorization of the flag State, except those necessary to relieve imminent danger to the lives of persons or those which derive from relevant bilateral or multilateral agreements.

6. Each State Party shall designate an authority or, where necessary, authorities to receive and respond to requests for assistance, for confirmation of registry or of the right of a vessel to fly its flag and for authorization to take appropriate measures. Such designation shall be notified through the Secretary-General to all other States Parties within one month of the designation.

7. A State Party that has reasonable grounds to suspect that a vessel is engaged in the smuggling of migrants by sea and is without nationality or may be assimilated to a vessel without nationality may board and search the vessel. If evidence confirming the suspicion is found, that State Party shall take appropriate measures in accordance with relevant domestic and international law.

Article 9
Safeguard clauses

1. Where a State Party takes measures against a vessel in accordance with article 8 of this Protocol, it shall:

(*a*) Ensure the safety and humane treatment of the persons on board;

(*b*) Take due account of the need not to endanger the security of the vessel or its cargo;

(*c*) Take due account of the need not to prejudice the commercial or legal interests of the flag State or any other interested State;

(*d*) Ensure, within available means, that any measure taken with regard to the vessel is environmentally sound.

2. Where the grounds for measures taken pursuant to article 8 of this Protocol prove to be unfounded, the vessel shall be compensated for any loss or damage that may have been sustained, provided that the vessel has not committed any act justifying the measures taken.

3. Any measure taken, adopted or implemented in accordance with this chapter shall take due account of the need not to interfere with or to affect:

(*a*) The rights and obligations and the exercise of jurisdiction of coastal States in accordance with the international law of the sea; or

(*b*) The authority of the flag State to exercise jurisdiction and control in administrative, technical and social matters involving the vessel.

4. Any measure taken at sea pursuant to this chapter shall be carried out only by warships or military aircraft, or by other ships or aircraft clearly marked and identifiable as being on government service and authorized to that effect.

III. Prevention, cooperation and other measures

Article 10
Information

1. Without prejudice to articles 27 and 28 of the Convention, States Parties, in particular those with common borders or located on routes along which migrants are smuggled, shall, for the purpose of achieving the objectives of this Protocol, exchange among themselves, consistent with their respective domestic legal and administrative systems, relevant information on matters such as:

(*a*) Embarkation and destination points, as well as routes, carriers and means of transportation, known to be or suspected of being used by an organized criminal group engaged in conduct set forth in article 6 of this Protocol;

(*b*) The identity and methods of organizations or organized criminal groups known to be or suspected of being engaged in conduct set forth in article 6 of this Protocol;

(*c*) The authenticity and proper form of travel documents issued by a State Party and the theft or related misuse of blank travel or identity documents;

(*d*) Means and methods of concealment and transportation of persons, the unlawful alteration, reproduction or acquisition or other misuse of travel or identity documents used in conduct set forth in article 6 of this Protocol and ways of detecting them;

(*e*) Legislative experiences and practices and measures to prevent and combat the conduct set forth in article 6 of this Protocol; and

(*f*) Scientific and technological information useful to law enforcement, so as to enhance each other's ability to prevent, detect and investigate the conduct set forth in article 6 of this Protocol and to prosecute those involved.

2. A State Party that receives information shall comply with any request by the State Party that transmitted the information that places restrictions on its use.

Article 11
Border measures

1. Without prejudice to international commitments in relation to the free movement of people, States Parties shall strengthen, to the extent possible, such border controls as may be necessary to prevent and detect the smuggling of migrants.

2. Each State Party shall adopt legislative or other appropriate measures to prevent, to the extent possible, means of transport operated by commercial carriers from being used in the commission of the offence established in accordance with article 6, paragraph 1 (*a*), of this Protocol.

3. Where appropriate, and without prejudice to applicable international conventions, such measures shall include establishing the obligation of commercial carriers, including any transportation company or the owner or operator of any means of transport, to ascertain that all passengers are in possession of the travel documents required for entry into the receiving State.

4. Each State Party shall take the necessary measures, in accordance with its domestic law, to provide for sanctions in cases of violation of the obligation set forth in paragraph 3 of this article.

5. Each State Party shall consider taking measures that permit, in accordance with its domestic law, the denial of entry or revocation of visas of persons implicated in the commission of offences established in accordance with this Protocol.

6. Without prejudice to article 27 of the Convention, States Parties shall consider strengthening cooperation among border control agencies by, inter alia, establishing and maintaining direct channels of communication.

Article 12
Security and control of documents

Each State Party shall take such measures as may be necessary, within available means:

(*a*) To ensure that travel or identity documents issued by it are of such quality that they cannot easily be misused and cannot readily be falsified or unlawfully altered, replicated or issued; and

(*b*) To ensure the integrity and security of travel or identity documents issued by or on behalf of the State Party and to prevent their unlawful creation, issuance and use.

Article 13
Legitimacy and validity of documents

At the request of another State Party, a State Party shall, in accordance with its domestic law, verify within a reasonable time the legitimacy and validity of travel or identity documents issued or purported to have been issued in its name and suspected of being used for purposes of conduct set forth in article 6 of this Protocol.

Article 14
Training and technical cooperation

1. States Parties shall provide or strengthen specialized training for immigration and other relevant officials in preventing the conduct set forth in article 6 of this Protocol and in the humane treatment of migrants who have been the

object of such conduct, while respecting their rights as set forth in this Protocol.

2. States Parties shall cooperate with each other and with competent international organizations, non-governmental organizations, other relevant organizations and other elements of civil society as appropriate to ensure that there is adequate personnel training in their territories to prevent, combat and eradicate the conduct set forth in article 6 of this Protocol and to protect the rights of migrants who have been the object of such conduct. Such training shall include:

(*a*) Improving the security and quality of travel documents;

(*b*) Recognizing and detecting fraudulent travel or identity documents;

(*c*) Gathering criminal intelligence, relating in particular to the identification of organized criminal groups known to be or suspected of being engaged in conduct set forth in article 6 of this Protocol, the methods used to transport smuggled migrants, the misuse of travel or identity documents for purposes of conduct set forth in article 6 and the means of concealment used in the smuggling of migrants;

(*d*) Improving procedures for detecting smuggled persons at conventional and non-conventional points of entry and exit; and

(*e*) The humane treatment of migrants and the protection of their rights as set forth in this Protocol.

3. States Parties with relevant expertise shall consider providing technical assistance to States that are frequently countries of origin or transit for persons who have been the object of conduct set forth in article 6 of this Protocol. States Parties shall make every effort to provide the necessary resources, such as vehicles, computer systems and document readers, to combat the conduct set forth in article 6.

Article 15
Other prevention measures

1. Each State Party shall take measures to ensure that it provides or strengthens information programmes to increase public awareness of the fact that the conduct set forth in article 6 of this Protocol is a criminal activity frequently perpetrated by organized criminal groups for profit and that it poses serious risks to the migrants concerned.

2. In accordance with article 31 of the Convention, States Parties shall cooperate in the field of public information for the purpose of preventing potential migrants from falling victim to organized criminal groups.

3. Each State Party shall promote or strengthen, as appropriate, development programmes and cooperation at the national, regional and international levels, taking into account the socio-economic realities of migration and paying special attention to economically and socially depressed areas, in order to combat the root socio-economic causes of the smuggling of migrants, such as poverty and underdevelopment.

Article 16
Protection and assistance measures

1. In implementing this Protocol, each State Party shall take, consistent with its obligations under international law, all appropriate measures, including legislation if necessary, to preserve and protect the rights of persons who have been the object of conduct set forth in article 6 of this Protocol as accorded under applicable international law, in particular the right to life and the right not to be subjected to torture or other cruel, inhuman or degrading treatment or punishment.

2. Each State Party shall take appropriate measures to afford migrants appropriate protection against violence that may be inflicted upon them, whether by individuals or groups, by reason of being the object of conduct set forth in article 6 of this Protocol.

3. Each State Party shall afford appropriate assistance to migrants whose lives or safety are endangered by reason of being the object of conduct set forth in article 6 of this Protocol.

4. In applying the provisions of this article, States Parties shall take into account the special needs of women and children.

5. In the case of the detention of a person who has been the object of conduct set forth in article 6 of this Protocol, each State Party shall comply with its obligations under the Vienna Convention on Consular Relations, where applicable, including that of informing the person concerned without delay about the provisions concerning notification to and communication with consular officers.

Article 17
Agreements and arrangements

States Parties shall consider the conclusion of bilateral or regional agreements or operational arrangements or understandings aimed at:

(*a*) Establishing the most appropriate and effective measures to prevent and combat the conduct set forth in article 6 of this Protocol; or

(*b*) Enhancing the provisions of this Protocol among themselves.

Article 18
Return of smuggled migrants

1. Each State Party agrees to facilitate and accept, without undue or unreasonable delay, the return of a person who has been the object of conduct set forth in article 6 of this Protocol and who is its national or who has the right of permanent residence in its territory at the time of return.

2. Each State Party shall consider the possibility of facilitating and accepting the return of a person who has been the object of conduct set forth in article 6 of this Protocol and who had the right of permanent residence in its territory at the time of entry into the receiving State in accordance with its domestic law.

3. At the request of the receiving State Party, a requested State Party shall, without undue or unreasonable delay, verify whether a person who has been the object of conduct set forth in article 6 of this Protocol is its national or has the right of permanent residence in its territory.

4. In order to facilitate the return of a person who has been the object of conduct set forth in article 6 of this Protocol and is without proper documentation, the State Party of which that person is a national or in which he or she has the right of permanent residence shall agree to issue, at the request of the receiving State Party, such travel documents or other authorization as may be necessary to enable the person to travel to and re-enter its territory.

5. Each State Party involved with the return of a person who has been the object of conduct set forth in article 6 of this Protocol shall take all appropriate measures to carry out the return in an orderly manner and with due regard for the safety and dignity of the person.

6. States Parties may cooperate with relevant international organizations in the implementation of this article.

7. This article shall be without prejudice to any right afforded to persons who have been the object of conduct set forth in article 6 of this Protocol by any domestic law of the receiving State Party.

8. This article shall not affect the obligations entered into under any other applicable treaty, bilateral or multilateral, or any other applicable operational agreement or arrangement that governs, in whole or in part, the return of persons who have been the object of conduct set forth in article 6 of this Protocol.

IV. Final provisions

Article 19
Saving clause

1. Nothing in this Protocol shall affect the other rights, obligations and responsibilities of States and individuals under international law, including international humanitarian law and international human rights law and, in particular, where applicable, the 1951 Convention and the 1967 Protocol relating to the Status of Refugees and the principle of non-refoulement as contained therein.

2. The measures set forth in this Protocol shall be interpreted and applied in a way that is not discriminatory to persons on the ground that they are the object of conduct set forth in article 6 of this Protocol. The interpretation and application of those measures shall be consistent with internationally recognized principles of non-discrimination.

Article 20
Settlement of disputes

1. States Parties shall endeavour to settle disputes concerning the interpretation or application of this Protocol through negotiation.

2. Any dispute between two or more States Parties concerning the interpretation or application of this Protocol that cannot be settled through negotiation within a reasonable time shall, at the request of one of those States Parties, be submitted to arbitration. If, six months after the date of the request for arbitration, those States Parties are unable to agree on the organization of the arbitration, any one of those States Parties may refer the dispute to the International Court of Justice by request in accordance with the Statute of the Court.

3. Each State Party may, at the time of signature, ratification, acceptance or approval of or accession to this Protocol, declare that it does not consider itself bound by paragraph 2 of this article. The other States Parties shall not be bound by paragraph 2 of this article with respect to any State Party that has made such a reservation.

4. Any State Party that has made a reservation in accordance with paragraph 3 of this article may at any time withdraw that reservation by notification to the Secretary-General of the United Nations.

Article 21
Signature, ratification, acceptance, approval and accession

1. This Protocol shall be open to all States for signature from 12 to 15 December 2000 in Palermo, Italy, and thereafter at United Nations Headquarters in New York until 12 December 2002.

2. This Protocol shall also be open for signature by regional economic integration organizations provided that at least one member State of such organization has signed this Protocol in accordance with paragraph 1 of this article.

3. This Protocol is subject to ratification, acceptance or approval. Instruments of ratification, acceptance or approval shall be deposited with the Secretary-General of the United Nations. A regional economic integration organization may deposit its instrument of ratification, acceptance or approval if at least one of its member States has done likewise. In that instrument of ratification, acceptance or approval, such organization shall declare the extent of its competence with respect to the matters governed by this Protocol. Such organization shall also inform the depositary of any relevant modification in the extent of its competence.

4. This Protocol is open for accession by any State or any regional economic integration organization of which at least one member State is a Party to this Protocol. Instruments of accession shall be deposited with the Secretary- General of the United Nations. At the time of its accession, a regional economic integration organization shall declare the extent of its competence with respect to matters governed by this Protocol. Such organization shall also inform the depositary of any relevant modification in the extent of its competence.

Article 22
Entry into force

1. This Protocol shall enter into force on the ninetieth day after the date of deposit of the fortieth instrument of ratification, acceptance, approval or accession, except that it shall not enter into force before the entry into force of the Convention. For the purpose of this paragraph, any instrument deposited by a regional economic integration organization shall not be counted as additional to those deposited by member States of such organization.

2. For each State or regional economic integration organization ratifying, accepting, approving or acceding to this Protocol after the deposit of the fortieth instrument of such action, this Protocol shall enter into force on the thirtieth day after the date of deposit by such State or organization of the relevant instrument or on the date this Protocol enters into force pursuant to paragraph 1 of this article, whichever is the later.

Article 23
Amendment

1. After the expiry of five years from the entry into force of this Protocol, a State Party to the Protocol may propose an amendment and file it with the Secretary-General of the United Nations, who shall thereupon communicate the proposed amendment to the States Parties and to the Conference of the Parties to the Convention for the purpose of considering and deciding on the proposal. The States Parties to this Protocol meeting at the Conference of the Parties shall make every effort to achieve consensus on each amendment. If all efforts at consensus have been exhausted and no agreement has been reached, the amendment shall, as a last resort, require for its adoption a two-thirds majority vote of the States Parties to this Protocol present and voting at the meeting of the Conference of the Parties.

2. Regional economic integration organizations, in matters within their competence, shall exercise their right to vote under this article with a number of votes equal to the number of their member States that are Parties to this Protocol. Such organizations shall not exercise their right to vote if their member States exercise theirs and vice versa.

3. An amendment adopted in accordance with paragraph 1 of this article is subject to ratification, acceptance or approval by States Parties.

4. An amendment adopted in accordance with paragraph 1 of this article shall enter into force in respect of a State Party ninety days after the date of the

deposit with the Secretary-General of the United Nations of an instrument of ratification, acceptance or approval of such amendment.

5. When an amendment enters into force, it shall be binding on those States Parties which have expressed their consent to be bound by it. Other States Parties shall still be bound by the provisions of this Protocol and any earlier amendments that they have ratified, accepted or approved.

Article 24
Denunciation

1. A State Party may denounce this Protocol by written notification to the Secretary-General of the United Nations. Such denunciation shall become effective one year after the date of receipt of the notification by the Secretary-General.

2. A regional economic integration organization shall cease to be a Party to this Protocol when all of its member States have denounced it.

Article 25
Depositary and languages

1. The Secretary-General of the United Nations is designated depositary of this Protocol.

2. The original of this Protocol, of which the Arabic, Chinese, English, French, Russian and Spanish texts are equally authentic, shall be deposited with the Secretary-General of the United Nations.

IN WITNESS WHEREOF, the undersigned plenipotentiaries, being duly authorized thereto by their respective Governments, have signed this Protocol.

Annex 3

Recommended Principles and Guidelines on Human Rights and Human Trafficking[1]

Recommended Principles on Human Rights and Human Trafficking

The primacy of human rights

1. The human rights of trafficked persons shall be at the centre of all efforts to prevent and combat trafficking and to protect, assist and provide redress to victims.

2. States have a responsibility under international law to act with due diligence to prevent trafficking, to investigate and prosecute traffickers and to assist and protect trafficked persons.

3. Anti-trafficking measures shall not adversely affect the human rights and dignity of persons, in particular the rights of those who have been trafficked, and of migrants, internally displaced persons, refugees and asylum-seekers.

Preventing trafficking

4. Strategies aimed at preventing trafficking shall address demand as a root cause of trafficking.

5. States and intergovernmental organizations shall ensure that their interventions address the factors that increase vulnerability to trafficking, including inequality, poverty and all forms of discrimination.

6. States shall exercise due diligence in identifying and eradicating public-sector involvement or complicity in trafficking. All public officials suspected of being

1 E/2002/68/Add.1, 20 May 2002.

implicated in trafficking shall be investigated, tried and, if convicted, appropriately punished.

Protection and assistance

7. Trafficked persons shall not be detained, charged or prosecuted for the illegality of their entry into or residence in countries of transit and destination, or for their involvement in unlawful activities to the extent that such involvement is a direct consequence of their situation as trafficked persons.

8. States shall ensure that trafficked persons are protected from further exploitation and harm and have access to adequate physical and psychological care. Such protection and care shall not be made conditional upon the capacity or willingness of the trafficked person to cooperate in legal proceedings.

9. Legal and other assistance shall be provided to trafficked persons for the duration of any criminal, civil or other actions against suspected traffickers. States shall provide protection and temporary residence permits to victims and witnesses during legal proceedings.

10. Children who are victims of trafficking shall be identified as such. Their best interests shall be considered paramount at all times. Child victims of trafficking shall be provided with appropriate assistance and protection. Full account shall be taken of their special vulnerabilities, rights and needs.

11. Safe (and, to the extent possible, voluntary) return shall be guaranteed to trafficked persons by both the receiving State and the State of origin. Trafficked persons shall be offered legal alternatives to repatriation in cases where it is reasonable to conclude that such repatriation would pose a serious risk to their safety and/or to the safety of their families.

Criminalization, punishment and redress

12. States shall adopt appropriate legislative and other measures necessary to establish, as criminal offences, trafficking, its component acts and related conduct.

13. States shall effectively investigate, prosecute and adjudicate trafficking, including its component acts and related conduct, whether committed by governmental or by non-State actors.

14. States shall ensure that trafficking, its component acts and related offences constitute extraditable offences under national law and extradition treaties.

States shall cooperate to ensure that the appropriate extradition procedures are followed in accordance with international law.

15. Effective and proportionate sanctions shall be applied to individuals and legal persons found guilty of trafficking or of its component or related offences.

16. States shall, in appropriate cases, freeze and confiscate the assets of individuals and legal persons involved in trafficking. To the extent possible, confiscated assets shall be used to support and compensate victims of trafficking.

17. States shall ensure that trafficked persons are given access to effective and appropriate legal remedies.

Recommended Guidelines on Human Rights and Human Trafficking

Guideline 1: Promotion and protection of human rights

Violations of human rights are both a cause and a consequence of trafficking in persons. Accordingly, it is essential to place the protection of all human rights at the centre of any measures taken to prevent and end trafficking. Anti-trafficking measures should not adversely affect the human rights and dignity of persons and, in particular, the rights of those who have been trafficked, migrants, internally displaced persons, refugees and asylum-seekers.

States and, where applicable, intergovernmental and non-governmental organizations, should consider:

1. Taking steps to ensure that measures adopted for the purpose of preventing and combating trafficking in persons do not have an adverse impact on the rights and dignity of persons, including those who have been trafficked.

2. Consulting with judicial and legislative bodies, national human rights institutions and relevant sectors of civil society in the development, adoption, implementation and review of anti-trafficking legislation, policies and programmes.

3. Developing national plans of action to end trafficking. This process should be used to build links and partnerships between governmental institutions involved in combating trafficking and/or assisting trafficked persons and relevant sectors of civil society.

4. Taking particular care to ensure that the issue of gender-based discrimination is addressed systematically when anti-trafficking measures are proposed

with a view to ensuring that such measures are not applied in a discriminatory manner.

5. Protecting the right of all persons to freedom of movement and ensuring that anti-trafficking measures do not infringe upon this right.

6. Ensuring that anti-trafficking laws, policies, programmes and interventions do not affect the right of all persons, including trafficked persons, to seek and enjoy asylum from persecution in accordance with international refugee law, in particular through the effective application of the principle of non-refoulement.

7. Establishing mechanisms to monitor the human rights impact of anti-trafficking laws, policies, programmes and interventions. Consideration should be given to assigning this role to independent national human rights institutions where such bodies exist. Non-governmental organizations working with trafficked persons should be encouraged to participate in monitoring and evaluating the human rights impact of anti-trafficking measures.

8. Presenting detailed information concerning the measures that they have taken to prevent and combat trafficking in their periodic reports to the United Nations human rights treaty-monitoring bodies.

9. Ensuring that bilateral, regional and international cooperation agreements and other laws and policies concerning trafficking in persons do not affect the rights, obligations or responsibilities of States under international law, including human rights law, humanitarian law and refugee law.

10. Offering technical and financial assistance to States and relevant sectors of civil society for the purpose of developing and implementing human rights-based anti-trafficking strategies.

Guideline 2: Identification of trafficked persons and traffickers

Trafficking means much more than the organized movement of persons for profit. The critical additional factor that distinguishes trafficking from migrant smuggling is the presence of force, coercion and/or deception throughout or at some stage in the process — such deception, force or coercion being used for the purpose of exploitation. While the additional elements that distinguish trafficking from migrant smuggling may sometimes be obvious, in many cases they are difficult to prove without active investigation. A failure to identify a trafficked person correctly is likely to result in a further denial of that person's rights. States are therefore under an obligation to ensure that such identification can and does take place.

States are also obliged to exercise due diligence in identifying traffickers, including those who are involved in controlling and exploiting trafficked persons.

States and, where applicable, intergovernmental and non-governmental organizations, should consider:

1. Developing guidelines and procedures for relevant State authorities and officials such as police, border guards, immigration officials and others involved in the detection, detention, reception and processing of irregular migrants, to permit the rapid and accurate identification of trafficked persons.

2. Providing appropriate training to relevant State authorities and officials in the identification of trafficked persons and correct application of the guidelines and procedures referred to above.

3. Ensuring cooperation between relevant authorities, officials and nongovernmental organizations to facilitate the identification and provision of assistance to trafficked persons. The organization and implementation of such cooperation should be formalized in order to maximize its effectiveness.

4. Identifying appropriate points of intervention to ensure that migrants and potential migrants are warned about possible dangers and consequences of trafficking and receive information that enables them to seek assistance if required.

5. Ensuring that trafficked persons are not prosecuted for violations of immigration laws or for the activities they are involved in as a direct consequence of their situation as trafficked persons.

6. Ensuring that trafficked persons are not, in any circumstances, held in immigration detention or other forms of custody.

7. Ensuring that procedures and processes are in place for receipt and consideration of asylum claims from both trafficked persons and smuggled asylum seekers and that the principle of non-refoulement is respected and upheld at all times.

Guideline 3: Research, analysis, evaluation and dissemination

Effective and realistic anti-trafficking strategies must be based on accurate and current information, experience and analysis. It is essential that all parties involved in developing and implementing these strategies have and maintain a clear understanding of the issues.

The media has an important role to play in increasing public understanding of the trafficking phenomenon by providing accurate information in accordance with professional ethical standards.

States and, where appropriate, intergovernmental and non-governmental organizations, should consider:

1. Adopting and consistently using the internationally agreed definition of trafficking contained in the Palermo Protocol.

2. Standardizing the collection of statistical information on trafficking and related movements (such as migrant smuggling) that may include a trafficking element.

3. Ensuring that data concerning individuals who are trafficked is disaggregated on the basis of age, gender, ethnicity and other relevant characteristics.

4. Undertaking, supporting and bringing together research into trafficking. Such research should be firmly grounded in ethical principles, including an understanding of the need not to re-traumatize trafficked persons. Research methodologies and interpretative techniques should be of the highest quality.

5. Monitoring and evaluating the relationship between the intention of anti-trafficking laws, policies and interventions, and their real impact. In particular, ensuring that distinctions are made between measures which actually reduce trafficking and measures which may have the effect of transferring the problem from one place or group to another.

6. Recognizing the important contribution that survivors of trafficking can, on a strictly voluntary basis, make to developing and implementing anti-trafficking interventions and evaluating their impact.

7. Recognizing the central role that non-governmental organizations can play in improving the law enforcement response to trafficking by providing relevant authorities with information on trafficking incidents and patterns taking into account the need to preserve the privacy of trafficked persons.

Guideline 4: Ensuring an adequate legal framework

The lack of specific and/or adequate legislation on trafficking at the national level has been identified as one of the major obstacles in the fight against trafficking. There is an urgent need to harmonize legal definitions, procedures and cooperation at the national and regional levels in accordance with international standards. The

development of an appropriate legal framework that is consistent with relevant international instruments and standards will also play an important role in the prevention of trafficking and related exploitation.

States should consider:

1. Amending or adopting national legislation in accordance with international standards so that the crime of trafficking is precisely defined in national law and detailed guidance is provided as to its various punishable elements. All practices covered by the definition of trafficking such as debt bondage, forced labour and enforced prostitution should also be criminalized.

2. Enacting legislation to provide for the administrative, civil and, where appropriate, criminal liability of legal persons for trafficking offences in addition to the liability of natural persons. Reviewing current laws, administrative controls and conditions relating to the licensing and operation of businesses that may serve as cover for trafficking such as marriage bureaux, employment agencies, travel agencies, hotels and escort services.

3. Making legislative provision for effective and proportional criminal penalties (including custodial penalties giving rise to extradition in the case of individuals). Where appropriate, legislation should provide for additional penalties to be applied to persons found guilty of trafficking in aggravating circumstances, including offences involving trafficking in children or offences committed or involving complicity by State officials.

4. Making legislative provision for confiscation of the instruments and proceeds of trafficking and related offences. Where possible, the legislation should specify that the confiscated proceeds of trafficking will be used for the benefit of victims of trafficking. Consideration should be given to the establishment of a compensation fund for victims of trafficking and the use of confiscated assets to finance such a fund.

5. Ensuring that legislation prevents trafficked persons from being prosecuted, detained or punished for the illegality of their entry or residence or for the activities they are involved in as a direct consequence of their situation as trafficked persons.

6. Ensuring that the protection of trafficked persons is built into anti-trafficking legislation, including protection from summary deportation or return where there are reasonable grounds to conclude that such deportation or return would represent a significant security risk to the trafficked person and/or her/his family.

7. Providing legislative protection for trafficked persons who voluntarily agree to cooperate with law enforcement authorities, including protection of their right to remain lawfully within the country of destination for the duration of any legal proceedings.

8. Making effective provision for trafficked persons to be given legal information and assistance in a language they understand as well as appropriate social support sufficient to meet their immediate needs. States should ensure that entitlement to such information, assistance and immediate support is not discretionary but is available as a right for all persons who have been identified as trafficked.

9. Ensuring that the right of trafficking victims to pursue civil claims against alleged traffickers is enshrined in law.

10. Guaranteeing that protections for witnesses are provided for in law.

11. Making legislative provision for the punishment of public sector involvement or complicity in trafficking and related exploitation.

Guideline 5: Ensuring an adequate law enforcement response

Although there is evidence to suggest that trafficking in persons is increasing in all regions of the world, few traffickers have been apprehended. More effective law enforcement will create a disincentive for traffickers and will therefore have a direct impact upon demand.

An adequate law enforcement response to trafficking is dependent on the cooperation of trafficked persons and other witnesses. In many cases, individuals are reluctant or unable to report traffickers or to serve as witnesses because they lack confidence in the police and the judicial system and/or because of the absence of any effective protection mechanisms. These problems are compounded when law enforcement officials are involved or complicit in trafficking. Strong measures need to be taken to ensure that such involvement is investigated, prosecuted and punished. Law enforcement officials must also be sensitized to the paramount requirement of ensuring the safety of trafficked persons. This responsibility lies with the investigator and cannot be abrogated.

States and, where applicable, intergovernmental and non-governmental organizations should consider:

1. Sensitizing law enforcement authorities and officials to their primary responsibility to ensure the safety and immediate well-being of trafficked persons.

2. Ensuring that law enforcement personnel are provided with adequate training in the investigation and prosecution of cases of trafficking. This training should be sensitive to the needs of trafficked persons, particularly those of women and children, and should acknowledge the practical value of providing incentives for trafficked persons and others to come forward to report traffickers. The involvement of relevant non-governmental organizations in such training should be considered as a means of increasing its relevance and effectiveness.

3. Providing law enforcement authorities with adequate investigative powers and techniques to enable effective investigation and prosecution of suspected traffickers. States should encourage and support the development of proactive investigatory procedures that avoid over-reliance on victim testimony.

4. Establishing specialist anti-trafficking units (comprising both women and men) in order to promote competence and professionalism.

5. Guaranteeing that traffickers are and will remain the focus of anti-trafficking strategies and that law enforcement efforts do not place trafficked persons at risk of being punished for offences committed as a consequence of their situation. 6. Implementing measures to ensure that "rescue" operations do not further harm the rights and dignity of trafficked persons. Such operations should only take place once appropriate and adequate procedures for responding to the needs of trafficked persons released in this way have been put in place.

7. Sensitizing police, prosecutors, border, immigration and judicial authorities, and social and public health workers to the problem of trafficking and ensuring the provision of specialized training in identifying trafficking cases, combating trafficking and protecting the rights of victims.

8. Making appropriate efforts to protect individual trafficked persons during the investigation and trial process and any subsequent period when the safety of the trafficked person so requires. Appropriate protection programmes may include some or all of the following elements: identification of a safe place in the country of destination; access to independent legal counsel; protection of identity during legal proceedings; identification of options for continued stay, resettlement or repatriation.

9. Encouraging law enforcement authorities to work in partnership with non-governmental agencies in order to ensure that trafficked persons receive necessary support and assistance.

Guideline 6: Protection and support for trafficked persons

The trafficking cycle cannot be broken without attention to the rights and needs of those who have been trafficked. Appropriate protection and support should be extended to all trafficked persons without discrimination.

States and, where applicable, intergovernmental and non-governmental organizations, should consider:

1. Ensuring, in cooperation with non-governmental organizations, that safe and adequate shelter that meets the needs of trafficked persons is made available. The provision of such shelter should not be made contingent on the willingness of the victims to give evidence in criminal proceedings. Trafficked persons should not be held in immigration detention centres, other detention facilities or vagrant houses.

2. Ensuring, in partnership with non-governmental organizations, that trafficked persons are given access to primary health care and counselling. Trafficked persons should not be required to accept any such support and assistance and they should not be subject to mandatory testing for diseases, including HIV/AIDS.

3. Ensuring that trafficked persons are informed of their right of access to diplomatic and consular representatives from their State of nationality. Staff working in embassies and consulates should be provided with appropriate training in responding to requests for information and assistance from trafficked persons. These provisions would not apply to trafficked asylum-seekers.

4. Ensuring that legal proceedings in which trafficked persons are involved are not prejudicial to their rights, dignity or physical or psychological well-being.

5. Providing trafficked persons with legal and other assistance in relation to any criminal, civil or other actions against traffickers/exploiters. Victims should be provided with information in a language that they understand.

6. Ensuring that trafficked persons are effectively protected from harm, threats or intimidation by traffickers and associated persons. To this end, there should be no public disclosure of the identity of trafficking victims and their privacy should be respected and protected to the extent possible, while taking into account the right of any accused person to a fair trial. Trafficked persons should be given full warning, in advance, of the difficulties inherent in protecting identities and should not be given false or unrealistic expectations regarding the capacities of law enforcement agencies in this regard.

7. Ensuring the safe and, where possible, voluntary return of trafficked persons and exploring the option of residency in the country of destination or third-country resettlement in specific circumstances (e.g. to prevent reprisals or in cases where re-trafficking is considered likely).

8. In partnership with non-governmental organizations, ensuring that trafficked persons who do return to their country of origin are provided with the assistance and support necessary to ensure their well-being, facilitate their social integration and prevent re-trafficking. Measures should be taken to ensure the provision of appropriate physical and psychological health care, housing and educational and employment services for returned trafficking victims.

Guideline 7: Preventing trafficking

Strategies aimed at preventing trafficking should take into account demand as a root cause. States and intergovernmental organizations should also take into account the factors that increase vulnerability to trafficking, including inequality, poverty and all forms of discrimination and prejudice. Effective prevention strategies should be based on existing experience and accurate information.

States, in partnership with intergovernmental and non-governmental organizations and where appropriate, using development cooperation policies and programmes, should consider:

1. Analysing the factors that generate demand for exploitative commercial sexual services and exploitative labour and taking strong legislative, policy and other measures to address these issues.

2. Developing programmes that offer livelihood options, including basic education, skills training and literacy, especially for women and other traditionally disadvantaged groups.

3. Improving children's access to educational opportunities and increasing the level of school attendance, in particular by girl children.

4. Ensuring that potential migrants, especially women, are properly informed about the risks of migration (e.g. exploitation, debt bondage and health and security issues, including exposure to HIV/AIDS) as well as avenues available for legal, non-exploitative migration.

5. Developing information campaigns for the general public aimed at promoting awareness of the dangers associated with trafficking. Such campaigns should be informed by an understanding of the complexities surrounding trafficking

and of the reasons why individuals may make potentially dangerous migration decisions.

6. Reviewing and modifying policies that may compel people to resort to irregular and vulnerable labour migration. This process should include examining the effect on women of repressive and/or discriminatory nationality, property, immigration, emigration and migrant labour laws.

7. Examining ways of increasing opportunities for legal, gainful and non-exploitative labour migration. The promotion of labour migration by the State should be dependent on the existence of regulatory and supervisory mechanisms to protect the rights of migrant workers.

8. Strengthening the capacity of law enforcement agencies to arrest and prosecute those involved in trafficking as a preventive measure. This includes ensuring that law enforcement agencies comply with their legal obligations.

9. Adopting measures to reduce vulnerability by ensuring that appropriate legal documentation for birth, citizenship and marriage is provided and made available to all persons.

Guideline 8: Special measures for the protection and support of child victims of trafficking

The particular physical, psychological and psychosocial harm suffered by trafficked children and their increased vulnerability to exploitation require that they be dealt with separately from adult trafficked persons in terms of laws, policies, programmes and interventions. The best interests of the child must be a primary consideration in all actions concerning trafficked children, whether undertaken by public or private social welfare institutions, courts of law, administrative authorities or legislative bodies. Child victims of trafficking should be provided with appropriate assistance and protection and full account should be taken of their special rights and needs.

States and, where applicable, intergovernmental and non-governmental organizations, should consider, in addition to the measures outlined under Guideline 6:

1. Ensuring that definitions of trafficking in children in both law and policy reflect their need for special safeguards and care, including appropriate legal protection. In particular, and in accordance with the Palermo Protocol, evidence of deception, force, coercion, etc. should not form part of the definition of trafficking where the person involved is a child.

2. Ensuring that procedures are in place for the rapid identification of child victims of trafficking.

3. Ensuring that children who are victims of trafficking are not subjected to criminal procedures or sanctions for offences related to their situation as trafficked persons.

4. In cases where children are not accompanied by relatives or guardians, taking steps to identify and locate family members. Following a risk assessment and consultation with the child, measures should be taken to facilitate the reunion of trafficked children with their families where this is deemed to be in their best interest.

5. In situations where the safe return of the child to his or her family is not possible, or where such return would not be in the child's best interests, establishing adequate care arrangements that respect the rights and dignity of the trafficked child.

6. In both the situations referred to in the two paragraphs above, ensuring that a child who is capable of forming his or her own views enjoys the right to express those views freely in all matters affecting him or her, in particular concerning decisions about his or her possible return to the family, the views of the child being given due weight in accordance with his or her age and maturity.

7. Adopting specialized policies and programmes to protect and support children who have been victims of trafficking. Children should be provided with appropriate physical, psychosocial, legal, educational, housing and health-care assistance.

8. Adopting measures necessary to protect the rights and interests of trafficked children at all stages of criminal proceedings against alleged offenders and during procedures for obtaining compensation.

9. Protecting, as appropriate, the privacy and identity of child victims and taking measures to avoid the dissemination of information that could lead to their identification.

10. Taking measures to ensure adequate and appropriate training, in particular legal and psychological training, for persons working with child victims of trafficking.

Guideline 9: Access to remedies

Trafficked persons, as victims of human rights violations, have an international legal right to adequate and appropriate remedies. This right is often not effectively available to trafficked persons as they frequently lack information on the possibilities and processes for obtaining remedies, including compensation, for trafficking and related exploitation. In order to overcome this problem, legal and other material assistance should be provided to trafficked persons to enable them to realize their right to adequate and appropriate remedies.

States and, where applicable, intergovernmental and non-governmental organizations, should consider:

1. Ensuring that victims of trafficking have an enforceable right to fair and adequate remedies, including the means for as full a rehabilitation as possible. These remedies may be criminal, civil or administrative in nature.

2. Providing information as well as legal and other assistance to enable trafficked persons to access remedies. The procedures for obtaining remedies should be clearly explained in a language that the trafficked person understands.

3. Making arrangements to enable trafficked persons to remain safely in the country in which the remedy is being sought for the duration of any criminal, civil or administrative proceedings.

Guideline 10: Obligations of peacekeepers, civilian police and humanitarian and diplomatic personnel

The direct or indirect involvement of peacekeeping, peace-building, civilian policing, humanitarian and diplomatic personnel in trafficking raises special concerns. States, intergovernmental and non-governmental organizations are responsible for the actions of those working under their authority and are therefore under an obligation to take effective measures to prevent their nationals and employees from engaging in trafficking and related exploitation. They are also required to investigate thoroughly all allegations of trafficking and related exploitation and to provide for and apply appropriate sanctions to personnel found to have been involved in trafficking.

States and, where appropriate, intergovernmental and non-governmental organizations, should consider:

1. Ensuring that pre- and post-deployment training programmes for all peacekeeping, peace-building, civilian policing, humanitarian and diplomatic staff

adequately address the issue of trafficking and clearly set out the expected standard of behaviour. This training should be developed within a human rights framework and delivered by appropriately experienced trainers.

2. Ensuring that recruitment, placement and transfer procedures (including those of private contractors and sub-contractors) are rigorous and transparent.

3. Ensuring that staff employed in the context of peacekeeping, peace-building, civilian policing, humanitarian and diplomatic missions do not engage in trafficking and related exploitation or use the services of persons in relation to which there are reasonable grounds to suspect they may have been trafficked. This obligation also covers complicity in trafficking through corruption or affiliation with any person or group of persons who could reasonably be suspected of engaging in trafficking and related exploitation.

4. Developing and adopting specific regulations and codes of conduct setting out expected standards of behaviour and the consequences of failure to adhere to these standards.

5. Requiring all personnel employed in the context of peacekeeping, peace-building, civilian policing, humanitarian and diplomatic missions to report on any instances of trafficking and related exploitation that come to their attention.

6. Establishing mechanisms for the systematic investigation of all allegations of trafficking and related exploitation involving personnel employed in the context of peacekeeping, peace-building, civilian policing, humanitarian and diplomatic missions.

7. Consistently applying appropriate criminal, civil and administrative sanctions to personnel shown to have engaged in or been complicit in trafficking and related exploitation. Intergovernmental and non-governmental organizations should, in appropriate cases, apply disciplinary sanctions to staff members found to be involved in trafficking and related exploitation in addition to and independently of any criminal or other sanctions decided on by the State concerned. Privileges and immunities attached to the status of an employee should not be invoked in order to shield that person from sanctions for serious crimes such as trafficking and related offences.

Guideline 11: Cooperation and coordination between States and regions

Trafficking is a regional and global phenomenon that cannot always be dealt with effectively at the national level: a strengthened national response can often result in the operations of traffickers moving elsewhere. International, multilateral and

bilateral cooperation can play an important role in combating trafficking activities. Such cooperation is particularly critical between countries involved in different stages of the trafficking cycle.

States and, where applicable, intergovernmental and non-governmental organizations, should consider:

1. Adopting bilateral agreements aimed at preventing trafficking, protecting the rights and dignity of trafficked persons and promoting their welfare.

2. Offering, either on a bilateral basis or through multilateral organizations, technical and financial assistance to States and relevant sectors of civil society for the purpose of promoting the development and implementation of human rights-based anti-trafficking strategies.

3. Elaborating regional and sub-regional treaties on trafficking, using the Palermo Protocol and relevant international human rights standards as a baseline and framework.

4. Adopting labour migration agreements, which may include provision for minimum work standards, model contracts, modes of repatriation, etc., in accordance with existing international standards. States are encouraged effectively to enforce all such agreements in order to help eliminate trafficking and related exploitation.

5. Developing cooperation arrangements to facilitate the rapid identification of trafficked persons including the sharing and exchange of information in relation to their nationality and right of residence.

6. Establishing mechanisms to facilitate the exchange of information concerning traffickers and their methods of operation.

7. Developing procedures and protocols for the conduct of proactive joint investigations by law enforcement authorities of different concerned States. In recognition of the value of direct contacts, provision should be made for direct transmission of requests for assistance between locally competent authorities in order to ensure that such requests are rapidly dealt with and to foster the development of cooperative relations at the working level.

8. Ensuring judicial cooperation between States in investigations and judicial processes relating to trafficking and related offences, in particular through common prosecution methodologies and joint investigations. This cooperation should include assistance in: identifying and interviewing witnesses with due

regard for their safety; identifying, obtaining and preserving evidence; producing and serving the legal documents necessary to secure evidence and witnesses; and the enforcement of judgements.

9. Ensuring that requests for extradition for offences related to trafficking are dealt with by the authorities of the requested State without undue delay.

10. Establishing cooperative mechanisms for the confiscation of the proceeds of trafficking. This cooperation should include the provision of assistance in identifying, tracing, freezing and confiscating assets connected to trafficking and related exploitation.

11. Exchanging information and experience relating to the implementation of assistance, return and integration programmes with a view to maximizing impact and effectiveness.

12. Encouraging and facilitating cooperation between non-governmental organizations and other civil society organizations in countries of origin, transit and destination. This is particularly important to ensure support and assistance to trafficked persons who are repatriated.

Selected Bibliography

Akande, D, 'International Law Immunities and the International Criminal Court," 98 *American Journal of International Law* 407 (2004)

Albrecht, H. J, 'Fortress Europe? – Controlling Illegal Immigration,' 10 *European Journal of Crime, Criminal Law and Criminal Justice* 1 (2002)

American Law Institute, *Restatement of the Law (Third): Foreign Relations Law of the United States*, 2 American Law Institute (1987)

Anderson, M, *et al.*, *Policing the European Union* (Oxford: Clarendon Press)(1995)

Anderson J.C, 'Respecting Human Rights: Multinational Corporations Strike Out," 2 *University of Pennsylvania Journal of Labour and Employment Law* 463 (2000)

Anderson, B, and J. O'Connell Davidson, *Is Trafficking in Human Beings Demand Driven? A Multi-Country Pilot Study* (Geneva: IOM)(2003)

Anti-Slavery International, *The Migration-Trafficking Nexus: Combating Trafficking through the Protection of Migrants' Human Rights* (London: Anti-Slavery International)(2003)

Asia Regional Cooperation to Prevent People Trafficking (ARCPPT), *The Role of Victim Support Agencies in the Criminal Justice Response to Human Trafficking: Lessons from Thailand, Cambodia, Lao PDR and Myanmar* (Bangkok: ARCPPT)(2004)

Bales, K, *New Slavery: A Reference Handbook* (Santa Barbara: ABC-CLIO Inc.)(2000)

Bantekas, I, 'International Law of Terrorist Financing,' 97 *American Journal of International Law* 315 (2003)

Barrett, G, 'Cooperation in Justice and Home Affairs in the European Union – An Overview and Critique,' in Barrett (ed.), *Justice Cooperation in the European Union: The Creation of a European Legal Space* (Dublin: Institute of European Affairs)(1997)

Bassiouni, M.C, 'Crimes against Humanity" in Bassiouni (ed.), *International Criminal Law*(2nd ed.)(New York: Transnational Publishers)(1999)

Beckman, M. D, 'The White Slave Traffic Act: The Historical Impact of a Criminal Law Policy on Women,' 72 *Georgetown Law Journal* 1111 (1984)

Beesey, A, 'Selling Sex on the Boundaries: The Crossroads of Sexual Desire and Economic Needs,' Paper Presented at the International Conference on Transborder Issues in the Greater Mekong Sub-region (June30- July 2, 2005)

Blackburn, R, *The Making of New World Slavery: From the Baroqu to the Modern 1492-1800* (London and New York: Verso)(1997)

Boister, N, 'Transnational Criminal Law?' 14 *European Journal of International Law* 953 (2003)

Boonpala, P, and J. Kane, *Trafficking of Children: The Problem and Responses Worldwide* (Geneva: ILO)(2001)

Brown, L, *Sex Slaves: Trafficking of Women in Asia* (London: Virago)(2001)

Bruggeman, W, *Illegal Immigration and Trafficking in Human Beings Seen as a Security Problem for Europe*, Paper delivered at the European Conference on Preventing and Combating Trafficking in Human Beings: Global Challenge for the 21st Century (18-20 September 2002)

Buergenthal, T, *International Human Rights in a Nutshell* (St. Paul: West Publishing Company)(1988)

Cassese, A, *International Criminal Law* (Oxford: Oxford University Press)(2003)

Cassese, A, 'When May Senior State Officials Be Tried for International Crimes? Some Comments on the Congo v. Belgium Case,' 13 *European Journal of International Law* 853 (2002)

Cassese, A, 'Crimes against Humanity' in Cassese, Gaeta and Jones (eds.), *The Rome Statute of the International Criminal Court: A Commentary, Volume I* (Oxford: Oxford University Pres)(2002)

Center for Reproductive Law and Policy, *Women of the World: Laws and Policies Affecting Their Reproductive Lives (East Central Europe)* (New York: Centre for Reproductive Law and Policy)(2000)

Center for the Study of Democracy (CSD), *Coalition Building in Transition Countries* (Sofia, Bulgaria: CSD)(2001)

Chalamwong, Y, 'Thailand', *Migration and The Labour Market in Asia: Recent Trends and Policies* (Paris: OECD)(2002)

Chiang, L, 'Trafficking in Women,' in Askin and Koening (eds.), *Women and International Human Rights Law Volume I* (New York: Transnational Publishers, Inc)(1999)

Chuang, J, 'Redirecting the Debate over Trafficking in Women: Definitions, Paradigms and Contexts,'11 *Harvard Human Rights Journal* 65 (1998)

Clapham, A, *Human Rights in the Private Sphere* (Oxford: Clarendon Press)(1993)

Cooper, B, 'A New Approach to Protection and Law Enforcement under the Victims of Trafficking and Violence Protection Act,' 51 *Emory Law Journal* 1041 (2002)

Corene, R, 'The Victimization of Women through Human Trafficking - An Aftermath of War?' 10 *European Journal of Crime, Criminal Law and Criminal Justice* 152 (2002)

Craig P, and G. de Burca, *EU Law: Text, Cases and Materials* (3rd ed)(Oxford: Oxford University Press)(2003)

Danilenko, G.M, 'The Statute of the International Criminal Court and Third States,' 21 *Michigan Journal of International Law* 445 (2000)

Demleitner, N, 'Forced Prostitution: Naming an International Offense,'18 *Fordham International Law Journal* 163 (1994)

Derks, A, *Combating Trafficking in South-East Asia: A Review of Policy and Programme Responses* (IOM Migration Research Series No. 2)(Geneva: IOM)(2000)

Drew, S, 'Human Trafficking: A Modern Form of Slavery?' 4 *European Human Rights Law Review* 481 (2002)

ECPAT Europe Law Enforcement Group, *Extraterritorial Legislation as a Tool to Combat Sexual Exploitation of Children* (Amsterdam: ECPAT)(1999)

Emerton, R, *Trafficking of Women into Hong Kong for the Purpose of Prostitution: Preliminary Research Findings* (Occasional Paper No. 3) (Hong Kong: Centre for Comparative and Public Law)(2000)

Farrior, S, 'The International Law on Trafficking in Women and Children for Prostitution: Making it Live Up to its Potential,' 10 *Harvard Human Rights Journal* 213 (1997)

Flynn, V, 'Europol - A Watershed in EU Law Enforcement Cooperation?' in Barett (ed.), *Justice Cooperation in the European Union: The Creation of a European Legal Space* (Dublin: Institute of European Affairs)(1997)

Fry, J. D, 'Terrorism as a Crime Against Humanity and Genocide,' 7 *UCLA Journal of International Law and Foreign Affairs* 169 (2002)

GAATW, "Appendix A: Human Rights Standard for the Treatment of Trafficked Persons", in *Human Rights and Trafficking in Persons: A Handbook* (Bangkok: GAATW)(2001)

Gallagher, A, 'Human Rights and the New UN Protocols on Trafficking and Migrant Smuggling: A Preliminary Analysis,' 23 *Human Rights Quarterly* 975 (2001)

Ghosh, B, *Huddled Masses and Uncertain Shores: Insights into Irregular Migration* (The Hague: Kluwer Law International)(1998)

Guymon, C.D, 'International Legal Mechanisms for Combating Transnational Organized Crime: The Need for a Multilateral Convention,' 18 *Berkeley Journal of International Law* 53 (2000)

Hague, C. H, 'Prostitution of Women and International Human Rights Law: Transforming Exploitation into Equality,' 8 *New York International Law Review* 23 (1995)

Hartsough, T, 'Asylum for Trafficked Women: Escape Strategies Beyond the T Visa,' 13 *Hastings Women's Law Journal* 77 (2002)

Healy, M. A, 'Prosecuting Child Sex Tourists at Home: Do Laws in Sweden, Australia and the United States Safeguard the Rights of Children as Mandated by International Law?' 18 *Fordham International Law Journal* 1852 (1995)

Held D, and A. McGrew, 'Introduction' in Held and McGrew (eds.), *Governing Globalization: Power, Authority and Global Governance* (Cambridge: Polity Press)(2002)

Henkin, L, 'That "S" Word: Sovereignty, and Globalization, and Human Rights, Et Cetera' 68 *Fordham Law Review* 1 (1999)

Hodgson, D, 'Sex Tourism and Child Prostitution in Asia: Legal Responses and Strategies,' 19 *Melbourne University Law Review* 512 (1994)

Holland, K. M, ' Equality and the Constitution: A Study in the Transformation of a Concept,' in Goldwin and Kaufman (eds.), *Slavery and Its Consequences: The Constitution, Equality and Race* (Washington D.C.: American Enterprise Institute for Public Policy Research)(1988)

Home Office, *Setting the Boundaries: Reforming the Law on Sex Offences* (London: Home Office)(2000)

Home Office, *Secure Border, Safe Haven: Integration with Diversity in Modern Britain* (London: HMSO)(2002)

Hughes, D. M, 'The "Natasha" Trade: The Transnational Shadow Market of Trafficking in Women,' 53 *Journal of International Affairs* 625 (2000)

Human Rights Watch, *Owed Justice: Thai Women Trafficked into Debt Bondage in Japan* (2001) at http://www.hrw.org/reports/2000/japan/3-context.htm

Human Rights Watch, *Hopes Betrayed: Trafficking of Women and Girls to the Post-Conflict Bosnia and Herzegovina for Forced Prostitution* (2002)

Human Rights Watch, *Out of Sight, Out of Mind: Thai Policy towards Burmese Refugees* (February 2004)

Hyland, K.E, 'Protecting Human Victims of Trafficking: An American Framework,' 16 *Berkeley Women's Law Journal* 29 (2001)

Inglis, S.C, 'Expanding International and National Protections against Trafficking for Forced Labour Using a Human Rights Framework,' 7 *Buffalo Human Rights Law Review* 55 (2001)

International Helsinki Federation for Human Rights (IHF), *A Form of Slavery: Trafficking in Women in OSÇE Member States* (Vienna: IHF)(2000)

Iselin, B, *Trafficking in Human Beings: New Patterns for an Old Phenomenon* (Paper Presented to "Trafficking in Persons: Theory and Practice in Regional and International Cooperation"), Bogota, Columbia (November 2003)

Jochnick, C, 'Confronting the Impunity of Non-State Actors: New Fields for the Promotion of Human Rights," 21 *Human Rights Quarterly* 56 (1999)

Jordan, A, 'Trafficking in Human Beings: The Slavery That Surrounds Us,' *Arresting Transnational Organized Crime: An Electronic Journal of U.S. Department of States.* Vol. 6, No.2 (2001), at http://usinfo.state.gov/journals/itgic/0801/ijge/gj05.htm

Karsznicki, K (National Prosecutor's Office), 'Trafficking in Human Beings in Light of Criminal Proceedings Conducted in Poland between 1995-2002, " *Report of the International Conference on Combating Trafficking in Human Beings: Prevention through Legal Solutions* (23-24 May 2003)

Kartusch, A, *Reference Guide Anti-Trafficking Legislative Review with Particular Emphasis on South Eastern Europe* (Warsaw: OSCE/ODIHR)(2001)

Kelly, L, and L. Regan, *Stopping Traffic: Exploring the Extent of, and Responses to, Trafficking in Women for Sexual Exploitation in the UK* (London: Home Office)(2000)

King, T,'The Modern Slave Trade,' 8 *U.C. Davis Journal of International Law and Policy* 293 (2002)

Koser, K, 'Negotiating Entry into 'Fortress Europe': the Migration Strategies of 'Spontaneous' Asylum Seekers,' in Muus (ed.), *Exclusion and Inclusion of Refugees in Contemporary Europe* (Utrecht: ERCOMER)(1997)

Lattimer, M, 'Enforcing Human Rights through International Criminal Law,' in Lattimer and Sands (eds.), *Justice for Crimes against Humanity* (Oxford: Hart Publishing)(2003)

Lederer, L. J, *Trafficking Route from Africa* (Baltimore: Protection Project)(2000)

Lederer, L.J, *Atlanta Trafficking Routes* (Baltimore: Protection Project)(2000)

Levan, P. D, 'Curtailing Thailand's Child Prostitution Through an International Conscience,' 9(3) *American University Journal of International Law and Policy* 872 (1994)

Li, V. F, 'Child Sex Tourism to Thailand: The Role of the United States as a Consumer Country,' 4 *Pacific Rim Law & Policy Journal* 505 (1995)

Limanowska, B, 'Trafficking in Women - Report from Poland,' in Klap, Kerk, and Smith (eds.), *Combating Traffic in Persons: SIM Special No. 17* (Utrecht: Netherlands Institute of Human Rights)(1995)

Maginnis, V, 'Limiting Diplomatic Immunity: Lessons Learned from the 1946 Convention on the Privileges and Immunities of the United Nations,' 28 *Brooklyn Journal of International Law* 989 (2003)

Malone, L. A, 'Economic Hardship as Coercion under the Protocol on International Trafficking in Persons by Organised Crime Elements,' 25 *Fordham International Law Journal* 54 (2001)

McKay, F, 'Civil Reparation in National Courts for Victims of Human Rights Abuse' in Lattimer and Sands (eds.), *Justice for Crimes against Humanity* (Oxford: Hart Publishing)(2003)

McCorquodale, R, 'The Individual and the International Legal System,' in Evans (ed.), *International Law* (Oxford: Oxford University Press)(2003)

McGuinness, D, and E. Barrington, 'Immigration, Visa and Border Controls in the European Union' in Barrett (ed.), *Justice Cooperation in the European Union: The Creation of a European Legal Space* (Dublin: Institute of European Affairs)(1997)

Meltzer, M, *Slavery: A World History Volumes I and II* (New York: Da Capo Press)(1993)

Meron, T, *Human Rights in Internal Strife: Their International Protection* (Cambridge: Grotius)(1987)

Meyring, B, 'Intergovernmentalism and Supranationality: Two Stereotypes for a Complex Reality,' 22 *European Law Review* (1997) 221

Miller, A, and A. N. Stewart, 'Report from the Roundtable on the Meaning of "Trafficking in Persons": A Human Rights Perspective,' 20 *Women's Rights Law Reporter* 11 (1998)

Mirecki, P (Ministry of Interior and Administration), 'Trafficking in Human Beings: Situation in Poland,' *Report of the International Conference on Combating Trafficking in Human Beings: Prevention through Legal Solutions* (23-24 May 2003)

Moore, J, 'From Nation State to Failed State: International Protection from Human Rights Abuses by Non-State Agents,' 31 *Columbia Human Rights Law Review* 81 (1999)

Morrison, J, *The Cost of Survival: The Trafficking of Refugees to the UK* (London: Refugee Council)(1998)

Morrison, J, and B. Crosland, *Trafficking and Smuggling of Refugees: The End Game in European Asylum Policy? (New Issues in Refugee Research, Working Paper No. 39)* (Geneva: UNHCR)(2001)

Mowbray, A, *The Development of Positive Obligations under the European Convention on Human Rights by the European Court of Human Rights* (Oxford: Hart Publishing)(2004)

Müller-Graff, P. C, 'The Legal Bases of the Third Pillar and Its Position in the Framework of the European Union,' 31 *Common Market Law Review* 493 (1994)

Mylonaki, E, 'The Manipulation of Organised Crime by Terrorists: Legal and Factual Perspectives,' 2 *International Criminal Law Review* 213 (2002)

Nelson, K.E, 'Sex Trafficking and Forced Prostitution: Comprehensive New Legal Approaches,' 24 *Houston Journal of International Law* 551 (2002)

Newman F.C, and K. Vasak, 'Civil and Political Rights," in Vasak (ed.), *The International Dimensions of Human Rights* (Westport: Greenwood Pres)(1982)

Niesner, E, and C. Jones-Pauly, *Trafficking in Women in Europe: Prosecution and Victim Protection in a European Context* (Bielefeld: Klein Verlag)(2001)

Obokata, T, 'Trafficking and Smuggling of Human Beings in Europe: Protection of Individual Rights or States' Interests?,' *Web Journal of Current Legal Issues* (Issue 5, 2001), at http://webjcli.nc.ncl.ac.uk

O'Keeffe, D, 'Can the Leopard Change its Spots? Visas, Immigration and Asylum- - Following Amsterdam' in O'Keeffe and Twomey (eds.), *Legal Issues of the Amsterdam Treaty* (Oxford: Hart Publishing)(1999)

Okolski, M, 'Migrant Trafficking and Human Smuggling in Poland,' in Laczko and Thompson (eds.), *Migrant Trafficking and Human Smuggling in Europe: A Review of the Evidence with Case Studies from Hungary, Poland and Ukraine* (Geneva: IOM) (2000)

O'Neill Richard, A, *International Trafficking in Women to the United States: A Contemporary Manifestation of Slavery and Organised Crime* (Washington D.C.: Center for Study of Intelligence(CIA))(2000)

Orentlicher, D. F, 'Settling Accounts: The Duty to Prosecute Human Rights Violations of a Prior Regime,' 100 *Yale Law Journal* 2537 (1991)

Orentlicher, D. F, 'Striking a Balance: Mixed Law Tribunals and Conflicts of Jurisdiction,' in Lattimer and Sands (eds.), *Justice for Crimes against Humanity* (Oxford: Hart Publishing)(2003)

Patterson, O, *Slavery and Social Death: A Comparative Study* (Cambridge: Harvard University Press)(1982)

Paust, J. J, 'The Other Side of Rights: Private Duties under Human Rights Law,' 5 *Harvard. Human Right Journal* 51 (1992)

Pearson, E, *Human Traffic, Human Rights: Redefining Victim Protection* (London: Anti-Slavery International)(2002)

Peers, S, *EU Justice and Home Affairs Law* (Harlow: Longman)(2000)

Phillips, W. D, *Slavery From Roman Times to the Early Transatlantic Trade* (Manchester: Manchester University Press)(1985)

Phongpaichit, P, S. Piriyarangsan, and T. Nualnoi, *Guns, Girls, Gambling Ganja: Thailand's Illegal Economy and Public Policy* (Chiang Mai: Silkworm Books)(1998)

Phongpaichit, P, 'Trafficking in People in Thailand,' in Williams (ed.), *Illegal Immigration and Commercial Sex: The New Slave Trade* (London: Frank Cass)(1999)

Phuong, C, 'Enlarging 'Fortress Europe': EU Accession, Asylum, and Immigration in Candidate Countries,' 52 *International & Comparative Law Quarterly* 641 (2003)

Pilkerton, C.M, 'Traffic Jam: Recommendations for Civil and Criminal Penalties to Curb the Recent Trafficking of Women from Post-Cold War Russia,' 6 *Michigan Journal of Gender and Law* 221 (1999)

Piotrowicz, R, 'European Initiatives in the Protection of Victims of Trafficking Who Give Evidence against Their Traffickers,' 14 *International Journal of Refugee Law* 263 (2002)

Piotrowicz, R, and C. Van Eck, 'Subsidiary Protection and Primary Rights,' 53 *International and Comparative Law Quarterly* 107 (2004)

Pomodoro, L, 'Trafficking and Sexual Exploitation of Women and Children', in Williams and Vlassis (eds.), *Combating Transnational Crime: Concepts, Activities and Responses* (London: Frank Cass)(2001)

Potts, L. G, 'Global Trafficking in Human Beings: Assessing Success of the United Nations Protocol to Prevent Trafficking in Persons,' 35 *George Washington International Law Review* 227 (2003)

Raghu, M, 'Sex Trafficking of Thai Women and the United States Asylum Law Response,'12 *Georgetown Immigration Law Journal* 145 (1997)

Ramasastry, A, 'Corporate Complicity: From Nuremberg to Rangoon, An Examination of Forced Labour Cases and Their Impact on the Liability of Multinational Corporations,' 20 *Berkeley Journal of International Law* 91 (2002)

Rassam, A. Y, 'Contemporary Forms of Slavery and the Evolution of the Prohibition of Slavery and the Slave Trade Under Customary International Law,' 39 *Virginia Journal of International Law* 303 (1999)

Ratner, S.R, and J. S. Abrams, *Accountability for Human Rights Atrocities in International Law: Beyond the Nuremberg Legacy* (Oxford: Oxford University Press)(1997)

Rawski, F, 'To Waive or Not to Waive: Immunity and Accountability in U.N. Peacekeeping Operations,' 11 *Connecticut Journal of International Law* 103 (2002)

Reanda, L, 'Prostitution as a Human Rights Question: Problems and Prospects of United Nations Action,'13 *Human Rights Quarterly* 202 (1991)

Rho-Ng, E, 'The Conscription of Asian Sex Slaves: Causes and Effects of U.S. Military Sex Colonialism in Thailand and the Call to Expand U.S. Asylum Law,' 7 *Asian Law Journal* 103 (2000)

Rijken, C, *Trafficking in Persons: Prosecution from a European Perspective* (The Hague: TMC Asser Press)(2003)

Rodley, N, 'Can Armed Opposition Groups Violate Human Rights,' in Mahoney and Mahoney (eds.), *Human Rights in the Twenty-First Century: A Global Challenge* (Dordrecht: Martinus Nijhoff Publishers)(1993)

Roujanavong, W, 'Thailand: The Situation of Trafficking in Women,' *Proceedings of the 1997 Regional Conference on Trafficking in Women and Children* (Bangkok)(1999)

Robinson, D, 'The Elements of Crimes Against Humanity' in Lee (ed.), *The International Criminal Court: Elements of Crimes and Rules of Procedure and Evidence* (New York: Transnational Publisher)(2000)

Roht-Arriaza, N, 'State Responsibility to Investigate and Prosecute Grave Human Rights Violations in International Law,' 78 *California Law Review* 449 (1990)

Roht-Arriaza, N, 'Punishment, Redress and Pardon: Theoretical and Psychological Approaches' in Roht-Arriaza (ed.), *Impunity and Human Rights in International Law and Practice* (Oxford: Oxford University Press)(1995)

Rubenstein, P, 'State Responsibility for Failure to Control the Export of Weapons of Mass Destruction,' 23 *California Western International Law Journal* 319 (1993)

Ruggiero, V, 'Trafficking in Human Beings Slaves in Contemporary Europe,' 24 *International Journal of Sociology of Law* 231 (1997)

Rybicki, R (Ministry of Interior and Administration), *Trafficking in Human Beings: Role of Governments – Polish Perspective* (Holy See, 15-16 May 2002)

Ryf, K.C, 'The First Modern Anti-Slavery Law: The Trafficking Victim Protection Act 2000,' 34 *Case Western Reserve Journal of International Law* 45 (2002)

Salt, J, and J. Stein, 'Migration as a Business: The Case of Trafficking,' 35 *International Migration* 467 (1997)

Salt, J. and J. Hogarth, 'Definitions of the Concepts of Trafficking, Smuggling, and Organized Crime,' in Laczko and Thompson (eds.), *Migrant Trafficking and Human Smuggling in Europe: A Review of the Evidence with Case Studies from Hungary, Poland and Ukraine* (Geneva: IOM)(2000)

Savona, E. U, *Corruption and Organised Crime in States in Transition: Joint Project between the Commission of the European Communities and the Council of Europe, Final Recommendation and Guidelines for Action* (Strasbourg: Council of Europe)(1998)

Schabas, W. A, 'Punishment of Non-State Actors in Non-International Armed Conflict,' 26 *Fordham International Law Journal* 907 (2003)

Scharf, M. P, 'Application of Treaty-Based Universal Jurisdiction to Nationals of Non-Party States,' 35 *New England Law Review* 363 (2001)

Schloenhardt, A, 'Organised Crime and the Business of Migrant Trafficking: An Economic Analysis,' 32 *Crime, Law and Social Change* 203 (1999)

Schreuer, C, 'The Waning of Sovereign State: Towards a New Paradigm for International Law?' 4 *European Journal of International Law* 447 (1993)

Seabrook, J, *No Hiding Place: Child Sex Tourism and the Role of Extraterritorial Legislation* (London: Zee Books) (2000).

Seabrook, J, *Travels in the Skin Trade: Tourism and the Sex Industry* (London: Pluto Press)(2001)

Secretariat of the Budapest Group, *The Relationship between Organised Crime and Trafficking in Aliens* (Vienna: International Centre for Immigration Policy and Dev elopment(ICMPD))(1999)

Senta, K, *Trafficking of Human Beings in Asia-Pacific Region* (Workshop of the UN Crime Prevention Network on Trafficking in Human Beings, Especially Women and Children)(May 2003)

Siron, N, and P. Van Baeveghem, *Trafficking in Migrants through Poland: Multidisciplinary Research into the Phenomenon of Transit Migration in the Candidate Member States of the EU, with a View to the Combat of Traffic in Persons* (Antwerp: Maklu)(1999)

Shannon, S, 'Prostitution and the Mafia: The Involvement of Organized Crime in the Global Sex Trade,' in Williams (ed.), *Illegal Migration and Commercial Sex: The New Slave Trade* (New York: Frank Cass)(1999)

Shelton, D, *Remedies in International Human Rights Law* (Oxford: Oxford University Press)(1999)

Skeldon, R, *Irregular Migration in the Greater Mekong Sub-Region : Policy Dimension of a Growing Issue* (Labour Migration and Trafficking within the Greater Mekong Sub-Region: Proceedings of Mekong Sub-Regional Expert Meeting and Explanatory Policy Paper)(Bangkok: ILO)(2001)

Skrobanek, S, 'Laws Relating to Traffic in Women - Case of Thailand,' *Combating Traffic in Persons*: *SIM Special No. 17* (Utrecht: Netherlands Institute of Human Rights)(1995)

Skrobanek, S, N. Boonpakdee and C. Jantateero, *Traffic in Women: Human Realities of the International Sex Trade* (London: Zed Books Ltd)(1997)

Slye, R.C, 'International Law, Human Rights Beneficiaries, and South Africa: Some Thoughts on the Utility of International Human Rights Law,' 2 *Chicago Journal of International Law* 59 (2001)

Smit, M (Bureau of the Dutch National Rapporteur on Trafficking), *Trafficking in Women: A Dutch Country Report* (April 2003)

Somerset, C, *What the Professionals Know: The Trafficking of Children into, and through, the UK for Sexual Purposes* (London: ECPAT UK)(2001)

Talleyrand, I, 'Military Prostitution: How the Authorities Worldwide Aid and Abet International Trafficking in Women,' 27 *Syracuse Journal of International Law and Commerce* 151 (2000)

Taylor, I, and R. Jamison, 'Sex Trafficking and the Mainstream of Market Culture,' 32 *Crime, Law & Social Change* 257 (1999)

Temkin, J, *Rape and Legal Process* (2nd ed) (Oxford: Oxford University Press)(2003)

Tessier, K, 'The New Slave Trade: The International Crisis of Immigrant Smuggling,' 3 *Global Legal Studies Journal* 261 (1995-1996)

Tiefenbrun, S, 'The Saga of Susannah a U.S. Remedy For Sex Trafficking in Women: The Victims of Trafficking and Violence Protection Act of 2002,' *Utah Law Review* 107 (2002)

Tiggey, M, et. al., *For Love or Money: Pimps and the Management of Sex Work (Police Research Series Paper No. 134)* (London: Home Office)(2000)

Toepfer, S. J, and B. S. Wells, 'The Worldwide Market for Sex: A Review of International and Regional Legal Prohibitions Regarding Trafficking in Women,' 2 *Michigan Journal of Gender & Law* 83 (1994)

Trapalis, V, 'Extraterritorial Jurisdiction: A Step Toward Eradicating the Trafficking of Women into Greece for Forced Prostitution,' 32 *Golden Gate University Law Review* 207 (2002)

Tumlin, K. C, *Trafficking in Children and Women: A Regional Overview* (Asia Regional High-level Meeting on Child Labour, Jarkarta, Indonesia, 8-10 March 2000) (Bangkok: Chulalongkorn University)(2000)

Turnbull, P, 'The Fusion of Immigration and Crime in the European Union: Problems of Cooperation and the Fight against the Trafficking in Women', in Williams (ed.), *Illegal Migration and Commercial Sex: The New Slave Trade* (New York: Frank Cass)(1999)

Twomey, P, 'Europe's Other Market: Trafficking in People,' 2 *European Journal of Migration and Law* 1 (2000)

UNICEF, *Children on the Edge*: *Protecting Children from Sexual Exploitation and Trafficking in East Asia and the Pacific* (Bangkok: UNICEF East Asia and Pacific)(2001)

UNICEF UK, *End Child Exploitation: Stop Traffic!* (London: UNICEF UK)(2003)

UNICRI, *International Cooperation in Combating Transnational Crime: New Challenges in the Twenty First Century: Background Paper for the Workshop on Combating Corruption,* A/CONF.187/9 (1999)

UNICRI, *Trafficking, Slavery and Peacekeeping: The Need for a Comprehensive Training Program (Conference Report)*(May 2002)

UNHCR, *Guideline on International Protection: Gender-Related Persecution in the Context of Article 1A(2) of the 1951 Convention and/or Its 1967 Protocol Relating to the Status of Refugees*, HCR/GIP/02/01 (2002)

U.S. Department of State, *Trafficking in Persons Report 2005*

U.S. Department of State, *Trafficking in Persons Report 2004*

U.S. Department of State, *Trafficking in Persons Report 2003*

Van den Wyngaert, C (ed.), *International Criminal Law: A Collection of International and European Instruments* (2nd ed) (The Hague: Kluwer Law International)(2000)

Ward, I, 'Identifying the European Other,' 14 *International Journal of Refugee Law* 219 (2002)

Weijers, M, 'Keep Your Women Home: European Union Policies on Trafficking in Women,' in Rossilli (ed.), *Gender Policies in the European Union* (New York: P. Lang)(2000)

Williams, P, 'Human Commodity Trafficking: An Overview,' in Williams (ed.), *Illegal Migration and Commercial Sex: The New Slave Trade* (New York: Frank Cass)(1999)

Williams, P, and G. Baudin-O'Hayon, 'Global Governance, Transnational Organized Crime and Money Laundering' in Held and McGrew (eds.), *Governing Globalization: Power, Authority and Global Governance* (Cambridge: Polity Press)(2002)

Women's Commission for Refugee Women and Children, *The Struggle between Migration Control and Victim Protection: The UK Approach to Human Trafficking* (New York: Women's Commission for Refugee Women and Children)(2005)

Websites

Anti-Slavery International, http://www.antislavery.org

Coalition against Trafficking in Women (Asia & Pacific), http://www.catw-ap.org/fspeech.htm

DEPDC, http://www.depdc.org/english/about_us1.htm

ECPAT UK, http://www.ecpat.org.uk/

Empower Foundation, http://www.empowerwomen.org/

European Commission (Justice and Home Affairs), http://www.europa.eu.int/comm/justice_home/fsj/crime/trafficking/fsj_crime_human_trafficking_en.htm

GAATW, http://www.gaatw.org/

Helsinki Foundation for Human Rights, http://www.hfhrpol.waw.pl/En/

International Helsinki Federation, http://www.ihf-hr.org/index.php

La Strada Foundation, http://free.ngo.pl/lastrada/index_en.html

United Nations High Commissioner for Human Rights, http://www.ohchr.org/english/issues/trafficking/index.htm

Index

International Studies in Human Rights

1. Bertrand G. Ramcharan: *Humanitarian Good Offices in International Law*. The Good Offices of the United Nations Secretary General in the Field of Human Rights. 1983 ISBN 90-247-2805-3
2. Bertrand G. Ramcharan: *International Law and Fact-Finding in the Field of Human Rights*. 1983 ISBN 90-247-3042-2
3. Bertrand G. Ramcharan: *The Right to Life in International Law*. 1985 ISBN 90-247-3074-0
4. Katarina Tomaševski and Philip Alston: *Right to Food*. 1984 ISBN 90-247-3087-2
5. Arie Bloed, Pieter van Dijk: *Essays on Human Rights in the Helsinki Process*. 1985 ISBN 90-247-3211-5
6. K. Tornudd: *Finland and the International Norms of Human Rights*. 1986 ISBN 90-247-3257-3
7. Berth Verstappen and Hans Thoolen: *Human Rights Missions. A Study of the Fact-Finding Practice of Non-Governmental Organizations*. 1986 ISBN 90-247-3364-2
8. Hurst Hannum: *The Right to Leave and Return in International Law and Practice*. 1987 ISBN 90-247-3445-2
9. H. Danelius and Herman Burgers: The United Nations Convention Against Torture. *A Handbook on the Convention Against Torture and Other Cruel, Inhuman or Degrading Treatment or Punishment*. 1988 ISBN 90-247-3609-9
10. David A. Martin: *The New Asylum Seekers: Refugee Law in the 1980's*. The Ninth Sokol Colloquium on International Law. 1988 ISBN 90-247-3730-3
11. Cecilia Medina: *The Battle of Human Rights. Gross, Systematic Violations and the Inter-American System*. 1988 ISBN 90-247-3687-0
12. Claus Gulmann, Lars Adam Rehof: *Human Rights in Domestic Law and Development*. Assistance Policies of the Nordic Countries. 1989 ISBN 90-247-3743-5
13. Bertrand G. Ramcharan: *The Concept and Present Status of the International Protection of Human Rights. Forty Years After the Universal Declaration*. 1989 ISBN 90-247-3759-1
14. Angela D. Byre: *International Human Rights Law in the Commonwealth Caribbean*. 1991 ISBN 90-247-3785-0
15. Natan Lerner: *Group Rights and Discrimination in International Law*. 1990 ISBN 0-79230-853-0
16. Shimon Shetreet: *Free Speech and National Security*. 1991 ISBN 0-79231-030-6
17. Geoff Gilbert: *Aspects of Extradition Law*. 1991 ISBN 0-79231-162-0
18. Philip E. Veerman: *The Rights of the Child and the Changing Image of Childhood*. 1992 ISBN 0-79231-250-3
19. Mireille Delmas-Marty: *The European Convention for the Protection of Human Rights*. International Protection versus National Restrictions. 1992 ISBN 0-79231-283-X
20. Arie Bloed and Pieter van Dijk: *The Human Dimension of the Helsinki Process*. The Vienna Follow-up Meeting and its Aftermath. 1991 ISBN 0-79231-337-2
21. Lyal S. Sunga: *Individual Responsibility in International Law for Serious Human Rights Violations*. 1992 ISBN 0-79231-453-0

22. Dinah Shelton and Stanislaw J. Frankowski: *Preventive Detention*. A Comparative and International Law Perspective. 1992 ISBN 0-79231-465-4
23. Michael Freeman and Philip E. Veerman: *Ideologies of Children's Rights*. 1992 ISBN 0-79231-800-5
24. Stephanos Stavros: *The Guarantees for Accused Persons Under Article 6 of the European Convention on Human Rights*. An Analysis of the Application of the Convention and a Comparison with Other Instruments. 1993 ISBN 0-79231-897-8
25. Allan Rosas, Diane Goodman and Jan Helgesen: *Strength of Diversity*. Human Rights and Pluralist Democracy. 1992 ISBN 0-79231-987-7
26. Andrew Clapham and Kees Waaldijk: *Homosexuality: A European Community Issue*. Essays on Lesbian and Gay Rights in European Law and Policy. 1993 ISBN 0-79232-038-7
28. Howard Charles Yourow: *The Margin of Appreciation Doctrine in the Dynamics of European Human Rights Jurisprudence*. 1995 ISBN 0-79233-338-1
29. Lars Adam Rehof: *Guide to the Travaux Préparatoires of the United Nations Convention on the Elimination of all Forms of Discrimination against Women*. 1993. ISBN 0-79232-222-3
30. Allan Rosas, Arie Bloed, Liselotte Leicht and Manfred Nowak: *Monitoring Human Rights in Europe*. Comparing International Procedures and Mechanisms. 1993 ISBN 0-79232-383-1
31. Andrew Harding and John Hatchard: *Preventive Detention and Security Law: A Comparative Survey*. 1993 ISBN 0-79232-432-3
32. Yves Beigbeder: *International Monitoring of Plebiscites, Referenda and National Elections*. Self-Determination and Transition to Democracy. 1994 ISBN 0-79232-563-X
33. Thomas David Jones: *Human Rights: Group Defamation, Freedom of Expression and the Law of Nations*. 1997 ISBN 90-411-0265-5
34. David M. Beatty: *Human Rights and Judicial Review: A Comparative Perspective*. 1994 ISBN 0-79232-968-6
35. Geraldine Van Bueren: *The International Law on the Rights of the Child*. 1995 ISBN 0-79232-687-3
36. Tom Zwart: *The Admissibility of Human Rights Petitions*. The Case Law of the European Commission of Human Rights and the Human Rights Committee. 1994 ISBN 0-79233-146-X
37. Helene Lambert: Seeking Asylum. Comparative Law and Practice in Selected European Countries. 1995 ISBN 0-79233-152-4
38. E. Lijnzaad: *Reservations to UN-Human Rights Treaties*. Ratify and Ruin? 1994 ISBN 0-7923-3256-3
39. L.G. Loucaides: *Essays on the Developing Law of Human Rights*. 1995 ISBN 0-7923-3276-8
40. T. Degener and Y. Koster-Dreese (eds.): *Human Rights and Disabled Persons*. Essays and Relevant Human Rights Instruments. 1995 ISBN 0-7923-3298-9
41. J.-M. Henckaerts: *Mass Expulsion in Modern International Union and Human Rights*. 1995 ISBN 90-411-0072-5
42. N.A. Neuwahl and A. Rosas (eds.): *The European Union and Human Rights*. 1995 ISBN 90-411-0124-1

43. H. Hey: *Gross Human Rights Violations: A Search for Causes*. A Study of Guatemala and Costa Rica. 1995 ISBN 90-411-0146-2
44. B.G. Tahzib: *Freedom of Religion or Belief*. Ensuring Effective International Legal Protection. 1996 ISBN 90-411-0159-4
45. F. de Varennes: *Language, Minorities and Human Rights*. 1996 ISBN 90-411-0206-X
46. J. Raikka (ed.): *Do We Need Minority Rights*? Conceptual Issues. 1996 ISBN 90-411-0309-0
47. J. Brohmer: *State Immunity and the Violation of Human Rights*. 1997 ISBN 90-411-0322-8
48. C.A. Gearty (ed.): *European Civil Liberties and the European Convention on Human Rights*. A Comparative Study. 1997 ISBN 90-411-0253-1
49. B. Conforti and F. Francioni (eds.): *Enforcing International Human Rights in Domestic Courts*. 1997 ISBN 90-411-0393-7
50. A. Spiliopoulou Akermark: *Justifications of Minority Protection in International Law*. 1997 ISBN 90-411-0424-0
51. A. Boulesbaa: *The U.N. Convention on Torture and the Prospects for Enforcement*. 1997 ISBN 90-411-0457-7
52. S. Bowen (ed.): *Human Rights, Self-Determination and Political Change in the Occupied Palestinian Territories*. 1997 ISBN 90-411-0502-6
53. M. O'Flaherty and G. Gisvold (eds.): *Post-War Protection of Human Rights in Bosnia and Herzegovina*. 1998 ISBN 90-411-1020-8
54. A.-L. Svensson-McCarthy: *The International Law of Human Rights and States of Exception*. With Special Reference to the *Travaux Préparatoires* and the Case-Law of the International Monitoring Organs. 1998 ISBN 90-411-1021-6
55. G. Gilbert: *Transnational Fugitive Offenders in International Law*. Extradition and Other Mechanisms. 1998 ISBN 90-411-1040-2
56. M. Jones and L.A. Basser Marks (eds.): *Disability, Divers-ability and Legal Change*. 1998 ISBN 90-411-1086-0
57. T. Barkhuysen, M.L. van Emmerik and P.H.P.H.M.C. van Kempen (eds.): *The Execution of Strasbourg and Geneva Human Rights Decisions in the National Legal Order*. 1999 ISBN 90-411-1152-2
58. S. Coliver, P. Hoffman, J. Fitzpatrick and S. Bowen (eds.): *Secrecy and Liberty: National Security, Freedom of Expression and Access to Information*. 1999 ISBN 90-411-1191-3
59. W.S. Heinz and H. Fruhling: *Determinants of Gross Human Rights Violations by State and State-Sponsored Actors in Brazil, Uruguay, Chile, and Argentina*. 1960-1990. 1999 ISBN 90-411-1202-2
60. M. Kirilova Eriksson: *Reproductive Freedom*. In the Context of International Human Rights and Humanitarian Law. 1999 ISBN 90-411-1249-9
61. M.B. Eryilmaz: *Arrest and Detention Powers in English and Turkish Law and Practice in the Light of the European Convention on Human Rights*. 1999 ISBN 90-411-1269-3
62. K. Henrard: *Devising and Adequate System of Minority Protection*. Individual Human Rights, Minority Rights and the Right to Self-Determination. 2000 ISBN 90-411-1359-2

63. K. Tomasevski: *Responding to Human Rights Violations*. 1946-1999. 2000 ISBN 90-411-1368-1
64. L.-V.N. Tran: *Human Rights and Federalism*. A Comparative Study on Freedom, Democracy and Cultural Diversity. 2000 ISBN 90-411-1492-0
65. C. Tiburcio: *The Human Rights of Aliens under International and Comparative Law*. 2001 ISBN 90-411-1550-1
66. E. Brems: *Human Rights: Universality and Diversity*. 2001 ISBN 90-411-1618-4
67. C. Bourloyannis-Vrailas and L.-A. Sicilianos: *The Prevention of Human Rights Violations*. 2001 ISBN 90-411-1672-9
68. G. Ulrich and K. Hastrup: *Discrimination and Toleration*. New Perspectives. 2001 ISBN 90-411-1711-3
69. V.O. Orlu Nmehielle: *African Human Rights System*. Its Laws, Practice and Institutions. 2001 ISBN 90-411-1731-8
70. B.G. Ramcharan: Human Rights and Human Security. 2002 ISBN 90-411-818-7
71. B.G. Ramcharan: The United Nations High Commissioner for Human Rights. The Challenges of International Protection. 2002 ISBN 90-411-1832-2
72. C. Breen: *The Standard of the Best Interests of the Child*. A Western Tradition in International and Comparative Law. 2002 ISBN 90-411-1851-9
73. M. Katayanagi: *Human Rights Functions of United Nations Peacekeeping Operations*. 2002 ISBN 90-411-1910-8
74. O.M. Arnadottir: *Equality and Non-Discrimination under the European Convention on Human Rights*. 2002 ISBN 90-411-1912-4
75. B.G. Ramcharan: *The Security Council and the Protection of Human Rights*. 2002 ISBN 90-411-1878-0
76. E. Fierro: *The EU's Approach to Human Rights Conditionality in Practice*. 2002 ISBN 90-411-1936-1
77. Natan Lerner: *Group Rights and Discrimination in International Law*. Second Edition. 2002 ISBN 90-411-1982-5
78. S. Leckie (ed.): *National Perspectives on Housing Rights*. 2003 ISBN 90-411-2013-0
79. L.C. Reif: *The Ombudsman, Good Governance and the International Human Rights System*. 2004 ISBN 90-04-13903-6
80. Mary Dowell-Jones: *Contextualising the International Covenant on Economic, Social and Cultural Rights: Assessing the Economic Deficit*. 2004 ISBN 90-04-13908-7

81 Li-ann Thio: *Managing Babel: The International Legal Protection of Minorities in the Twentieth Century*. 2005 ISBN 90-04-14198-7

82. Klaus Dieter Beiter: *The Protection of the Right to Education by International Law: Including a Systematic Analysis of Article 13 of the International Covenant on Economic, Social and Cultural Rights*. 2005 ISBN 90-04-14704-7
83. Janneke Gerards: *Judicial Review in Equal Treatment Cases*. 2005 ISBN 90-04-14379-3
84. Virginia A. Leary and Daniel Warner (eds.): *Social Issues, Globalisation and International Institutions: Labour Rights and the EU, ILO, OECD and WTO*. 2006 ISBN-90-04-14579-6

85. J.K.M. Gevers, E.H. Hondius and J.H. Hubben (eds.) *Health Law, Human Rights and the Biomedicine Convention: Essays in Honour of Henriette Roscam Abbing*, 2005 ISBN 90 04 14822 1
86. Claire Breen, *Age Discrimination and Children's Rights*, 2005 ISBN 90 04 14827 2
87. B.G.Ramcharan, *Human Rights Protection in the Field*, 2005 ISBN 90 04 14847 7
88. Geoff Gilbert, *Responding to International Crime*, Second Edition, 2006 ISBN 90 04 15276 8
89. Tom Obokata, *Trafficking of Human Beings from a Human Rights Perspective: Towards a Holistic Approach*, 2006 ISBN 90 04 15405 1

This series is designed to shed light on current legal and political aspects of process and organization in the field of human rights

---

MARTINUS NIJHOFF PUBLISHERS – LEIDEN • BOSTON

www.ingramcontent.com/pod-product-compliance
Lightning Source LLC
LaVergne TN
LVHW012051011026
849162LV00017B/134

* 9 7 8 9 0 0 4 1 5 4 0 5 6 *